'I am delighted that such a comprehensive, mot
book has been produced that focuses on the d
sustainable careers in ı

Music is such an important part of all our lives; almost everyone, from all nations or cultures, is engaged in some way with music on a daily basis. And yet, in terms of career development, little support or guidance is usually given to those who are musically gifted; those who put in countless hours of hard practice from a young age; those who often commit their entire lives to the creation, performance, and recording of music for all our benefit.

This book is therefore an extremely welcome addition to the literature, containing as it does a wealth of highly relevant and detailed case studies and exercises, plus inspirational ideas and sound advice.

So whether your passion is for classical, jazz or popular music, if you want to make a success of your career and your future, then this book is essential reading!'

Paul Kirkham, Managing Director at the Institute of Contemporary Music Performance

'Actively choosing a career in music is, in today's fast-changing and highly competitive environment, both an incredibly difficult decision to make and yet for many aspiring and dedicated young musicians the only real career option they seriously consider. Hallam and Gaunt's impressive publication provides undoubtedly the most important contribution to the literature available to such young people at the cusp of professional training for the music industry, and should be considered an indispensable tool for individuals, music teachers, schools and entrants to further and higher education programmes of music education and training alike. Its practical exercises and pragmatic advice – not least the opening guidance on the use of the book – as well as the gateway it provides to a host of other related literature, provide an exemplary tool that supports the development of a host of vital skills, both transferable to other walks of life and invaluable to a lifelong career in music. An outstanding achievement.'

Dr Claire Mera-Nelson, Director of Music, Trinity Laban Conservatoire of Music and Dance

'Hallam and Gaunt present accessible, down-to-earth guidance to (primarily classical) musicians as they prepare for a career, spanning the sometimes bewildering breadth and depth and rates of change of contemporary musical life. Rich examples, reflections, quotes and exercises give the volume real-world currency for advanced music learners. *Preparing for success* is a valuable contribution to an emerging body of literature that brings home the idea that it takes more than a focus on playing well to become a music professional in the twenty-first century.'

Professor Huib Schippers, Director, Queensland Conservatorium, Griffith University

'*Preparing for Success: A practical guide for young musicians* is an excellent practical guide for anyone thinking seriously about pursuing a career in the music profession.

The journey to becoming a musician (and the reality of entering the profession) has changed significantly in recent years. There are now a myriad of training and education options available for young musicians and this publication provides an excellent signpost to the options available, the importance of life-long learning, navigating a complex profession and being realistic about success.

The desire to become a musician usually emerges from a desire to transfer your love of playing music into a career, but there are often many hurdles to overcome in order to be ready to tackle the challenges of a demanding and complex profession. With this in mind, *Preparing for Success* importantly details the holistic needs of musicians – these include ensuring adequate health and wellbeing, developing entrepreneurial skills and preparing young musicians to be resilient in the face of the inevitable ups and downs that are part and parcel of a portfolio career that requires young musicians to be ready to deal with ambiguity and to be flexible, with the capacity to respond to the demands of a fast-changing profession.

Overall, *Preparing for Success* encourages young musicians to be clear about their sense of purpose, of knowing what exactly they hope to achieve and by when. As with any publication dealing with supporting people to better performance, the book also engenders reflection about what it means to be self-analytical, to develop a high level of emotional intelligence and to be clear about understanding both your strengths and musical identity.

I thoroughly recommend this book for any young musician starting to consider a professional musical career. When I started my own professional study some twenty years ago, my main focus was on mastering the violin. What I now know is that a broader consideration of wider learning activities, the importance of mentoring and an analysis of the complexities of managing a portfolio career (as detailed in *Preparing for Success*) would have been invaluable.'

Michelle Wright, Director, Cause4

PREPARING FOR SUCCESS

PREPARING FOR SUCCESS

A PRACTICAL GUIDE FOR YOUNG MUSICIANS

SUSAN HALLAM AND HELENA GAUNT

Institute of Education, University of London
Issues in Practice

Leading education
and social research
Institute of Education
University of London

First published in 2012 by the Institute of Education,
University of London, 20 Bedford Way, London WC1H 0AL

www.ioe.ac.uk/publications

© Susan Hallam and Helena Gaunt 2012

British Library Cataloguing in Publication Data:

. A catalogue record for this publication is available from the
British Library

ISBN 978 0 85473 903 5

Typeset by Quadrant Infotech (India) Pvt Ltd

Printed and bound by CPI Group (UK) Ltd, Croydon, CR0 4YY

Contents

List of figures

List of tables

ACKNOWLEDGEMENTS

The authors would like to thank the following professional and student musicians, and other professionals associated with music, who contributed to this book through being interviewed, supplying essential information, or commenting on chapter drafts:

Julian Anderson
Stefanie Anderson
Emmanuel Antwi
Alexi Ayliff-Vellianitis
Dr Russel Ayling
Lucy Baish
Drew Balch
Louise Bartle
Katie Bennington
Lucy Bernstein
Ed Blunt
Gail Brand
William Bruce
David Bush
Jack Carroll
Nell Catchpole
Ian Clarke
Simon Couzens
Sue Cowan
Dr Andrea Creech
Dr Guy Dammann
Elizabeth Dearsley
Joshua Dickson
Anna Durance
Dr Colin Durrant
Kate Eaton
Sian Edwards
Max Elton

Zoe Feltham
Samuel Kubrick Finney
David Foister
Hannah Gill
Dick Hallam
Clare Hammond
Martin Hathaway
L I Henderson
Paul Hughes
Lucy Hunt
Sky Ingram
Ashanti Kemp
Kirill Khassine
Associate Professor Don Lebler
Pamela Lidiard
Elizabeth Mannion
Joanna McGowan
Malcolm McKeand
Lisandra Mendes
Natalie Miller
George Millward
Nicolle Nair
Preetha Narayanan
Poppy Neame
Patryca Nowacka
Kate Paterson
Luke Paterson
R Patterson

Adam Pyle
Mark Rainbow
Alex Rayner
Helen Reid
William Ring
Ian Ritchie
Mike Roberts
Jon Roskilly
Sigrun Saevarsdottir
Fabian Schmidt
Pedro Segundo
Ann Sloboda
Professor John Sloboda
Dr Gareth Dylan Smith

Alexander Soares
Christoper Suckling
Toby Sweetman
Cherelle Thompson
Dr Emma Webster
Faye Weston
R Wiles
Alan Williams
Chris Williams
Simon Wills
Scott Wilson
Guy Wood
Raymond Yiu
Armin Zanner

Special thanks go to Geoff Coates, who assisted with research for the book. This was made possible by funds for a National Teaching Fellowship, awarded to Dr Helena Gaunt in 2009 by the Higher Education Academy.

The authors and publisher gratefully acknowledge the permission granted to reproduce copyright material in this book.

Figure 1.1 from Creech, A., Papageorgi, I., Duffy, C., Morton, F., Haddon, E., Potter, J. (2007), *From Undergraduate to Professional Musicians: Supporting critical transitions*. Paper presented at the Society for Research into Higher Education, Brighton, UK. Reprinted with permission from Andrea Creech.

Case Study 7.2 from Duncan, Katrina, 'Cross-curricular Creative Projects'. Online. www.anewdirection.org.uk/file_download.aspx?id=7203. Reprinted with permission from A New Direction.

Case Study 7.3 from Youth Music (2008) 'Case Study: At Risk - Good Vibrations Gamelan in Prison'. Online. http://dev1.youthmusic. uk/case_studies/Good_vibrations_gamelan_in_prison.html. Reprinted with permission from Youth Music.

Every effort has been made to trace copyright holders and to obtain their permission for the use of copyrighted material. The publisher apologises for any errors or omissions in the above list and would be grateful if notified of any corrections that should be incorporated in future reprints or editions of this book.

ABOUT THE AUTHORS

Professor Susan Hallam is Professor of Education at the Institute of Education, University of London (IOE) and currently Dean of the Faculty of Policy and Society. She pursued careers as both a professional musician and a music educator before completing her psychology studies and becoming an academic in 1991. Her research interests include: disaffection from school; ability grouping and homework; and issues relating to learning in music, practising, performing, musical ability, musical understanding and the effects of music on behaviour and studying. She is the author of several books, including *Instrumental Teaching: A practical guide to better teaching and learning* (1998), *The Power of Music* (2001) and *Music Psychology in Education* (2005). Susan is editor of *The Oxford Handbook of Psychology of Music* (2009) and has many other scholarly articles to her name. She is past editor of *Psychology of Music*, *Psychology of Education Review* and *Learning Matters*. She has twice been Chair of the Education Section of the British Psychological Society, and is past treasurer of the British Educational Research Association, an auditor for the Quality Assurance Agency and an Academician of the Learned Societies for the Social Sciences.

Dr Helena Gaunt is the Assistant Principal (Research and Academic Development) at the Guildhall School of Music & Drama in London, and a National Teaching Fellow (2009). Her current research focuses on: one-to-one and small group tuition in conservatoires; orchestral musicians in the twenty-first century; and the role of improvisation (verbal and musical) in developing professional expertise. Alongside research, she is a professional oboist, and has been a member of the Britten Sinfonia. Helena is a co-editor of *Music Performance Research* and a member of the Editorial Board of the *British Journal of Music Education*. She chairs the Innovative Conservatoire (ICON) group and the Forum for Instrumental/Vocal Teaching for the International Society of Music Education (ISME).

CHAPTER 1
PURSUING A CAREER IN MUSIC

INTRODUCTION

This chapter sets out the contents of this book and how to use it. It also:
- gives an overview of how professional music is changing in the twenty-first century
- identifies the range of skills, knowledge and attitudes that may be important in being successful as a musician
- explores different education and training options available.

Music expresses that which cannot be said and on which it is impossible to be silent.

Victor Hugo

Pursuing a career in music is one of the most challenging and satisfying things you can do. Because music expresses something fundamental about our humanity, it is almost impossible to make it a profession without putting heart and soul into it. You probably would not be reading this book if you were not serious about becoming a professional musician.

Each person finds his or her own personal connection to music. There is a difference, though, between enjoying music as a hobby or being good at it, and making it your profession. However talented you are, however much family and friends around you may admire your ability, sustaining a successful career of any kind in music requires exceptional commitment and hard work. You need to be passionate about music, and sure that this is the only professional route you really care about. Equally you need to be realistic about your prospects. There are many exciting avenues to explore within the music industry. However, if you want to become a successful classical performer, for example, and do not have the self-discipline to practise for several hours each day, and have not already taken significant steps in this direction, you will almost inevitably end up disappointed. Ensuring that your plans match your musical abilities and professional skills is vital.

Case Study 1.1 sets out some examples of professional musicians in different fields talking about why they have chosen this as a career.

CASE STUDY 1.1: MUSICIANS TALKING ABOUT WHY THEY DO WHAT THEY DO

Professional drummer and teacher

'For most musicians we are kind of lucky, but we also haven't got a lot of choice. I wouldn't be that happy doing anything else, and I'd be a bit rubbish at anything else, because I'd be constantly distracted by wanting to do this.'

Recent conservatoire graduate

'For me, the most natural way of communicating is music. It's my strongest attribute and has always been part of my family. I couldn't live without music. I'd hate to have a normal job.'

Artistic director of Music in Prisons

'My first adventure into Her Majesty's Prisons…was a memorable one and stands out as one of the most powerful and important musical and personal moments in my life to date. A man who had served many years inside came to the performance with a piece of music he had written but never heard, hoping that we might be able to play it for him. We performed it, and to this day I can remember my feeling as we were playing it and his response to that. Instantly, this man had genuine respect and kudos among his peers – something I know to be important in life but what I quickly realised to be vital to anyone's survival in prison. He had been elevated, and looked proud and was very pleased to take the praise.

'We were told that the performance had a big impact, and the group was asked if anyone might like to come and teach music for two hours a week on a regular basis. I said yes…25 years on and although quite different, my passion is still there. Increased knowledge has only brought more of a desire to make what the man and the audience felt available to more people, as I believe music and the process of creating it makes a massive difference to people's lives.'[1]

Orchestral musician

'I think it is a lot to do with being able to express yourself, and being accepted, because I wasn't very good at talking…I was terrified of talking to people on the phone. I don't know why, I just was…So I think playing the bass…fitted me naturally…because of not being confident socially, wanting to be accepted into a group, wanting to express myself musically. And I do feel I am a completely different person when I am playing the bass. I feel so confident and so outward…I feel myself when I am playing the bass, and not many other times…The job that I have is constantly challenging. It never ever gets to the point where you think, I am bored with this now, I can do it, it's easy. Doing education work, you can never predict what you're going to be presented with when you get there.'

Jazz musician and music therapist

'I'm only happy when I'm involved in the making of music, the thinking about music, the defence of music, the promotion of music, and also using music as a force for absolute positive good…I can turn round at whatever age I shuffle off and say "I didn't waste my time". Everything that I do is about being a musician. It's a philosophy really. I believe in music first and foremost as the principal communicative art form; artists and dancers and actors and writers would probably disagree and that's fine, but it means everything I do I'm fully enthused and engaged by.'

HOW TO USE THIS BOOK

The aim of this book is to provide a useful resource to help you build a realistic professional vision, support your development, and understand what it takes to make a successful career. As well as providing lots of information, it offers practical tools and exercises. At the end of each chapter are some suggestions for further reading, which goes into more depth on a specific topic, together with a short description of the focus of each piece, to help you decide whether it will be relevant.

The chapters in the book divide into three main areas:

- exploring essential aspects of the learning process as a musician, such as motivating yourself, setting goals, making the most of tuition, practising and rehearsing, learning from your experience
- nurturing your creativity and expanding your experience and professional horizons
- mapping out the professional landscape and outlining vital parts of getting a career started.

Each chapter provides an overview of key issues, and illustrates these with case studies of experience and recent findings from research. It also points out common barriers to success. In addition, there are lots of practical exercises that offer ways to connect what you have read to your own experience and to support your development in meeting the challenges of becoming a professional musician.

This is not a book that needs to be read from cover to cover. It will probably be more effective if you dip into different chapters when they feel appropriate. Particularly when you are in search of ways to understand your experience, solve problems or identify next goals, this will be a good time to work on the practical exercises, perhaps with a mentor or friend.

EXERCISE 1.1: USING THIS BOOK

To begin with, drawing on the content of this book as a whole, Table 1.1 (see below) sets out ten fundamental principles that we consider essential in preparing for success as a professional musician in the twenty-first century.

Read through these and give yourself a rating from 1 to 5 for how much you think you are already engaging with each one: 1 = a great deal, 5 = not at all. This will immediately show you where you are strong and will indicate some things you should think about developing further.

Choose one area where you are strong and one where you are less sure. For each of these, look at the suggestions in the right-hand column of Table 1.1 to see which chapters will offer further insights and resources.

TABLE 1.1: TEN WAYS TO PREPARE FOR SUCCESS IN BECOMING A PROFESSIONAL MUSICIAN

Ways to prepare for success	Relevant chapters in this book
1. Take responsibility for your development and follow what you are passionate about Be active as a learner. Work on a personal development plan and keep it updated, seeking input from mentors, friends and other professional musicians. Clarify the core musical skills that are important for your success and develop these as much as you can. Be prepared for new learning opportunities, both formal and informal, and get as good as you can at learning in different contexts. Be honest about what you find difficult, but do not avoid these things. Seek out opportunities that will be both enjoyable and challenging. Ask for feedback from people who will be constructive. Be aware of how inconsistent and subjective assessment in music can be.	Chapters 1, 2, 3, 4, 7, 11

2. Understand what motivates you and why, what brings satisfaction and builds your confidence. Question and nurture your connection to your art and to your audiences Remember why you do what you do. Work out what motivates you as a musician and how your aspirations can best align with your musical and professional skills. What helps you to sustain your motivation? Which contexts are most appropriate for your work? Who are your audiences and how do you connect with them? Be informed about possibilities and explore new contexts.	Chapters 1, 2, 9

3. Develop collaborative and interpersonal skills
Collaboration is an enormous part of making music – whether you are a composer, an ensemble player, a soloist, or creating devised work, teaching, researching, programming or organising. In the past, we often used to think about expertise as something individual, but this is rapidly changing. Interpersonal skills (for example of listening, supporting, empathising, challenging) are vital both at a musical level and in all kinds of communication. Even if collaboration is only a small part of your specific musical practice, these skills will be vital in the process of finding and managing work.

Chapters 6, 7, 11

4. Find a circle of trusted teachers, mentors and friends to support your development. Get involved in groups and communities that interest you or might be useful. All musicians rely on extensive networks: performers, creative collaborators, employers, agents, programmers and critical friends (friends who can be trusted to give honest and constructive feedback and act as a sounding board). Seek out high-quality teachers, mentors and critical friends whom you trust and whose opinion you value. Having a strong set of relationships of this kind will speed up your learning, open doors and provide important knowledge and skills, and psychological support. A programme of study creates its own community. Use it to build peer support and to generate ideas and artistic collaborations. Other networks are also important, providing access to professional contexts, additional skills and personal support. Engaging proactively in such communities will also help to clarify your musical and professional identity.	Chapters 4, 7, 10, 11

5. Explore, take risks, extend beyond your existing boundaries
Aspects of your work that encourage you to take risks and explore new things will stimulate your creativity and innovative ideas, and extend your flexibility as a musician. The more we develop intense expertise in a narrow field, the more difficult we are likely to find it to translate that expertise and apply it in other contexts. This can be frustrating if, for example, you have focused exclusively on performing and find that you are not getting enough work in that field. Seek out opportunities to develop improvisation skills in any musical style. Use these to build your confidence in dealing with the unknown, and making decisions on the spur of the moment. Improvisation is also a great way of building collaborative skills.

Chapters 5, 6, 7, 9

6. Engage with technology   Chapters 1, 3, 5, 10

Technology is an increasingly central part of professional practice in music. Think about the ways in which it can be a useful part of your practice. You might use it to:

- record, create, compose, document, analyse and archive music
- communicate, share and sell music
- organise and promote events
- support and monitor your learning
- help you to reflect.

Be aware that your experience of technology may be greater than that of your teachers, and you may have to find other routes to develop your knowledge and skill.

7. Support your health and well-being   Chapters 8, 9

The twentieth century saw an unprecedented rise in instances of musicians suffering from physical injury, stress and burnout. Keeping healthy and avoiding such difficulties is vital. As a performer, treat yourself as an athlete, be aware that both mind and body are an integral part of what you do and rely on each other. Fine-tune their development together. Consider the particular stresses of your field of work, and take charge of your work–life balance.

8. Be organised and reliable, and manage yourself effectively   Chapters 8, 10, 11

Most musicians have a varied working life, and many find that they do not have particularly regular routines. This emphasises the importance of being able to manage your own time and organise your schedule, often with conflicting priorities. Pay attention to essential components of professionalism, such as:

- keeping an organised diary
- being on time
- planning ahead
- communicating any difficulties in good time
- being prepared
- making time to reflect
- building in 'down time'.

9. Treat your work as a business – manage the finances and   Chapter 10
issues of intellectual property, and develop entrepreneurial
skills

A study of conservatoire musicians has shown that financial issues are perceived as one of the strongest barriers to success.[2] Recognise the importance of finance. Learn to budget realistically and plan ahead. What are the costs of studying on different programmes and in different countries? Consider what grants, scholarships and bursaries are available. Be aware of taxation law and keep appropriate accounts. Be informed about issues relating to copyright, intellectual property and performing rights. Know what your work is worth and make sure, for example, that your own creative outputs are protected. Consider ways of earning money that will also develop relevant skills.

10. Develop resilience, expect ups and downs Everyone has difficulties, setbacks and moments of doubt. Successful musicians are those who are able to cope with these, learn from them and move on. It is very easy for musicians to be overly self-critical or to be overwhelmed by a sense of competition in which they will never succeed. One student said: 'people can go through real lows, because they just criticise themselves so much... and then everything about even their playing...just goes splat...I almost left in my second year, because I think I was being so self-critical it was ridiculous, and I wasn't getting any enjoyment out of it anymore...I have been so self-critical that I can't even take any encouragement, because I've really just thought that things were so rubbish.'[3] Focus on seeking out constructive feedback. Learn to deal realistically with negative experiences or destructive feedback and avoid getting obsessed with them. All serious musicians know that they will have to take some knocks. Work out how to engage with challenges in ways that help you to sustain a healthy level of self-esteem without avoiding important difficulties.	Chapters 2, 11

CONTEMPORARY LIFE AND THE MUSIC INDUSTRY

Essential for any musician is having an overview of the music industry and what being a professional musician may entail. The music industry is changing fast. People often talk about this as if it were a new phenomenon. Yet there is nothing particularly unusual about it – the pace of change in general in the world is growing at an astonishing rate, and music is no exception. In the nineteenth century the industrial output of the world trebled. In the twentieth century it grew by 35 times. In some countries, life expectancy has nearly doubled since 1900, transforming people's aspirations and their desire to get more out of life. In general, community structures are moving towards more 'mobile, globally interconnected, innovative, urbanized societies'.[4] The capacity for change is now one of the main drivers in societies, and also brings with it some of the most troubling dilemmas.

Similarly, the music industry has developed dramatically over the last centuries. One only has to think about the invention of vinyl, CDs and then downloads to realise the extent of this. And the pace of change is accelerating. In the twenty-first century the ability to share music informally or formally via the internet has sparked a quantum shift in the ways that musicians can find and interact with audiences. Tools such as Myspace and YouTube are being used by artists to promote and sell their tracks, blog and stream about gigs, and upload sound and video clips to attract and interact with fans. Cultural diversity, cross-arts collaborations, and widening opportunities to participate creatively in music are transforming the landscape. Live performance continues to attract audiences, but the contexts of live performance are more varied. As one director of a major arts venue has suggested about contemporary performance, 'You feel that all bets are off, and no rules apply'.[5]

Background Briefing 1.1 sets out some important facts about the contemporary music industry. These reinforce the wealth of opportunities there can be for musicians, and just how much live performance there is in the UK, for example, and its growing economic contribution to the country.

BACKGROUND BRIEFING 1.1: FACTS AND FIGURES IN THE CONTEMPORARY MUSIC INDUSTRY

In the UK, the Performing Right Society 2010 *Economic Insight* report valued the UK music industry at £3.9 billion in 2009, a 5 per cent increase on the 2008 figure. 2009 also saw a 9.4 per cent increase in the monetary value of live music performance on the previous year.

The same report also showed that UK recorded music revenues (as measured by the British Recorded Music Industry retail value of the recorded music industry) stabilised in 2009 (0 per cent growth) after years of decline. The 2008 data showed a 6 per cent fall in the value of recorded music for that year (compared with a 13 per cent growth in the value of live music).[6]

Engagement with music online has exploded, particularly since the advent of broadband internet at the very beginning of the twenty-first century. YouTube, founded in 2005, has promoted free publication of all kinds of music production. For example, a search of 'remix' delivered about 4,720,000 results in early 2011.

What does this all amount to for a career in music? First of all this is a time of extraordinary possibilities for engaging with music. Music and the arts are desperately needed in the contemporary world, economically, through their focus on creativity and innovation, and in their contribution to addressing some of the world's biggest human challenges. For example, in his book *Group Genius: The creative power of collaboration*, Keith Sawyer draws attention to the creative skills and practices of improvising musicians and actors, and how it is these kinds of skills that underpin successful innovation in any domain.[7]

The arts are an essential part of how we are able to make sense of our world as human beings. In 2008, in the UK, an influential report on excellence in the arts for the Department for Culture, Media and Sport (DCMS) suggested:

> *Just as the new society we live in has immense potential for the creation of art, so art has never before been so needed to understand the deep complexities of Britain today.*[8]

This report also emphasised the importance of innovation and risk-taking in the arts, arguing that these are integral to making art relevant in our diverse and complex modern societies.[8] Clearly there are high expectations of, and potential for, musicians.

EXERCISE 1.2: DEFINING EXCELLENCE IN DIFFERENT KINDS OF PROFESSIONAL WORK

The DCMS report defined excellence in culture as: 'when an experience affects and changes an individual. An excellent cultural experience goes to the root of living.'[8] How good a definition is this in your opinion? How do you see excellence realised in musicians' work, for example through:

- solo artists or ensemble musicians
- creative collaborators across the arts
- musicians working through technology and the internet
- music teachers and leaders in community contexts?

What are the similarities and differences between these contexts?

At the same time, the music industry can feel quite an unstable place, with lots of new and unproven areas of practice emerging, while long-established traditions lose ground and influence. There is no doubt that some fields of work are shrinking. The recording industry is a classic example. Downloads and digital file-sharing mean that sales of CDs and DVDs are diminishing, and whereas live tours were generally used to promote an album, they are more likely now to be used to promote a range of other merchandise.

At the same time, the internet is enabling an increase in sales of music that is less mainstream. The pattern used to be that the bulk of sales came from a few most popular items. Now, many more sales come from a larger number of less popular CDs and DVDs, each of which finds its own smaller market. This means that there is considerably more scope for work with a niche market, and less need for megastars, whose recordings dominate the sales. It is not surprising then that novel business ideas and ground-breaking practices are much in evidence. Some smaller-scale examples are given in Background Briefing 1.2.

BACKGROUND BRIEFING 1.2: INNOVATIVE INITIATIVES IN THE MUSIC INDUSTRY

1. Across the world, populations are ageing and there is growing recognition of the need to focus on how we can improve quality of life and healthy ageing in older people. Research is demonstrating that participating in music can have significant impact on the well-being of older people. What comes with this is urgent need for more musicians with the leadership skills to facilitate this kind of work, whether it be choirs, bands, ukulele orchestras, individual lessons or creative composition.[10]

2. Plushmusic.tv is a platform for live classical, jazz and world music. It enables users to watch and buy quality high-definition videos and audio, to directly support international artists, and to discover a world of music. As well as viewing performances, users can explore masterclasses that provide insights into musical processes and the development of artistry, and can join the website's network.[11]

3. As video games become more advanced, there is an increasing demand for high-quality video game music. This presents another valuable opportunity for composers and music producers of all kinds, and offers the potential to experiment with new techniques and creative contexts.

EXERCISE 1.3: NAVIGATING A LIFE IN THE CHANGING MUSIC PROFESSION

The momentum of change can feel profoundly unsettling for musicians.

Consider the following questions:

- How is it possible to keep pace with change, to keep a sense of balance between long-established traditions and practices, fundamental musical values and innovation?
- What skills do contemporary musicians need compared with 100, 50, 20 or even 10 years ago?
- What kind of professional structures are needed to enable musicians to function effectively in society?
- Will some musical genres and practices die out as others develop and grow?

We know that many musicians find that their work affects them at a profoundly personal level, as well as at a professional level. One example, a statement from the head of an education team for an opera festival and studio for developing new work, is given below:

> *I think art and creativity have a very important role because they touch your inside, your identity, your emotions and the way you look at things…I love the freedom that art brings. It allows you to cross [unwritten] boundaries or barriers that are blocking your view or keeping you from 'playing'…At the centre of it all is 'relationship'. Your relationship with yourself, your relationship with others and the way you connect the two.[1]*

The aim of this exercise is to get you to consider: why are you a musician? What is it about music that is essential to you? These may seem like simple questions. It is worth taking some time, however, to explore your answers. How you respond is likely to have a major influence on your aspirations and on how you go about achieving your goals.

Table 1.2 suggests a range of things that might come to mind when you think about why you are a musician. Rank these 12 statements from 1–12, starting with the one that is most important to you. There are no right answers, and you may want to add more. Before you do this exercise, you may want to think of some particular things that have happened, or people you have come into contact with who have been especially significant. What was important about these experiences? If possible, talk with a friend who is also passionate about music, and share your responses. You may well find that you have different ideas. You may also notice that some of the suggestions relate to music itself (intrinsic aspects of the work) and some relate to external factors, such as other people's opinions (extrinsic aspects). Note that motivation that is intrinsic is likely to sustain you longer, and produce more satisfying results in the long term, than extrinsic motivation – although this can be useful in the short term. For more discussion of motivation, see Chapter 2.

The chances are also that your thoughts may change over time, so this is an exercise to try several times over a period of years. What we do know is that passion is vital to the process of acquiring the skills you need to become successful. Understanding what drives you will help to sustain the hard work and perseverance required, particularly when things seem tediously repetitive or you experience setbacks. The clearer you are about what makes you tick as a musician, the easier it is likely to be to achieve your goals and find appropriate contexts in which to work. You may want to look again at the examples of musicians who work in quite different areas of music and the passion behind their motivation, shown in Case Study 1.1 above.

TABLE 1.2: UNDERSTANDING WHAT MOTIVATES YOU

Why do you want to work in music?	Your ranking (1–12, where 1 is the most important to you)
Music is a way of expressing myself that doesn't rely on words.	
I love working with other musicians.	
I enjoy the physical sensations of playing.	
Music gives me a way to be creative.	
Music is a way to communicate with other people.	
Music is a way of making a difference to other people, of enabling other people's voices to be heard and valued.	
People admire what I do as a musician.	
Members of my family always wanted me to be a musician.	

Through music I can begin to make sense of the world.

Being a musician is glamorous and I like the lifestyle.

Music is a good way of making money.

I love the buzz of performing.

DEVELOPING SKILLS AS A MUSICIAN – DEPTH AND BREADTH

One thing we know for sure is that most musicians now do things professionally that they had not expected to do. Similarly, student musicians are likely to apply their skills and experience in ways that their teachers have not even thought of.

It is not surprising then that research shows that being a music student and the transition to professional life demand the development of a broad array of skills and experiences. Refined musical skills are, of course, essential. These need, however, to be complemented by other vital qualities, such as imagination, personal confidence, versatility, interpersonal skills, and the ability to recognise opportunities and generate work from them. Most importantly, musicians need to develop resilience to manage uncertainty and fast-moving opportunities; they need to become lifelong learners. Background Briefing 1.3 sets out further detail from two recent research studies.

In this context, it is noticeable that many universities and conservatoires are taking a more holistic view of musicians' skills, and aim to equip students with a range of generic skills as well as discipline-specific expertise. In undergraduate performance programmes, for example, health and well-being, music administration, small business management and entrepreneurialism often feature.

BACKGROUND BRIEFING 1.3: RESEARCH DEMONSTRATING THE IMPORTANCE OF LIFELONG LEARNING AND 'RESILIENCE' FOR MUSICIANS

A biographical study of 32 musicians from varied backgrounds across the world explored key incidents and important aspects of their artistic and professional development.[12] Some of the musicians were performers, some were teachers or music educators, and some were following a portfolio career.

Key findings from this study included the following:

- Changes in the socio-cultural landscape are immediately changing the nature of the workplace for musicians.

- Flexible portfolio careers are an increasingly common experience. They require the sophisticated application of a wide range of musical and generic/transferable skills, and a more entrepreneurial attitude towards work.

- In responding creatively to more diverse cultural and professional contexts, musicians are finding themselves taking on a greater variety of roles.

- Working collaboratively, and with people from other disciplines in cross-arts, cross-cultural and cross-sector contexts, is an increasingly central part of professional life.

Investigating Musical Performance: Comparative studies in advanced musical learning was an ESRC-funded research project that explored how professional and student musicians perceive their skills and how they acquire them. Some 244 undergraduate and portfolio career musicians (from classical, popular, jazz and Scottish traditional genres) took part in the survey and interview study. In looking at what was required to make a successful transition from a student to a professional musician, the model of a 'resilient' musician emerged[13] (see Figure 1.1).

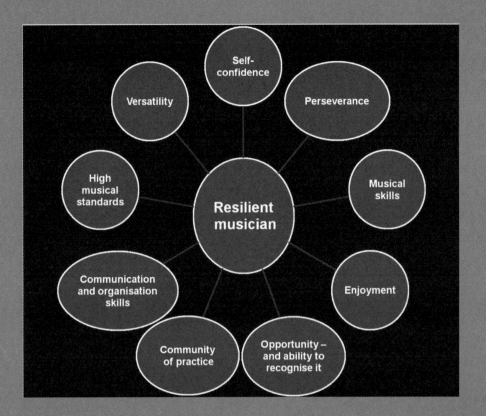

Figure 1.1
The resilient musician

EDUCATION AND TRAINING OPTIONS

There are now unprecedented opportunities to study music as a way of preparing to be a professional musician. Formal programmes focus on a range of interests, including:

- musical performance, composition, improvisation, recording, devised performance
- musicology, music theory and analysis, ethnomusicology and organology
- music technology and acoustics
- aesthetics and criticism
- music psychology

- teaching and pedagogy, music therapy (postgraduate only) and music in the community.

In the UK, for example, there were 1,226 undergraduate courses that included music on offer through the Universities and Colleges Admissions Service for 2011/12. Many of these combined music with another subject, such as a language or cultural studies. A total of 160 courses offered Music Performance as a single subject; 252 courses focused on Music Technology; and nine focused on Music Education.[14]

EXERCISE 1.4: CHOOSING A PROGRAMME OF STUDY

When choosing a programme of study, it is essential to think about the types of experience, standards and qualifications it offers and how these fit with your particular career ambitions. In addition, it is important to consider how breadth and depth of skills are balanced in a programme, and how this is likely to meet your needs and possible professional directions. To begin with, consider the following questions:

- What is the purpose of the programme and what musical, collaborative, imaginative, entrepreneurial and organisational skills will you develop through it?
- How much does the programme focus on a single area of excellence or on several areas in order to create multi-skilled musicians?
- How may the programme enable you to forge an individual path through it? What areas of choice will you have?
- Will you be able to combine the intense hours of research or personal practice needed to achieve professional standards along with exploring new territories?
- What connections are there between the programme and the creative and cultural industries, through teaching staff, work placements and professional mentoring?

Conservatoires, which traditionally have offered the most obviously vocationally focused programmes in classical music, are also changing. Nearly all now offer jazz at undergraduate and postgraduate level, and three offer undergraduate courses in popular music. Other pathways that have become established include traditional (folk) music, music theatre, arts management, leadership in artistic innovation and community outreach, digital arts in performance, and music education with qualified teacher status.

In addition, the growing body of international students across most degree programmes in music is increasing possibilities for cross-fertilisation between musical genres, and people's experience of what it is to be a musician.

As well as thinking about the quality of the institution and the teaching staff as a whole, it is important to consider how teaching and learning are structured within a programme. Traditionally, different genres of music have been taught in quite different ways. Rock musicians have often developed in informal contexts and through self-teaching and playing in bands. Western classical musicians have almost always had individual and/or small group lessons over many years. Indian classical musicians tend to have spent extended periods of time with a guru teacher, immersed in their whole lifestyle. Musicians who are academics may have mixed some instrumental learning with lectures and seminar teaching. These different approaches can have a profound impact on how you learn. One-to-one tuition, for example, enables an intense focus on the development of specific instrumental skills and understanding of repertoire. It can be harder, though, to develop your autonomy as a learner in this context, or to explore different outlets for your individual artistic and professional voice.[15]

Increasingly, modes of teaching and learning traditionally associated with particular musical genres are cross-fertilising. One-to-one tuition may feature in popular music programmes. Equally, self-directed and peer learning may feature in Western classical performance programmes. In addition, some programmes are capitalising on the potential of new technologies, for example enabling you to practise aural skills at your own pace using software such as Aurelia or EarMaster, or following up face-to-face contact with an interactive online forum or online feedback. Online portfolios allow you to accumulate pieces of work in a variety of formats, including audio and video recordings, and in many cases to publish selected parts to external audiences in order to support your emerging professional career.

Similarly, music programmes use diverse assessment methods, and it is important to consider these when looking at what is on offer. In some cases, formal assessments are designed to focus on judging performance or achievement level at the end of a period of study ('assessment *of* learning'). In other cases, however, assessment is increasingly being designed to assist the learning process: 'assessment *for* learning'. In these cases, assessment is likely to take place in several stages, rather than simply making a final, summative judgement, and will include providing rich feedback to inform future learning, and will often include peer as well as tutor or 'expert' feedback. In some cases, assessment is designed so that in itself it offers an important learning process: 'assessment *as* learning'. It is important to note that types of assessment and level of feedback used have a profound impact on learning, and give a clear idea of exactly what is valued within it. Looking at these can therefore be an excellent way of informing your choice between otherwise apparently similar programmes.

Preparation 1.1 sets out some further questions to think about in the process of choosing a programme of study.

PREPARATION 1.1: QUESTIONS TO ASK YOURSELF IN CHOOSING A PROGRAMME OF STUDY

- What are your main interests in music? Which particular skills are important for these interests? What are your additional areas of interest?
- What are your existing musical skills? How do these relate to the interests you want to pursue? Where are your existing areas of strength and weakness?
- What other skills do you want to develop?
- Where may particular programmes lead professionally? What doors can they open? How widely recognised is the qualification they bring within the creative and cultural industries?
- Who are the teachers on the programme and how well do their expertise and experience match your needs?
- How do the ways in which you have developed skills in the past compare with the teaching and learning modes on offer in programmes which interest you? What approaches to teaching and learning will be most useful to you? Be prepared to look at approaches which might take you out of your comfort zone as well as at those which are familiar.
- How long do you want to study for? What length of study is normally required to develop the particular skills you are focusing on?
- What length of study is realistic for you financially, and what sources of funding do you have to support your study? Will it work better for you to study full-time or part-time?
- Who can help you to review different programmes or who can advise you about which might best suit you?

SUCCESS FROM THE START – ADOPTING A PROFESSIONAL APPROACH

Music is a competitive industry, full of opportunities for those who can harness them. We used to think that talent was an innate quality, something people were either born with or not. Research now shows that much more in fact depends on the amount of time put into learning a craft and building professional skills (see also Chapter 2).

It is relatively rare for musicians to move from being students to professionals overnight. Transition is usually gradual. It is vital, therefore, to adopt a professional approach from the start. Lots of musicians begin to build professional networks and earn a living through music while studying. First impressions are often lasting impressions. Teachers may become colleagues or may be in a position to offer work. Peers become professional colleagues. It can be very difficult to change a reputation for being unprofessional.

Looking after the business side of professional work is also important. Attending to the procedures for taxation and subcontracting work, for example, avoids sudden financial problems. Similarly, protecting intellectual property and understanding the basic opportunities and constraints of copyright and performing rights will help to maximise income and ensure that unpleasant legal problems do not arise. Finally, the more professional, curious and open-minded people are in their approach as students, the more they benefit from studying, and from the opportunities that appear. This in turn helps to keep them motivated.

CHAPTER SUMMARY: PURSUING A CAREER IN MUSIC

It is not sufficient to be a great musician to pursue a career in music – you need to be willing to work hard and to grasp opportunities.

You need to understand how to learn, develop your creativity, and motivate yourself.

You need to be able to learn from the experiences that you have, so that you improve and do not endlessly repeat mistakes.

You need to understand the music industry and to be able to find – or create – your niche in it.

Above all, you need to love – and be passionately committed to – music.

FURTHER READING

Kenyon, N. (forthcoming 2012) 'Performance Now'. In C. Lawson and R. Stowell (eds), *The Cambridge History of Musical Performance*. Cambridge: Cambridge University Press. This chapter provides a compelling account of just how diverse performance is now becoming in terms of venues, content, audiences and what counts as performance at all. It includes lots of examples.

Sawyer, K. (2007) *Group Genius: The creative power of collaboration*. New York: Basic Books. Sawyer draws on his understanding of how both jazz musicians and improvising theatre groups work together, and demonstrates how collaboration and the ability to improvise lie at the heart of success in business and in enabling innovation of different kinds. The book gives a powerful indication of the value of these aspects of musicians' skills beyond the field of the arts.

Smilde, R. (2006) *Lifelong Learners in Music: 32 portraits of musicians as lifelong learners*. Groningen: Hanzehogeschool Groningen. Online. http://tinyurl.com/cny79zk (accessed 3 February 2011). These portraits are of musicians of different ages, working in quite different fields. Each portrait traces an individual's journey of development and highlights key influences or turning points in their career. Several have changed direction from their original path.

NOTES

1. Renshaw, P. (2010) *Engaged Passions: Searches for quality in community contexts*. Delft: Eburon Academic Publishers, 154.

2. Creech, A., Gaunt, H. and Hallam, S. (2009) 'Plans and Aspirations of Young Musicians: An investigation into aspirations and self perceptions in the conservatoire'. Paper presented at the conference The Reflective Conservatoire: Building Connections, Guildhall School of Music & Drama, London, March.

3. Gaunt, H. (2010) 'One-to-one Tuition in a Conservatoire: The perceptions of instrumental and vocal students'. *Psychology of Music*, 38(2), 178–208.

4. Leadbeater, C. (2001) *Living on Thin Air: The New Economy*. London: Penguin, 233–4.

5. Kenyon, N. (2012) 'Performance Now' in C. Lawson and R. Stowell (eds), *The Cambridge History of Musical Performance*. Cambridge: Cambridge University Press.

6. Performing Right Society (2010) *Economic Insight*, 20. Online. www.prsformusic.com/economics (accessed 24 January 2011).

7. Sawyer, K. (2007) *Group Genius: The creative power of collaboration*. New York: Basic Books.

8. McMaster, B. (2008) *Supporting Excellence in the Arts: From measurement to judgement*. Report commissioned by the Department for Culture, Media and Sport, 5. Online. www.culture.gov.uk/images/publications/supportingexcellenceinthearts.pdf (accessed 1 January 2011).

9. Sandbrook, B. (2010) Presentation for 'Becoming a 21st Century Musician', a multi-stakeholder roundtable discussion, hosted by Awards for Young Musicians, Musicians Benevolent Fund and Youth Music, London, 7 September.

10. Hallam, S., Creech, A., Gaunt, H., Pincas, A., Varvarigou, M. and McQueen, H. (2011) 'Promoting social engagement and well being in older people through community supported participation in musical activities'. Paper presented for a symposium on 'Ageing and the Arts

and Humanities – A New Research Programme', held at the VII European International Congress Healthy and Active Ageing for All Europeans (International Association for Gerontology and Geriatrics), Bologna, Italy, 14–17 April.

11. Plushmusic.tv. Online. www.plushmusic.tv (accessed 23 December 2010).

12. Smilde, R. (2009) *Musicians as Lifelong Learners: Discovery through biography*. Delft: Eburon Academic Publishers.

13. Creech, A., Papageorgi, I., Duffy, C., Morton, F., Haddon, E., and Potter, J. (2007) 'From Undergraduate to Professional Musician: Supporting critical transitions'. Paper presented at the Society for Research into Higher Education, Brighton, UK.

14. Universities and Colleges Admissions Service. Online. www.ucas.com (accessed 7 January 2011).

15. Creech, A., Papageorgi, I., Duffy, C., Morton, F., Haddon, E., Potter, J., de Bezenac, C., Whyton, T., Himonides, E. and Welch, G. (2008) 'From music student to professional: The process of transition'. *British Journal of Music Education*, 25(3): 315–31.

CHAPTER 2
LEARNING, SETTING GOALS AND MOTIVATING YOURSELF

INTRODUCTION

This chapter sets out the key issues related to learning, with a particular stress on self-motivation.

It considers:

- the processes of learning and how they can be optimised
- the importance of developing a strong musical identity and future possible selves in sustaining motivation
- how success and failure are explained
- the importance of setting goals in the short, medium and long term as a means of enhancing motivation, self-discipline and determination.

LEARNING

The music profession is diverse. It includes musicians who:

- make music in a wide range of different genres
- make music in different combinations (alone, in small groups or in large groups)
- have full-time employment in music, a portfolio career or work full-time in another occupation
- teach
- compose, arrange music and contribute in various ways to its technological production (for example sound engineers, producers)
- write about, analyse and critique music.

To develop high levels of expertise in any of these areas requires time to be invested in acquiring knowledge about music and in developing a range of skills which enable that knowledge to be used.

Learning is a natural process for human beings. We learn all the time. Frequently we learn without making a conscious effort to do so. For instance, the sound of a particular piece of music can be learnt through repeatedly hearing it while actively focusing on completing other tasks. On other occasions we make a deliberate effort to learn, for instance when we learn to play a new piece of music from notation, acquire a new element of technique, or listen intently to music with a view to understanding its composition.

Developing familiarity with music through listening in everyday life, over time, leads to the acquisition of sophisticated listening skills. Those with no formal musical training can recognise melodies as well as trained musicians; in some cases, the skills of non-musicians are greater than those who have received professional training. When young people were asked to memorise the same Japanese pop song, by ear, over four ten-minute practice sessions and reproduce it after each session, those without formal musical training, particularly those who performed regularly at karaoke sessions, memorised the song better than those who had received formal training. The musicians reported particular difficulties in learning the song without notation to support the process.[1]

BACKGROUND BRIEFING 2.1: THE BRAIN AND LEARNING

Information processing in the brain is undertaken largely through interactions between its 100 billion neurons, each of which has the processing capacity of a small computer. Each neuron has approximately 1,000 connections with other neurons through axons and dendrites. When we learn, there are changes in the growth of each neuron's axons and dendrites and the number of synapses connecting neurons. When an event is important enough or is repeated sufficiently often, synapses and neurons fire repeatedly, leading to changes in the strength of existing connections and the coating of the axon of each neuron (myelinisation), thereby enhancing efficiency. Pruning also occurs, where the number of synaptic connections is reduced. As these processes occur over time in response to our activities, the brain self-organises.

These processes have been demonstrated in much research concerned with the development of musical expertise, showing that the longer the engagement with musical learning, the greater the neurological changes. These changes are also specific to the particular musical learning undertaken and are reflected in the different brain substrates of string players, drummers, conductors, and so on. Each individual has a unique brain substrate, which reflects their prior learning. These permanent changes in the brain take considerable time to develop. Those who are involved in music for the longest time exhibit the greatest levels of change.

When we learn something, we change. We may know something that we didn't know before, be able to do something that we couldn't do before, understand something that had previously been incomprehensible, or have experienced a new emotion or a new activity. Each of these learning experiences involves change in the learner and brings about changes in the brain. To bring about the permanent and substantial change in brain functioning that underpins the development of musical and other types of expertise takes considerable time (see Background Briefing 2.1).

The human brain has a relatively small real-time processing capacity, and can only attend to a limited amount of information at any one time. As we learn, musical knowledge and skills become automated, which means that they can be carried out easily without conscious thought – in much the same way that we walk and talk. As fewer processing resources are required in retrieving knowledge and using skills in carrying out tasks (e.g. reading music, physically making the sounds) when skills are automated, more resources are available to attend to higher-level activities, for instance musical interpretation or co-ordinating performance with colleagues. High levels of automaticity can only be acquired through extended engagement with a particular activity.

One feature of the operation of high levels of automaticity is that while the individual is able to reflect on the quality of the overall performance, he or she may find it very difficult to describe precisely how it was achieved. A player may be able to produce a sound with a 'floating' quality, but even if they can give some indication of the general technique they adopted (e.g. a light bow stroke with a string instrument), they will almost certainly not be able to describe the exact physical movements that produced it. It is in the nature of skill development that, as performance becomes more and more skilful, the way it was produced becomes less and less open to conscious reflection. Musicians come to play, improvise and carry out many of the activities of composition in much the same way that they make physical movements or use language – with little conscious effort. This means that they can focus on the overall outcome that they are hoping to achieve.

To become a successful musician requires the acquisition of a substantial body of knowledge and a wide range of skills. The acquisition of knowledge and skills is inextricably linked. For instance, in learning to read music, connections have to be made between knowledge of the position of the notes on the stave, their sound and how to produce that sound. Table 2.1 sets out the kinds of skills that are needed to become an expert musician. These include aural, cognitive, technical, musicianship, performance, creative, evaluative and self-regulatory skills. The last two of these are particularly important, as learning is more effective when the learner is familiar with, and can utilise, a range of evaluative and self-regulatory strategies. Being able to assess the nature of a particular task, being aware of personal strengths and weaknesses, having a range of learning strategies, being familiar with the nature of the required outcomes and being able to monitor progress towards the goal are all important in learning.[2,3] Developing such 'meta-cognitive' skills is crucial in acquiring high levels of expertise. In music, those attaining the highest levels have well-developed meta-cognitive and self-monitoring skills. They are better able to detect errors and the status of their own learning. They know why they make errors, and are able to identify solutions and monitor progress. They can judge the difficulty of what it is they have to learn, select appropriate strategies for tackling the difficulty, and monitor their progress. They are also opportunistic in making use of whatever sources of support are available. Such skills can be learnt and are crucial for becoming a successful musician.[2,3]

TABLE 2.1: MUSICAL SKILLS

Aural skills support the development of:
- rhythmic accuracy and a sense of pulse
- good intonation
- the facility to know how music will sound without having to play it
- playing by ear
- improvisational skills.

Cognitive skills support the development of:
- reading music
- transposition
- understanding keys
- understanding harmony
- understanding the structure of the music
- the memorisation of music
- composing
- understanding different musical styles and their cultural and historic contexts.

Technical skills support the development of:
- instrument-specific skills
- technical agility
- articulation
- expressive tone quality.

Musicianship skills support the development of:
- expressive playing
- sound projection
- control
- conveying musical meaning.

Performance skills support the development of:
- communication with an audience
- communication with other performers
- being able to co-ordinate a group
- presentation to an audience.

Creative skills support the development of:
- interpretation
- improvisation
- composition.

Evaluative skills support the development of:
- listening with understanding
- being able to describe and discuss music
- being able to make comparisons between different types of music and performances
- being able to critically assess personal performance, improvisation and composition
- the skills for monitoring progress.

Self-regulatory skills support the development of:
- managing the process of learning
- managing practice
- enhancing concentration
- enhancing motivation.

EXERCISE 2.1: IDENTIFYING STRENGTHS AND WEAKNESSES

What are your musical aspirations? Which musical skills do you need to meet your aspirations? Make a list of the skills that you already have and those you would like to acquire. You may like to use the skills listed in Table 2.1 to help you.

What are your main strengths and weaknesses as a musician? What strategies have you got for building on your strengths and addressing your weaknesses? Draw up a plan for implementing these strategies.

ACQUIRING KNOWLEDGE AND SKILLS

There are generally acknowledged to be two kinds of knowledge: procedural (skills) and declarative (factual).

There are three main phases in the acquisition of both types of knowledge (see Table 2.2):

- In the first stage of the development of procedural knowledge (skills), learning is largely under cognitive, conscious control. The learner has to understand what is required to undertake the task and carries it out while consciously providing self-instruction, for instance consciously thinking about which fingering pattern is needed to make a particular sound.
- In the associative stage, the learner begins to put together a sequence of responses, which become more fluent over time. Errors are detected and eliminated. Feedback from the sounds produced and a teacher play a particularly important role here in enhancing the quality of what is learnt.
- Finally, after much practice, automisation develops and the skills can be used fluently and quickly.[4]

TABLE 2.2: STAGES OF PROCEDURAL AND DECLARATIVE SKILL ACQUISITION

Procedural knowledge (skills)	Declarative knowledge (factual)
Cognitive-verbal-motor stage	Acclimation
Associative stage	Competence
Autonomous stage	Proficiency/expertise

In acquiring a new body of factual knowledge, there is initially development of an understanding of the scope of the field of study, where the learner is introduced to specific facts, rules, terminology or conventions, definitions, simple concepts and principles. Simple links between the component parts of the knowledge domain are made. This is called the 'acclimation phase'. In the 'competence phase', more complex interrelationships are established as the knowledge base is expanded and refined, so that it can be used to solve problems. Finally, the knowledge domain is secure, and speed and accuracy in retrieving information – and in using it – improve.[5] Although what is learnt in acquiring factual skills is very different from skill knowledge, the processes of acquisition are very similar. Both require time and effort.

In music, the acquisition of procedural and declarative knowledge occurs simultaneously, with new knowledge and skills constantly being added to the repertoire. As mastery of more advanced skills or complex knowledge is acquired, earlier learning is continuously practised and greater automaticity is achieved in the skills that were learnt first. As one set of skills or area of knowledge is becoming increasingly automated, others will be at the earlier stages. The development of the knowledge base and the skills needed to work with that knowledge are inextricably intertwined. For instance, knowledge of notation and its use in reading music develops alongside playing skills. Knowledge, whether factual or skill based, is stored in long-term memory and can be retained over many years. Motor skills are particularly resistant to forgetting.

THE DEVELOPMENT OF EXPERTISE

The way that learners increase their knowledge and skills in a field of study has been conceptualised as the development of expertise. The acquisition of musical expertise takes time and begins in the womb as the foetus begins to hear sounds in the environment (the human auditory system is functional 3–4 months before birth). The process of musical enculturation begins from that point, as the child comes to know the tonal system of the culture within which they are growing up. Individuals may develop an understanding of, and become proficient in, two musical systems in the same way that they can become bilingual. This is known as being 'bi-musical'. To achieve this, they have to commit the time necessary for enculturation into two systems to take place.

The extent to which anyone develops musical expertise depends on the opportunities that are available to them for listening to different kinds of music, learning to play an instrument, sing, improvise, compose, and so on. The more time that is spent engaging with musical activities, the greater the level of expertise attained.[6,7] The time need not be totally spent in solitary, individual practice, although this is likely to constitute a substantial proportion of it for many musical genres. Participating in a wide range of musical activities can make a major contribution to the acquisition of the musical skills outlined in Table 2.1 (see also Chapters 3, 5 and 6). There are also differences in the time required to develop musical expertise, depending on the particular instruments or activity, the difficulty and extent of the repertoire to be learnt and the demands of the various strands of the music profession. For instance, there is a limited repertoire for some instruments, for example the tuba or double bass in contrast to the piano or violin. Learning to perform a major concerto from memory will take longer than learning to play a short folk tune or popular song. Composing a symphony will take longer, and will present a more complex challenge, than creating an advertising jingle.

The expertise that we develop is specific to a particular field of knowledge, although some skills may transfer to other fields. However, even within fields this may not be easy. A highly skilled musician may experience considerable difficulty when required to play in another genre. For instance, Sudnow,[8] an adult, professional, classically trained musician, documented how difficult, frustrating and time consuming it was to acquire expertise in jazz improvisation (see also Chapter 5).

Thinking of learning as the development of expertise challenges the notion that high-level achievement depends on inherited ability. Instead, it suggests that the length of time spent learning is a better predictor of how skilled we become. Developing very high levels of expertise in any field of study takes a great deal of time. For instance, in classical music, to achieve levels that will lead to international standing in playing an instrument, the individual usually begins to play at a very early age, with increasing amounts of practice being undertaken. This can be as much as 50 hours a week by adolescence.[9] To sustain this high level of commitment requires considerable motivation. Even when skills have been acquired, time is still required to maintain them.

Those with high levels of musical expertise are able to carry out musical tasks with greater ease and speed than those who have not devoted time to music. However, having high levels of expertise can be limiting in some ways. Experts can become rigid in their thoughts and practices (see Key Point Summary 2.1). Even those whose expertise is creative in nature can become fixed in their approach or style, although, overall, the quality of their work may improve over time. There are exceptions to this, where exposure to a different genre or other new ideas can generate a new approach, but this is not common. Once an accepted and successful way of performing, improvising or composing is found, and is rewarded by public acclaim, it tends to be sustained throughout an individual's career. In the twenty-first century this may not be sufficient. Musicians will need to be more creative and versatile, and will need to adapt to the demands of the market.

KEY POINT SUMMARY 2.1: CHARACTERISTICS AND LIMITATIONS OF EXPERTS[10,11]

Characteristics

Experts:

- have high levels of automaticity in relation to knowledge and skills in their field
- have an extensive body of knowledge
- can complete tasks quicker than novices
- have well-developed self-monitoring and meta-cognitive skills
- can focus attention on higher-level skills, e.g. interpretation, communication, because lower-level skills have become automated
- have skills that are relatively resistant to disruption, because of their high level of automatisation
- can perceive large, meaningful patterns in their field (e.g. recognise familiar patterns, identify difficult sections)
- organise available information in their field into larger units, which makes processing faster and easier (read groups of notes rather than single notes, copy sequences of sounds rather than individual notes)
- have superior memory in their field (for sounds, notation)
- see and represent problems in their field at a deeper, principled level, taking longer to understand them (e.g. when composing, are able to generate a representation of the outcome they wish to attain and predict where difficulties will arise and how to solve them).

Limitations

Experts:

- may become entrenched in their thinking and may be unable to recognise, accept or adapt to new ways of thinking or working
- may be inflexible
- can be overconfident
- may overlook important details, as they always focus on the bigger picture
- have difficulty taking the role of the novice, which can create problems when they are trying to explain to others.

EXERCISE 2.2: ASSESSING WHAT HAS HELPED DEVELOP YOUR MUSICAL SKILLS

Take some time to think about the activities which contributed to the musical expertise that you have already acquired. What was most important in assisting you in acquiring your skills? Was it individual practice or work with others in an ensemble? Which motivated you? Are there other activities that you could engage with, which would enhance your skills? How can you access these?

MOTIVATION

To develop and maintain the high level of expertise that is crucial for pursuing a career in music requires motivation. Musicians need to be able to understand and manage their own motivation. The key elements of motivation, as they relate to music, fall into four main groups:

- music acting to satisfy personal needs
- developing and maintaining a positive musical identity
- acquiring appropriate approaches to learning music
- having a supportive environment (see Key Point Summary 2.2).

Musicians derive considerable personal fulfilment from making music, in addition to the social rewards that it offers. They also have other life motivations that may influence their career choices and trajectories, for instance finding a partner, having a family. The balance between the different elements of motivation as set out in Key Point Summary 2.2 and other life plans inevitably influence career trajectories, which may also change over time. In addition, not all musical activities are intrinsically motivating; for instance, some musicians do not enjoy solitary practice. This issue will be explored in Chapter 3. There may also be points in a musician's career where there are few tangible rewards and she or he may feel like giving up. Developing strategies for self-motivation is important when this occurs.

KEY POINT SUMMARY 2.2: KEY MOTIVATIONAL THEMES IN MUSIC

Music acting to satisfy personal needs, including:

- the satisfaction derived from music itself (a love of music), which seems to meet emotional and pleasure-seeking needs and leads to music being valued
- fulfilment of the need for achievement, curiosity and developing the self
- satisfaction derived from positive social responses to successful playing and performance.

Developing and maintaining a positive musical identity, including:

- setting and achieving high musical standards
- the acquisition and retention of a positive musical self-concept
- sustaining belief in a personal ability to make music
- maintaining overall self-belief
- demonstrating resilience when there is frequent negative feedback
- developing the capacity to manage strong feelings and impulses.

Acquiring appropriate approaches to learning music, including:

- the adoption of mastery goals (a focus on constant improvement; the desire to learn new skills, master new tasks or understand new things)
- seeking choice of repertoire
- the adoption of strategies to explain success or failure which focus on effort, practice and strategy use, rather than lack of ability
- being able to make realistic plans
- having a range of practice strategies, an understanding of how to practise effectively, and being able to manage practice.

Having a supportive environment, including:

- teachers who have acted, or continue to act, as role models
- support from family, friends and colleagues
- musical groups and institutions which offer opportunities for learning and constructive feedback.

SELF-MOTIVATION

Musicians can learn to manage their motivation to some extent, although the perceptions which they have of themselves as musicians – and what they perceive it is possible for them to achieve – are inevitably influenced by the interactions that they have with other people, including family, friends, colleagues and those more expert than themselves, for instance teachers. These interactions influence identity or self-concept, the way that we think about ourselves and our relationships with others, and play a crucial role in motivation. Where comparisons are made with high-attaining others, identity and self-concept are likely to be deflated. In highly competitive environments such as the music profession, musical identities and self-concepts are particularly vulnerable. Identities are not static. They are constructed, and over time they are challenged, negotiated and renegotiated as the individual interacts with others.

During study in higher education, music students go through a transitional process where they identify with like-minded others and develop and strengthen their perception of themselves as musicians. During this process, a wide range of events can act as turning points, influencing future aspirations, plans and self-perceptions. For instance, successful performance at a masterclass or in a competition may support aspirations to be a performer. In contrast, negative self-comparisons made with the performance of others may lead to a decision to pursue a full-time career that does not involve performing.

Individuals also have beliefs about their likelihood of success in relation to particular tasks or areas of work. This is known as 'self-efficacy'. Motivation for a particular activity is at its peak when strong self-efficacy beliefs are combined with some uncertainty about the outcome, i.e. when a person feels competent but challenged. The highest levels of motivation also depend on an individual having made the choice to participate in a particular activity and valuing that activity. Self-determination in relation to your career trajectory, and the sub-goals required to attain that trajectory, are crucial in ensuring that you maintain the highest levels of motivation.

EXERCISE 2.3: ESTABLISHING YOUR MUSICAL IDENTITY

We can have many different identities, for instance as brother/sister, son/daughter, musician, pianist, folk musician, pop singer, rebel/conformist, optimist/pessimist, being kind/cruel, and so on. What identities do you have? Which of these are the most important to you? Which do you wish to develop? Are these different identities sometimes in conflict with each other? If so, how can you make changes in your life so that they sit more easily alongside each other?

GOALS AND AIMS

The goals and aims that musicians strive to attain are related to their identity, self-concept, self-efficacy and what they believe is possible for them – their possible selves. Self-perceptions are crucial in the way that identities and possible selves develop. If a musician perceives himself or herself as successful, attributes this success to high ability and wishes to pursue a career in music, they have what is known as a 'positive possible future self' as a musician.[12] Possible selves can be powerful motivators, providing long-term goals and encouraging the setting up of interim goals which need to be achieved en route. If a musician does not have a positive possible self in one branch of the music profession, in the long, medium or short term they are unlikely to succeed. Setting up positive possible selves for musicians early on is important, combined with dedication, commitment, determination and a willingness to make sacrifices. Self-belief is particularly important, as musicians encounter considerable criticism and greater competition than is the case in many professions.[13] Individuals can also have negative or feared possible selves. These are selves which they believe are possible or even likely for them, which they wish to avoid. These might include being unable to make a living as a musician, or not succeeding as a soloist.

Setting goals provides a focus for attention, enhances motivation and can sustain the development of positive possible selves. Goals can be set in the short, medium or long term. To sustain motivation, the mastery of each small goal and sub-goal needs to be acknowledged. Setting goals and receiving rewards for achieving them helps to maintain motivation. Rewards might include the sense of achievement at having mastered something, the enjoyment of performing well, the acclaim of others, taking a break from practising. Goals can sometimes conflict with each other and their fulfilment can be disrupted by others. Musicians may have to make trade-offs between goals at different levels and undertake some activities to attain a particular goal which they may not find particularly enjoyable, for instance playing music that they do not like in order to become a member of a particular musical group.

Because identity and self-concept depend in part on the feedback that musicians receive from others (either explicitly or through non-verbal communication), the way that feedback is interpreted is particularly important. Musicians' motivation and subsequent behaviour is influenced by their interpretation of situations and events. How individuals explain their successes and failures is particularly important in maintaining self-esteem.[14] This process is influenced by the extent to which musicians perceive that they have control over their lives.

Everyone is motivated to establish, maintain and promote a consistent and usually positive self-image, so individuals develop a variety of coping strategies to maintain self-worth – some of which may be self-defeating. For instance, they might reduce effort in relation to a particular task, so if failure follows, they can argue that this does not reflect a lack of ability but a lack of effort. To maintain self-esteem, musicians can attribute failure to the particular context that they were in at the time. This might include factors relating to the performance environment, difficulties with the instrument, lack of rehearsal time, and so on. This type of explanation will enable them to maintain belief in their own expertise and skills.

Overall, what contributes to maintaining self-esteem and motivation is attributing successful outcomes to personal effort and skills and attributing unsuccessful outcomes to external factors. Attributing failure to lack of ability has a particularly negative impact on motivation (see Case Study 2.1 for examples). Musicians' beliefs about the nature of learning and ability are also important in success – musicians need to believe that they can continue to master new skills, learn throughout their careers, and that their achievements are not limited by a fixed musical ability.[15]

CASE STUDY 2.1: WAYS OF ATTRIBUTING SUCCESS AND FAILURE

Paul had always been successful in examinations and attributed this to his hard work, commitment and ability to focus on the task in hand. When in his second year at conservatoire he passed one of his examinations but with a very low grade, he attributed this to the fact that he had not put in sufficient time and effort to ensure mastery of the materials. He determined that he would work even harder during the following year, ensuring that he had understood what was required, and seeking support from staff and other students to ensure that he was making appropriate progress.

Tricia was a highly successful young performer, who attributed her success to her high level of musical ability. On entering conservatoire, she began to realise that there were others who were able to perform at a higher standard. They were often selected for performing opportunities in preference to her. She began to have doubts about her ability and to lose confidence. When offered the opportunity to perform in a highly prestigious concert, she became very anxious and the performance was not as good as she would have liked. She concluded that she did not have sufficient 'ability' and left the conservatoire to pursue a different career.

When Dylan began to experience difficulties in his lessons, with his teacher becoming ever more critical of his efforts, he began to lose motivation. To preserve his conception of himself as an outstanding musician, he blamed his lack of progress on lack of practice. This led to a vicious circle of decline, with ever-increasing criticism in lessons and less and less work and effort on his part.

In contrast, Rosie attributed the criticism she was receiving to her practice being ineffective and to not always understanding what was required. She worked on improving her practising strategies, increased actual practice time and ensured that she was clear about what was expected of her. As a result, her progress improved, her teacher was impressed with the way that she had tackled the problems, and their working relationship was enhanced.

EXERCISE 2.4: THINKING ABOUT YOUR 'POSSIBLE SELVES'

Do you have a positive possible self as a musician? If so, is it related to one particular area of music? What goals do you have in the short, medium and long term to help you attain your positive possible self? Have you set up sub-goals as well? Make a list of these with a timescale for achieving each. Make sure that this is realistic and can be achieved but is not so easy that you have no sense of challenge.

Do you have a feared possible self? If so, what can you do to avoid this feared self becoming a reality?

MOTIVATION AND TRANSITION INTO THE MUSIC PROFESSION

There are a number of different routes into the music profession, depending on the nature of the particular career pursued.

Some musicians follow a path from formal lessons to a music degree at university or conservatoire and during this begin to get work, teaching, playing in ensembles or solo engagements with the help of their teachers. Some take other subjects at university or have other jobs but continue with musical activities through playing at weekends or in the evenings. Some begin working in music straight from school, often being unemployed or supported by parents. Whatever the means of entering the music profession, musicians become further established through developing their skills, adapting to the norms and conventions of the music world, and learning the value of collaboration and of building networks.

Musicians need to become lifelong learners, continuing to acquire and enhance skills in a range of ways, including:

- informally, through self-teaching or learning with peers
- privately arranged sessions
- workshops
- new experiences, such as conducting, composing, playing new instruments, working in different genres
- training in community music.

It is important to be able to learn to adapt to circumstances, although this is not always easy. A total commitment to music is needed and a compulsion to engage with it despite any difficulties that may be experienced.[16] Whatever the means of transition into the profession, you must take responsibility for your progression, be versatile, have self-belief, plan, persevere and have good interpersonal skills. You need to learn to work independently, manage your practice and performance, and deal with critical evaluation of your work. If you are going to perform, you need high levels of self-belief to cope with the critical and competitive environment in the music profession.

Music is not valued equally in all cultures. In some it is viewed as decadent and is forbidden. In others it is highly valued, and those involved in its composition or execution are highly revered members of society. Economic, demographic and political factors have a major impact on the opportunities that may be available for musical engagement at amateur and professional levels.[17] Over time, the value placed on music by society and the sub-groups within it can change. These cultural and societal factors impact on musicians, their careers and their motivation. In planning a career, current and likely future changes need to be taken into account.

EXERCISE 2.5: OVERCOMING CHALLENGES

If you are currently in full-time education, what challenges do you anticipate facing when you leave it? What strategies do you have for overcoming these challenges?

For those leaving further or higher education and entering the music profession there are a number of possible obstacles. These include:

- too few opportunities to perform
- too few work opportunities
- failure at auditions
- professional competition
- a lack of self-confidence
- financial hardship
- difficulties in self-promotion
- insufficient knowledge of the workings of the music profession

- lack of personal contacts in the music business
- a lack of time management skills
- health problems
- inadequate knowledge of repertoire
- being overspecialised
- having an inappropriate specialism
- bad luck
- inexperience.

CASE STUDY 2.2: A CLASSICAL PERFORMER

Jonathan started playing the trumpet while at school, having lessons through the local authority music service with a generalist brass teacher. In addition to having individual lessons, he participated in a range of musical groups at school, the local brass band (where he played cornet), a local authority music school and, as his expertise developed, the local authority youth orchestra.

On aspiring to become a professional performing musician, he changed teacher to a specialist trumpet teacher and later studied at the Royal Academy of Music. While at the Academy, he took every opportunity to gain experience, playing in a wide variety of musical groups and exploring different genres. He also took on some instrumental teaching.

On leaving the Academy, he developed a portfolio career, performing with symphony, chamber and opera orchestras, playing in big bands, in the theatre and recording studios, doing instrumental teaching in state and private schools, and conducting and coaching young people in a variety of musical groups.

MAINTAINING MOTIVATION THROUGHOUT A CAREER

Having successfully made the transition into the music profession, musicians need to maintain motivation throughout their career. The extent to which musicians are successful in doing this depends partly on the nature of the work that they undertake but also on the other roles that they have to fulfil, for instance in relation to their families. There may be challenges in relation to motivation for different groups of musicians. While orchestral musicians, in general, seem to enjoy their work, they can become frustrated if they do not have the opportunity to fulfil their artistic ideas. Of particular importance are the skills, both musical and personal, of the conductor. Performances over time can be transformed by the appointment of conductors who are inspirational and who can co-ordinate the work of the players so that the performance is as good as it can possibly be.[18] When this is the case, musicians feel fulfilled. Motivation can wane when poor conductors lead to the production of poor performances.

CASE STUDY 2.3: A POPULAR MUSIC SINGER

Janie began singing from a very early age, encouraged by her mother, who always sang around the house. She emulated singers that she heard on the radio and through her parents' collection of recordings.

At primary school, the quality of her singing was noted and she was frequently chosen to sing solos in the school choir. Aged 7 she decided that she wanted to become a musician. She began to learn to play the piano but was put off by a strict teacher, who emphasised the playing of scales and exercises more than making music. Her parents supported her in changing from playing the piano to learning the guitar. As she progressed on the guitar, she began to accompany herself singing. At secondary school, encouraged to compose as part of the school curriculum, she began to write songs as well as singing them.

Aged 16 she left school to attend the local further education college and take a course in the Performing Arts. Here, she and friends formed a group and began to do gigs locally, also publicising their work on the internet. A degree in the Performing Arts supported the ongoing development of a wide range of musical skills until the group was able to make professional-level recordings, increasing their fan base and work opportunities.

Portfolio musicians have more control over the direction of their careers and can instigate changes over time. Frequently, they reach their performing peak while young, taking on greater responsibilities as a teacher later, although this is not always the case. To be successful, they need to have a strong identity as a musician which has developed early on. The transitions between different career periods hold risks for musicians in terms of emotional crisis. These are greater the more highly skilled and creative the performer. Reducing the number of performances – or ceasing to perform altogether – removes powerful rewards in terms of audience response and more general critical acclaim.

One challenge which faces most musicians is having to undertake work that does not match their aspirations.[19] Musical careers may be characterised by struggle. Attempting to reconcile tensions between being employed, striving to attain high artistic standards and needing to be versatile within a rapidly changing profession is difficult. However, there are currently increasing opportunities for creativity, with opportunities for collaborative artistic leadership where musicians can become the agents of their own careers, planning and organising ongoing learning opportunities.

CHAPTER SUMMARY: LEARNING, SETTING GOALS AND MOTIVATING YOURSELF

Developing the skills to become a professional musician takes time and commitment.

As expertise develops, many skills become automated, freeing up processing to focus on musical issues.

Experts are faster and more efficient than novices, but can become fixed in their thinking and practices.

Experts have highly developed evaluative and self-regulatory skills.

Musical identity and self-concept play a crucial role in motivation.

Having clear goals, and strategies for attaining them, is important for maintaining motivation.

To succeed in the music profession requires determination, agency and opportunity.

FURTHER READING

Hallam, S. (2009) 'Motivation to learn'. In S. Hallam, I. Cross and M. Thaut (eds), *Handbook of Psychology of Music*. Oxford: Oxford University Press, 285–94. This chapter provides an overview of recent research on musical motivation, including a model of how the relationships between the individual and the environment interact to enhance or diminish motivation.

Hallam, S. (in press) 'Maintaining motivation through the lifespan'. In G. Welch and I. Papageorgi (eds), *Investigating Musical Performance*. London: Ashgate. This chapter sets out what we know about sustaining motivation throughout the lifespan as a professional musician. It also considers what motivates amateur musicians and how developing resilience is important for sustaining well-being.

NOTES

1. Mito, H. (2004) 'Role of daily musical activity in acquisition of musical skill'. In J. Tafuri (ed.), *Research for Music Education: The 20th Seminar of the ISME Research Commission*, Las Palmas, Spain, 4–10 July 2004.

2. Hallam, S. (1995) 'Professional musicians' orientations to practice: Implications for teaching'. *British Journal of Music Education*, 12(1), 3–20.

3. Hallam, S. (2001) 'The development of metacognition in musicians: Implications for education'. *British Journal of Music Education*, 18(1), 27–39.

4. Fitts, P.M. and Posner, M.I. (1967) *Human Performance*. Belmont, CA: Brooks Cole.

5. Alexander, P.A. (1997) 'Mapping the multidimensional nature of domain learning: The interplay of cognitive, emotional and strategic forces'. In M.L. Maehr and P.R. Pintrich (eds), *Advances in Motivation and Achievement*, 10, 213–50. Greenwich, CT: JAI Press.

6. Ericsson, K.A., Krampe, R.T. and Tesch-Romer, C. (1993) 'The role of deliberate practice in the acquisition of expert performance'. *Psychological Review*, 100(3), 363–406.

7. Hallam, S. (1998) 'Predictors of achievement and drop out in instrumental tuition'. *Psychology of Music*, 26(2), 116–32.

8. Sudnow, D. (1978) *Ways of the Hand: The organisation of improvised conduct*. London: Routledge and Kegan Paul

9. Sosniak, L.A. (1985) 'Learning to be a concert pianist'. In B.S. Bloom (ed.), *Developing Talent in Young People*, 19–67. New York: Ballantine.

10. Glaser, R. and Chi, M.T.H. (1988) 'Overview'. In M.T.H. Chi, R. Glaser and M.J.Farr (eds), *The Nature of Expertise*. Hillsdale, New Jersey: Lawrence Erlbaum Associates.

11. Chi, M.T.H. (2006) 'Two approaches to the study of expert characteristics'. In K.A. Ericsson, N. Charness, P.J. Feltovich and R.R. Hoffman (eds), *The Cambridge Handbook of Expertise and Performance*. Cambridge: Cambridge University Press.

12. Markus, H. and Ruvolo, A. (1989) 'Possible selves: Personalized representations of goals'. In L.A. Pervin (ed.), *Goal Concepts in Personality and Social Psychology*. Hillsdale, New Jersey: Lawrence Erlbaum Associates.

13. MacNamara, A., Holmes, P. and Collins, D. (2006). 'The pathway to excellence: The role of psychological characteristics in negotiating the challenges of musical development'. *British Journal of Music Education*, 23(3), 285–302.

14. Weiner, B. (1986) *An Attributional Theory of Motivation and Emotion*. New York: Springer-Verlag.

15. Dweck, C.S. and Leggett, E.L. (1988) 'A social cognitive approach to motivation and personality'. *Psychological Review*, 95(2), 256–373.

16. Coulson, S. (2010) 'Getting "capital" in the music world: Musicians' learning experiences and working lives'. *British Journal of Music Education*, 27(3), 255–70.

17. Simonton, D.K. (1997) 'Products, persons and periods'. In D.J. Hargreaves and A.C. North (eds), *The Social Psychology of Music*. Oxford: Oxford University Press.

18. Boerner, S., Krause, D.E. and Gebert, D. (2001) 'In der Kunst "untergehen" – in der Kunst "aufgehen"? Empirische Ergebnisse zur Funktionalität einer direktiv-charismatischen Führung im Orchester'. *Zeitschrift Führung + Organisation*, 70(5), 285–92.

19. Smilde, R. (2009) *Musicians as Lifelong Learners: Discovery through biography*. Delft: Eburon Academic Publishers.

CHAPTER 3
PRACTISING AND PREPARING FOR PERFORMANCE

INTRODUCTION

This chapter focuses on issues relating to practising. It considers the importance of practice and the need to make time spent practising as effective as possible, to avoid unnecessary physical strain.

It outlines a range of practising strategies, including:

- how to plan and organise practice to get the optimal benefit from it

- how to self-manage motivation to practice

- how to develop meta-cognitive skills, so that tasks can be realistically assessed, appropriate strategies adopted, progress monitored and outcomes evaluated.

IS PRACTICE NECESSARY?

All musicians need to practise. Practice serves a number of functions, which depend on the level of expertise of the musician and the preparations required for particular performances. For inexpert musicians, practice is required to develop a range of musical skills: the technical skills for playing the instrument; listening skills to monitor whether the music is being played appropriately; and skills concerned with reading and performing music. For professional musicians, practice involves maintaining existing skills, learning new music and preparing for performance.

There is considerable variability in the amount of time that individual musicians spend practising and the way that they practise. This variability is demonstrated by considering the practice of latter-day virtuosi.

Kreisler had very strong views about practising. He said of excessive practising:

> It benumbs the brain, renders the imagination less acute, and deadens the alertness. For that reason I never practise before a concert.[1]

Kreisler described the virtuoso Kubelik, who practised for 12 hours on the day of a concert, giving a technically perfect performance which, in Kreisler's opinion, was 'a blank'. Kreisler's preparation depended on mental, rather than physical, preparation:

> I never practise. In the accepted sense of the term, in the formal use of the word, I have never practised in my whole life. I practise only as I feel the

> *need. I believe that everything is in the brain. You think of a passage and you know exactly how you want it.*[1]

Kreisler was not the only virtuoso to have had a negative view of practice. Sarasate was known to have performed without practising, and Paganini was never heard to practise.[1] Flesch believed in practice but in moderation:

> *If you can't learn to become a violinist in four hours of daily practice, you never will.*[1]

But Flesch went on to suggest that those four hours had to be spent practising effectively.

Nowadays, with audience expectations of technical perfection in performance, professional musicians have to practise regularly to maintain their technique. But, they do not all find practice a stimulating activity. Nigel Kennedy, one of today's virtuosi, described his daily four hours of technical practice:

> *Time has to be spent doing it, so I do it. You don't have to use a lot of grey cells to do most of that work, so I usually put a quiz show or hockey game on the TV and just hack my violin. Finger exercises mostly, physical co-ordination stuff. Everyone has their own weaknesses and strengths, so I've made up my own exercises to deal with my problems.*[2]

For some musicians, practice is clearly a chore.

The amount of time spent practising by musicians differs considerably. It is only possible to practise on some instruments for a short space of time without causing physical damage (see also Chapter 8). Singers have to take particular care to protect their voices, and all musicians are at risk of creating long-term problems for themselves if they over-practise.

THE NATURE OF PRACTICE

Practice can include a range of different activities, for instance:
- acquiring, developing or maintaining aspects of technique
- learning new music
- memorising music for performance
- developing interpretation
- developing improvisational skills
- preparing for performance.

The particular purpose of any practice session will dictate the way that practice proceeds. If the aim of practice is to learn a new piece of music, it may involve working out fingerings, breathing and phrasing, and making decisions about interpretation. Or it may concern mastering the work from a technical point of view, perhaps analysing why something is not working well, or undertaking repetitious practice to increase speed or facility. If the purpose is to maintain or improve technical skill, the session will almost certainly involve some form of repetition, perhaps in the form of playing scales, exercises or studies. If it involves developing improvisational skills, it may involve listening to recordings, analysing and copying the work of existing artists, and developing and working on ideas.

Practice is particularly important for developing 'automaticity' (see Chapter 2). Many of the skills involved in playing a musical instrument are carried out by expert players with little conscious effort. They have been repeated sufficiently often for them to be undertaken automatically, rather as many aspects of driving a car become automated as experience is gained. The advantage of skills becoming relatively automatic is that attention can then be focused on other aspects of performance, for instance playing musically, synchronising playing with others or following a conductor. The development of automaticity requires repetition. Repetition does not occur only in practice. Every time that the individual plays their instrument, skills are being repeated and enhanced.

Practice may also be necessary to prepare for performance itself. This may go beyond actually mastering the music. It may involve learning to play the piece from memory or preparing for the act of performing, for example carrying out mock performances, imagining the performance situation and attempting to play under those circumstances. Such performance practice serves two purposes:

- It can give feedback regarding aspects of performance that are insecure and need more technical practice.
- It can help to reduce nervous tension, by giving the performer an opportunity to experience and manage the feelings that they will encounter when performing for an audience.

Practice might also involve activities that are less directly concerned with developing skills on the instrument, for instance improvisation, working on aural skills, improving sight-reading, analysing the structure of a work to facilitate memorisation or the development of interpretation, or simply playing with musical ideas. Key Point Summary 3.1 outlines the main activities of practice.

KEY POINT SUMMARY 3.1: PRACTICE ACTIVITIES

Technical skills may relate to:

- warming up
- repetitive technical work (to develop automaticity and consolidate or maintain technique)
- scale or exercise practice
- analysing and finding solutions to technical problems.

Cognitive skills may relate to:

- enhancing the reading of notation
- the development of sight-reading skills
- the development of analytic skills.

Aural skills may relate to:

- the development of aural and critical listening skills
- playing by ear
- improvisation.

Performance skills may relate to:

- preparation of a previously unlearnt piece
- revision of a previously learnt piece
- development of interpretation
- memorisation of a piece
- preparing for performance itself.

EXERCISE 3.1: PRACTICE ACTIVITIES

Typically, what activities do you undertake when you practise? What is the purpose of these activities? Do you think that they are effective in achieving your goals? Are there other skills that you need to focus on?

The next time you practise, make a note of how long you spend on each activity. The outcome might surprise you!

EFFECTIVE PRACTICE

In recent years it has become apparent that over-practising can lead to physical injury. For that reason it is important that time spent practising is as effective as possible. There is also considerable agreement among professional musicians that between three and four hours is the maximum useful solitary practice that one can do in a day, because the intense concentration required cannot be sustained for longer than that. In addition, practising intensely for longer than about 45 to 60 minutes without a break is not productive. This solitary practice is distinguished from playing or rehearsal with others, where the level of concentration required may be less intense over long periods.

Effective practice can be defined as that which achieves the desired end-product, in as short a time as possible, without interfering with longer-term goals. In other words, effective practice is 'what works' in learning what needs to be learnt, with the further proviso that 'what works' in the short term must not interfere with progression in the long term, for example by creating undue muscular tension or physical damage.

This definition assumes that effective practice might take many forms, depending on the nature of the task to be undertaken, the context within which the task is to be learnt, the level of expertise already acquired, and individual differences. It also implies that the individual musician requires considerable knowledge of their own strengths and weaknesses and the different strategies which can be adopted to complete task requirements. Strategies that can be developed to promote effective practice can be divided into two broad categories: task-oriented strategies; and person-oriented strategies. These enable the individual to maintain motivation and concentration, and to prepare for performance.

EXERCISE 3.2: TIME SPENT PRACTISING AND REHEARSING

How much solitary practice do you typically do in a week? How is it divided up? Do you do more than four hours daily? Do you take regular breaks? Are you involved in regular rehearsals with others, which enable you to consolidate skills? How much time do you spend in such ensemble work? Try keeping a practice and rehearsal diary for a week. See how much time you actually spend in individual practice and rehearsals.

TASK-ORIENTED STRATEGIES

While musicians exhibit considerable individual diversity in their practice, some general trends have emerged.[3] The specific strategies adopted depend on the purpose of the practice and the musician's needs at the time.

LEARNING A NEW PIECE OF MUSIC

When a musician learns a new piece of music, they must have a range of strategies for doing so. This requires knowledge of personal strengths and weaknesses, and of what is possible, and a vision of how they wish the final performance to sound. A plan of the way that practice will then proceed needs to be developed. Progress towards the performance goal will need to be monitored. If progress is unsatisfactory, alternative strategies will need to be employed. Constant monitoring of progress will be required, with adjustments made to sub-goals as and when necessary. When the work has been mastered, the prepared performance will need to be evaluated and adjustments made. After public performance, further evaluation will be required, with consideration of how it might be improved for future performances (see Tips and Reminders 3.1).

Typically, musicians learning a new work acquire an overview of the piece.[4] How this is acquired varies. Some musicians will already have listened to a range of recordings or live performances of the piece, to acquire a mental representation of its sound. Others prefer to acquire an overview through playing the piece, not necessarily on the instrument on which it is to be performed. This initial engagement with the music enables the important musical themes and the nature of the technical difficulties which the work presents to be established. Slow, careful work follows, to analyse problems, develop appropriate fingerings, breathing, etc. Specific strategies are then adopted, to practise difficult sections. These can involve repetition or variable techniques, such as changing rhythms, bowings, articulation, etc. The nature of practice changes as a work is mastered. When practice commences on a piece of music, the sections practised tend to be short. The sections chosen initially are based on the musical structure of the work: the greater the difficulty, the shorter the sections. As the work nears completion, the sections practised become longer and links between sections are practised. As the technical aspects of the work are mastered, more attention is given to the musical and interpretative aspects (see Tips and Reminders 3.1).

TIPS AND REMINDERS 3.1: EFFECTIVE STRATEGIES FOR LEARNING A NEW WORK

Effective practice requires the musician to:

- establish long-term goals
- set goals for each practice session
- establish sub-goals as work proceeds
- monitor progress towards the goals
- change sub-goals and long-term goals as necessary in the light of the monitoring process.

The learning or revising of already learnt music includes:

- obtaining an initial overview of what is to be learnt, to acquire an aural template to monitor progress
- identification of technical difficulties
- consideration of musical ideas
- careful analysis of problems
- identification of ways of overcoming problems
- the implementation of specific strategies to overcome difficulties, which may vary according to the instrument being played
- rehearsing short then long sections
- fusing the sections together after technical practice
- developing interpretation
- playing the work as a whole
- video-recording a mock performance, critically listening and watching with a view to improving performance.

IDENTIFYING YOUR STRENGTHS AND WEAKNESSES

Each individual musician has a different pattern of strengths and weaknesses.[5] These will be in evidence throughout their musical career. The musician needs to develop strategies for coping with them. The detailed aspects of practice therefore need to be tailored to individual needs. Some musicians need to undertake lengthy warming-up exercises before they begin to practise; for others, where physical dexterity is a strength, this may not be necessary. Some musicians may find some aspects of technique particularly difficult, while others master them quickly. There is no simple recipe for what constitutes effective practice, although, overall, learning seems to proceed more effectively when there is a musical goal, with a continued awareness of the need for technical security. The musician must also have a range of practice strategies to help overcome weaknesses (e.g. using a metronome, repetition, analysis, varying bowings, breathing or articulation, improvising, making up exercises, mental practice). The strategies adopted also depend on the nature of the task.

TECHNICAL PRACTICE

Practice to enhance generalisable technical and musical skills may include work on scales, technical exercises, or studies. To make technical practice more interesting, some musicians improvise in such a way as to rehearse the techniques required or devise their own exercises. Others vary the way that they play scales to maintain their concentration and motivation, for instance by using different rhythmic patterns, starting at different points in the scale, or using different articulations.

There is a range of ways in which technical practice can be made interesting to sustain motivation while undertaking it. Each individual needs to explore what is most effective for them. It is important to remember that technical practice is only a means to an end – making music – not an end in itself.

MENTAL PRACTICE

To avoid developing physical injuries, use can be made of mental practice. This involves rehearsing music mentally without actually playing it. While this cannot be effective in relation to some skills, for instance enhancing intonation, it can play a major role in thinking through difficult rhythmic or tonal passages, consolidating complex finger patterns, memorising music for performance, or clarifying ideas for interpretation. Mental practice is effective, as it stimulates the same brain activity as actual practice.

Some skills are most effectively developed through playing in ensembles, for instance sight-reading. Playing in situations where the learner is forced to keep up – even if this means not being able to play every note – speeds up the rate of processing. For pianists, taking on a role as an accompanist is effective for similar reasons.

EXERCISE 3.3: PRACTISING STRATEGIES

What are the strengths and weaknesses that you have as a musician? Which of these are important for your planned career trajectory? What strategies do you need to adopt to improve those elements of your technique which are weak but crucial for your future prospects?

What practice strategies do you have? Use the musical practice checklist (Table 3.1) to assess what you already do. Make a list of the ways that you could increase the range of strategies that you have. Try implementing them over a period of time, making a note of which ones seem to suit you best.

TABLE 3.1: MUSICAL PRACTICE CHECKLIST

	Agree	Not sure	Disagree
When learning a new piece of music, I always get an overview of it before starting detailed practice			
I ensure that I know what I am aiming for when I learn a new piece			
I listen to recordings of works that I am to learn			
I listen to recordings of a wide variety of music			
I attend concerts on a regular basis			
I attend masterclasses on a regular basis			
I identify the musically important sections in a new piece			
I take time to think about interpretation of pieces			
I mentally rehearse music as I am learning it			
I identify difficult sections when I start to learn a new piece			
I practise difficult sections slowly, gradually speeding them up when speed is required			

I have a range of practising strategies for practising difficult sections			
I use a metronome to support my learning when appropriate			
I mark things on the music to help me remember			
I record myself doing a mock performance, so I can assess my progress and see what requires further work			
When memorising for performance, I ensure that I have internalised the sound of the entire work			
When memorising for performance, I make use of visual memory of the notation			
When memorising for performance, I make use of memory for movement			
When memorising a long work, I analyse its structure and remember key elements			
I always do warm-up exercises			
I practise with the metronome when I need to be rhythmically secure			
I keep a record of my progress in relation to the development of technique			
I devise my own exercises to help me maintain and develop technique			
When I experience a difficulty, I analyse why I am finding it difficult			
I record myself practising and use the tape to improve the efficiency of my practice			
I work with computer software where it is helpful to my practice			
I have clear long-term goals for my practice			
I always set specific goals for each practice session			
I plan my practice			

I try to make sure that I always have a performance coming up			
I use opportunities in ensembles to develop my skills			
I take regular breaks when practising			
I try to make sure that I have the best environment for practising			

CASE STUDY 3.1: DEVELOPING EFFECTIVE PRACTISING STRATEGIES

Although he was putting a lot of time into his practice, Tristan was not making sufficient progress between his lessons. His teacher was exhorting him to practise more, but he was already doing seven hours of practice a day.

Following discussion with a fellow student who had attended a workshop about practising effectively, he video-taped his practice for a week. Looking critically at the videos, he realised that he was mindlessly playing in his practice, without focusing on the difficulties. He adopted two main strategies to make his practice more effective.

In relation to the general technical difficulties that he was having, he began to analyse the problems systematically. Operating at this deeper level, he found solutions to most of them and was able to incorporate the changes into his playing. He developed some exercises of his own to enable him to continue to maintain those elements of his technique that he felt were weak.

Similarly, in his pieces he focused on the technically difficult areas, spending less time just playing through them. Where he was unable to sort the problems out for himself, he was able to discuss the issues with his teacher, who was now much happier with his general progress and much more willing to offer support where problems were persistent.

MEMORISING MUSIC FOR PERFORMANCE

Sometimes musicians are required to perform from memory. Some musicians perform from memory when they are not required to do so, because they feel that:

- it improves presentation
- they can communicate more easily with the audience
- they develop a deeper knowledge of the music
- they have greater freedom in performance.

Some musicians never play from memory in public, because they are irrationally afraid of forgetting.[6]

The length of time required for memorising music and the strategies required for doing so vary, depending on the length and complexity of the music. Some musicians have highly developed aural skills, enabling them to play easily by ear. For them, memorising short pieces is simply a question of listening to what is to be learnt, perhaps by recording it themselves first and, once the sound has been committed to memory, repeating it using their aural skills. Where the music to be memorised is long and complex, musicians tend to adopt a range of strategies. The most secure way of learning to play from memory is to adopt multiple coding – in other words, to have memorised the material in a number of different ways.[6] Codes which can be used include aural, visual, kinaesthetic (movement) and cognitive. The most common approach adopted to learning to play from memory is a process of repeated repetition and testing, which enables the piece to be played automatically. This facilitates:

- knowing the sound (aural memory), which can then be used to play by ear
- kinaesthetic memory (knowing the physical movements required to make the sounds)
- visual representation, which can vary from sketchy representations of the placing of the notes on the page to almost photographic memory of every note.

For security, these are often supplemented by cognitive analysis, for example counting the number of times a particular phrase occurs and consciously remembering different exit points, examining the structure of the music, noting key changes, and looking for sequences. Most of these activities are undertaken as insurance against a lapse of automated memories. Successful performance from memory tends to make use of all of these strategies at some level. Successfully performing from memory also increases confidence, so that the task becomes less daunting in the future.

To increase your confidence in playing from memory, you might try:

- learning a very short piece
- learning to play a short piece by ear

- listening to a recording of the piece, so that you have memorised the sound
- mentally rehearsing a piece – playing through it in your head
- systematically analysing the structure of the piece, so that your knowledge is deeper
- identifying where there is the potential for confusion, if sections are similar
- testing your memory weekly as you rehearse something
- giving 'mock' performances of pieces in their entirety to friends or to your teacher.

EXERCISE 3.4: PERFORMING FROM MEMORY

Do you have to perform from memory? What strategies do you use when learning music from memory? Are they secure? What other strategies could you use?

PERSON-ORIENTED STRATEGIES

Establishing appropriate support strategies in relation to practice is crucial for musicians. To be successful in playing a musical instrument or singing professionally requires practice. Without practice, even the most talented will not succeed. The skills of managing time, motivation and concentration are therefore among the most important that a prospective musician must acquire. Once acquired, they are also useful in a range of other activities and provide a valuable resource throughout the individual's life.

Musicians need to have an awareness of the conditions necessary for them to practise effectively and how to bring these about. These include:

- optimising concentration
- being aware of when it is necessary to take a break
- coping with distractions
- planning practice times
- ensuring that there is somewhere suitable to practise and that the working environment is conducive
- ensuring that equipment is working properly

- arranging for sufficient time to practise in relation to other commitments.

MOTIVATION TO PRACTISE

Motivating yourself to practise if you enjoy all aspects of practice is easy. It is less easy if you dislike practice or elements of it. Motivation can be intrinsic, extrinsic or a combination of the two. A person is intrinsically motivated when he or she undertakes an activity which is enjoyed and valued for its own sake. In the case of practice, this may be for the love of playing, or the sense of achievement when a work or technical problem is mastered. Extrinsic motivation occurs when an activity is valued for the rewards it will bring, e.g. praise, playing well in a concert, passing an examination. Musicians exhibit both types of motivation and mixed motives are often in evidence.[7]

TIPS AND REMINDERS 3.2: STRATEGIES TO PROMOTE MOTIVATION TO PRACTISE

Find a pattern of practice that suits your lifestyle and other commitments.

Set targets with particular goals to be met in the short, medium and long term.

Ensure that your goals are challenging but not unattainable.

If getting started is difficult, specify a short time for practice – this will often be exceeded when your interest is engaged.

Develop ways of making your practice more interesting, e.g. compose your own exercises, practise scales in different ways.

Learn to use alternative modes of practice, e.g. analysis, improvisation, listening to music, mental practice.

When still developing technical skills, keep a record of practice, the length of time spent and what was practised.

Ensure that you have sufficient performing engagements to stimulate a need to practise.

Get involved in playing in musical groups. This acts to support the development of many musical skills.

Some musicians find practice extremely tedious and are exclusively motivated by external rewards. They develop strategies to try to reduce the amount of time spent practising or to make practice more interesting, using improvisation to improve aspects of technique or spending time analysing music, rather than playing it.

Others love practising and can think of no more pleasurable way of spending their time. For most musicians, practice is enjoyable when it involves interesting or challenging tasks, but can become routine when it is undertaken solely to maintain technique.[5] There are some strategies that can be used to promote motivation. These are set out in Tips and Reminders 3.2.

SUSTAINING CONCENTRATION IN PRACTICE

Lack of concentration in practice can be precipitated by external factors, for instance disruptions. However, the problem frequently relates to a lack of focus. Strategies that may help when concentration is waning include:

- working on something which is challenging, interesting and requires conscious, cognitive effort
- setting targets to be achieved in a short space of time
- trying to memorise short sections
- playing with the metronome
- varying the activities undertaken, so that your interest is sustained
- taking regular breaks
- building in rewards for achieving certain targets.

THE PRACTISING ENVIRONMENT

The ideal practising environment is quiet, has a comfortable temperature and does not provide too many immediate distractions. If practising is undertaken within an institution, practice facilities may be good but there may be problems with booking rooms in advance or a practice rota, limiting the amount of available practice time. There may be noise from adjacent practice rooms and fellow students may disrupt practice. If this is the case, you need to find optimal times to practise and plan ahead accordingly. Despite environmental difficulties, if a piece has to be learnt quickly, then practice can be undertaken in almost any environment.

LEARNING HOW TO LEARN (META-COGNITION)

The nature of being a musician means that much of the work is undertaken by the musician working independently.[5] Musicians therefore have to develop the means of learning independently. This is part of meta-cognitive development. Meta-cognition relates not only to specific learning strategies, but also to those strategies which may support the individual in their learning, for example concentration.

Meta-cognition refers to knowledge of a range of skills concerned with self-awareness of learning processes. These include awareness of:

- one's own strengths and weaknesses
- strategies for approaching particular tasks
- how to assess task requirements
- planning skills
- problem-solving skills
- monitoring skills
- evaluating skills
- reflective skills.

These skills must be acquired for musicians to be able to learn independently. However, to be used appropriately, they need to be embedded within a musical knowledge base. It is, for instance, impossible to evaluate progress in learning to play a piece of music unless you have considerable knowledge about the nature of the end product that you wish to achieve. This requires a substantial knowledge base, which is acquired through listening to much music.

EXERCISE 3.5: ANALYSING YOUR PRACTICE

Record yourself practising (sound or video). Listen to or watch the recording. Do you waste time when you are practising? Do the skills you are working on improve? How could you enhance your practising, so that skills improve more quickly? Could you mentally rehearse some elements that you practised in order to reduce the possibility of physical injury?

WHAT DO WE MEAN BY PERFORMANCE?

What constitutes 'performance' is socially defined and, as such, changes over time. Currently, most Western professional musicians tend to view performance in terms of public concerts given to an audience. However, with the increasing use of technology, most performances are no longer 'live' and performance is often in a studio where there is no immediate audience. As a recording is likely to reach a far wider audience than would be possible through live public performance, over time, musicians' conception of performance, and the way that they prepare for it, is likely to change.

The essence of musical performance is that it involves communication between the performer and the listener. However, we know very little about the nature of this communication. Those writing about performance tend not to consider this issue. They either consider how one should interpret particular works, the appropriate style of playing to be adopted, the value of authentic performances, or the cultural differences in music itself, which may determine differing performance environments. Little attention has been paid to understanding the performance situation itself.

The ways in which music is performed and understood within any one culture or subculture depends on shared understandings within that culture. In Western society there are many differing styles of music, which reflect differing subcultures, for example classical, jazz, folk, rock, pop. Each type of music is performed in particular ways in differing kinds of environments, although there are some similarities. Performance can be viewed in terms of a hierarchy of formal to less formal situations, which create different levels of stress in the performer – the least stressful being private performance, where one plays to oneself.

In musical performance, for communication to occur, there must be shared understanding of the meaning of the music among the participants in performance. Failure in communication might occur where shared meanings are not immediately available, for instance where music is unfamiliar or from a different culture. The listener's understanding of the work must be similar to that which the composer and performer intended.

While it seems clear that to give an effective musical performance one needs to communicate with an audience, we know very little about how this is achieved and the processes involved. Those elements that have been identified are related to:

- interpretation
- exaggeration of expression
- bodily movements.

INTERPRETATION

Interpretation is an important element in the level of communication established between a performer and an audience. While we may be impressed with technical mastery, particularly of a difficult work, this is not considered sufficient in performance. If it was, computers could be programmed to deliver 'perfect' technical performances and there would be no need for live performance or even alternative recordings of the same work. In comparison to human performance, computer simulations sound dull and lifeless.

Human performance varies, because it goes beyond the information in the printed score. When musicians play, each performance differs in subtle ways from any other performance. In fact, even within a single bar, there can be subtle variations of timing, loudness, tone quality, and intonation. It is these variations which contribute towards an expressive performance.[8]

Ideas for interpretation can be developed prior to learning to play the music or can evolve as the music is learnt.[9] Both approaches can provide performances of equal merit. Where interpretation is developed prior to learning a piece, it is usually based on extensive listening to that work, or to other works by the same composer or songwriter. Some musicians reject this approach, as they feel that it may influence their own interpretation to an unacceptable degree.

EXPRESSION

The communication of expression can only be effective when listeners can detect variations in performance and interpret them. The most effective communicators are more consistent in their use of expression and exaggerate it more.[10] The least effective communicators are inconsistent and violate 'rules' that the majority of performers obey. The use of expressive variation in the music which is exaggerated may actually help listeners to understand the structure of a piece of music.

MOVEMENT

The visual aspects of performance are also important. Davidson[11] has shown that body movements made by performers while playing contribute to the expressivity of the performance as judged by observers. Particular movements are related to specific structural features of the music. The movements seem to draw the observers' attention to particular aspects of the music.

ENHANCING MUSICAL COMMUNICATION SKILLS

To enhance your musical communication skills, you should:

- think of the communication of meaning as the central purpose of performing
- ensure that you have a musical message or intention which you wish to communicate
- listen to a number of interpretations of the music you are to perform, so that you can make an informed decision about what you are attempting to communicate
- ensure that you understand the structure of the work and think about how you might communicate this
- consider how you are going to develop interpretation
- experiment with different ways of playing the same music
- experiment with imitating different styles of playing
- consider using stories or analogies to develop ideas about meaning
- consider a wide range of possible meanings for every piece
- consider the range of emotions that any piece might demonstrate
- learn about the context of the music, the composer, the songwriter, his or her life and times
- reflect on the meaning that the composer or songwriter might have intended
- explore the background to the piece and its place in relation to other works by the same composer or songwriter
- exaggerate the playing of expression
- use movement to assist in the communication of musical meaning
- use video recordings of mock performances to enable you to assess the effectiveness of your musical communication.

SPECIFIC PREPARATION FOR PUBLIC PERFORMANCE

There are wide differences between musicians in their feelings about performance. Some musicians are so unconcerned regarding the performance situation that they feel the need to 'psych themselves up' in order to perform well; others experience debilitating nerves and use beta blocker drugs when performances are important or perceived as particularly stressful. Some feel that adequate preparation of the music is sufficient to ensure a good performance; others take nervousness into account when planning fingering, bowing, breathing and technical movement, and avoid taking risks which might not come off in performance. Where professional musicians have performed under conditions calculated to evoke high emotional arousal, their performance is generally judged to be better than when they perform under relaxed conditions. As one musician put it: 'without some anxiety performances would be very boring'. Some sort of 'spark' needs to be generated.[4] It is a question of arriving at the optimal level of anxiety. Experienced performers learn to let their arousal peak sharply just before the performance, whereas less-experienced performers suffer anxiety which builds over a long period of time and reaches its peak during the performance itself (see also Chapter 8).

Nervousness is not always consistent or necessarily predictable. Repeated performances of the same concert can result in different nervous reactions. Some musicians report going through spells of nervousness and, for a time, of 'being afraid of being afraid'. For this reason it is important that musicians are aware of the kinds of strategies that they can utilise to help them manage performance anxiety.

To support the management of performance anxiety, the following can be helpful.

LIFESTYLE

- Develop a lifestyle that ensures your overall physical and mental well-being.
- Perform relatively frequently, so that it becomes a familiar activity.

IN THE PLANNING STAGE

- Try to select opportunities for performance which will build up confidence.
- Ensure that the performance situation is appropriate for your level of expertise.
- Select the repertoire to demonstrate your strengths as well as to provide musical integrity.
- Ensure that the music is appropriate for the particular performing context.

IN THE PREPARATION STAGE

- Allow ample time for preparation.
- Ensure that the music is thoroughly known.
- Over-learn, as over-learnt skills are less susceptible to the effects of anxiety.
- To avoid boredom accompanying over-learning, concentrate on issues of interpretation and communication with the audience, as the performance draws near.
- Focus in your practice on interpreting the music.
- Ensure that the music is regularly and thoroughly rehearsed with any others involved in the performance (e.g. accompanist).
- Visualise the performing situation and experience sensations of nervousness by undertaking a mock performance to help develop coping strategies.
- Explore possibilities for mock performances in front of friends or family.
- Arrange to rehearse in the performance venue or other similar venues.
- Ensure that you can perform when there are distractions and non-optimal circumstances, e.g. different temperatures.
- Make sure that your instrument is in good working order and that nothing is likely to break in the immediate future.
- Ensure that you are confident about issues of presentation, dress, walking on, acknowledging applause. Practise these if necessary.
- As the performance draws near, try to reduce other sources of stress.
- Develop strategies that can be deployed if physical symptoms become overwhelming.
- Imagine and role-play the worst possible thing that could happen in performance.

IMMEDIATELY PRIOR TO THE PERFORMANCE

- Make sure that you allow adequate time for getting to the venue, changing, tuning your instrument, so that more stress is not created.
- Acknowledge to yourself that everyone feels nervous.

- Acknowledge to yourself that nervousness makes an important positive contribution to performance, by increasing alertness and concentration.

- Acknowledge that minor errors are not important. Most people make them and the audience is more interested in the overall impression conveyed by the music than the odd wrong note.

- Focus on the task in hand, how you are going to communicate your interpretation to the audience, doing well for the composer or some other distracting activity, e.g. breathing deeply.

CASE STUDY 3.2: OVERCOMING PERFORMANCE ANXIETY

Eleanor had a difficult experience when performing a solo in a concert in her hometown. She had been working very hard, doing a series of chamber music concerts and, although she knew the piece she was to perform very well, she had not put in the performance preparation that she usually did, as the performance environment was not very prestigious.

During the performance, she experienced severe nervousness, leading to her being unable to control her bowing arm. The quality of sound became very stuttering, and although she tried to relax the muscles, overall, she was very dissatisfied with the performance. Following this, she became 'afraid of being afraid'. Every performance became a major challenge to overcome her nervousness.

Eleanor came across some readings about stage fright and realised that she needed to ensure that her nervousness peaked immediately before the actual performance. After this, she allowed herself to feel nervous in advance, focused her attention on performance preparation, so that she was confident that she could easily manage the technical demands of the piece, and spent time thinking about what she wanted to communicate to the audience.

Immediately prior to the performance she adopted a coping strategy, playing down her own importance and raising that of the music and the enjoyment that she wanted the audience to experience. This was successful in ensuring that her performance was optimised. She continued to experience nervousness prior to concerts, but used this to energise the performance and fix her attention on musical communication with the audience.

FOR ACTION DURING THE PERFORMANCE

- Focus on communicating musical meaning to the audience.
- Enact strategies for overcoming physical symptoms, if necessary.
- If you make errors, don't allow them to disrupt what is coming next.

AFTER THE PERFORMANCE

- Reflect on the performance, how you felt about it, what went well, what you might do better next time.
- Plan future performances in the light of experiences.

EXERCISE 3.6: ANALYSING YOUR PERFORMANCE

Video-record yourself in an actual performance (get a friend to do it) or in a mock performance. What strikes you about your performance? Do you need to work to create more of a 'spark' and to psych yourself up for performance, or do you need to implement strategies to overcome performance anxiety?

Think of performances that have gone really well. What contributed to these outstanding performances? How can you replicate that?

CHAPTER SUMMARY: PRACTISING AND PREPARING FOR PERFORMANCE

Practice is vital in learning to play a musical instrument.

There is individual variation in the amount of time required for practice and the nature of the practice required.

Practice needs to be tailored to suit individual needs.

Musicians need to acquire a range of task-oriented and person-oriented strategies.

Practice is more effective when it focuses on musical issues.

The functions of music within society can provide many and varied performance opportunities for musicians.

The essence of musical performance is communication, which occurs between the composer, the performer and audience.

Musicians can help themselves to become effective musical communicators, by focusing on interpretation, the exaggeration of expressive features and the use of movement.

Preparing for public performance requires an awareness of one's own characteristics and performing history and of the performance environment.

FURTHER READING

Jorgensen, H. and Hallam, S. (2009) 'Practising'. In S. Hallam, I. Cross and M. Thaut (eds), *Oxford Handbook of Music Psychology*. Oxford: Oxford University Press, 265–73. This chapter provides an overview of the research on practising, including its importance and the strategies that can be used to enhance it.

Williamon, A. (ed.) (2004) *Musical Excellence: Strategies and techniques to enhance performance*. Oxford: Oxford University Press. This book is an excellent resource if you wish to explore in more depth the research relating to studying music in higher education. It has chapters on practising and performing, and a range of strategies that you can adopt to promote your health and well-being.

NOTES

1. Schwarz, B. (1983) *Great Masters of the Violin*. London: Robert Hale.

2. Pfaff, T. (1989) 'Monster music: Violinist Nigel Kennedy is ready for anything'. *Strings*, Spring, 36–9.

3. Jorgensen, H. and Hallam, S. (2009) 'Practising'. In S. Hallam, I. Cross and M. Thaut (eds), *Oxford Handbook of Music Psychology*. Oxford: Oxford University Press, 265–73.

4. Hallam, S. (1995) 'Professional musicians' orientations to practice: Implications for teaching'. *British Journal of Music Education*, 12(1), 3–20.

5. Hallam, S. (2001) 'The development of metacognition in musicians: Implications for education'. *British Journal of Music Education*, 18(1), 27–39.

6. Hallam, S. (1997) 'The development of memorisation strategies in musicians: Implications for instrumental teaching'. *British Journal of Music Education*, 14(1), 87–97.

7. Hallam, S. (2009) 'Motivation to learn'. In S. Hallam, I. Cross and M. Thaut (eds), *Oxford Handbook of Music Psychology*. Oxford: Oxford University Press, 285–94.

8. Shaffer, L.H. (1992) 'How to interpret music'. In M.R. Jones and S. Holleran (eds), *Cognitive Bases of Musical Communication*. Washington, DC: American Psychological Association.

9. Hallam, S. (1995) 'Professional musicians' approaches to the learning and interpretation of music'. *Psychology of Music*, 23, 111–28.

10. Sloboda, J.A. (1983) 'The communication of musical metre in piano performance'. *Quarterly Journal of Experimental Psychology*, 35A, 377–96.

11. Davidson, J.W. (1993). 'Visual perception of performance manner in the movement of solo musicians'. *Psychology of Music*, 21(2), 103–13.

CHAPTER 4
MAKING THE MOST OF INDIVIDUAL LESSONS

INTRODUCTION

This chapter explores the power of individual lessons and how you can use this opportunity most productively. It focuses on:

- different approaches to individual lessons and what they may achieve
- what research indicates about the strengths and challenges of individual lessons
- strategies for getting the most out of individual lessons and building effective interpersonal relationships with teachers.

THE POWER OF INDIVIDUAL LESSONS

In some musical cultures, individual lessons have no place at all. In others, they have been at the heart of the learning process for centuries. Cross-fertilisation of approaches to teaching and learning in different genres means that individual lessons are being used in a wider range of contexts. Most musicians also experience important one-to-one interactions in their musical development through informal coaching or mentoring situations, if not through formal lessons. Much of what is covered in this chapter is also relevant to these contexts.

Before focusing on individual lessons, it is worth pointing out a common misconception, particularly among people who experience a lot of individual tuition: that an individual teacher will be the answer to everything, solving all problems and taking responsibility for your development. Tempting though it can be to view the relationship in this way, it can easily generate a passive approach to learning, reducing your own creativity as the student, reducing your motivation, and reducing your ability to learn from different situations. When they work well, individual lessons produce a fantastic creative partnership. If, however, you feel that you are starting to put in less effort yourself in lessons, then it may simply be that you are starting to depend too much on your teacher.

In some fields, peer learning and developing within a group are more highly prized than individual lessons, because the learning environment can be richer and can develop faster.[1] For example, a drum teacher in popular music has suggested:

> *Lessons happen in groups up to 12. The groups are great: you get the ones who aren't keeping up, but mostly they're excellent for people watching what other people do. Sometimes as a teacher I've explained something every way I can, but one of the other guys will have another way of explaining it. Ninety per cent of the time I'd say that it's better than individual lessons.*

Whatever your own preferences and experiences, extending your personal ability to learn effectively in different situations is an excellent way to prepare for life beyond formal education (lifelong learning) and to build resilience as a musician. Many of the best professional musicians have developed the ability to learn continually from others in different ways and different contexts. As one player said about working in an orchestral section: 'every day of your life you go to work and you get a lesson free without a word being said'.

THE EMOTIONAL IMPACT OF INDIVIDUAL LESSONS

Relatively little research has as yet been done into individual lessons in music. What is certain, however, is that students' experiences vary considerably. Many people – not least those who have gone on to be successful classical musicians – report positively about them, finding that they provide essential inspiration, access to musical and technical skills, and personal support. Others have felt disempowered by them, and have even been put off pursuing a career in music as a result. The examples in Case Study 4.1 demonstrate just how powerful the impact of individual lessons can be, both positively and negatively.

In recent years, research about learning in higher education more generally has begun to show that learning is an emotional experience. It depends on the overall environment, existing levels of knowledge and expertise, and the processes and strategies being used to enable learning, as well as on the subject content being introduced (see Chapter 2). Relationships that develop between students and teachers are therefore particularly important. This may be true, for example, even in the context of large lectures, where a single teacher works with 200–300 students at a time.[2] In one-to-one interactions, the significance of the relationship is amplified considerably.

CASE STUDY 4.1: STUDENT EXPERIENCES OF LEARNING IN INDIVIDUAL LESSONS

Student 1: 'I am one of the very lucky people who have found a teacher that I work well with, and a lot of people actually never find that. And she has been more than just a professor of the [instrument] for me, she has been there for me when, any number of crises happened…people dying…with relationships, kind of anything, she's always been there, dedicated, just sort of ready to talk and help me.'

Student 2: '[The teacher would] never put his [instrument] down. He would always have to have his [instrument], and sort of play absolutely amazingly, and try and get me to do it and I couldn't. I would just feel stupid.'

Student 3: 'I go to a lesson and play just ok-ish, and by the end of the lesson I am playing really well, and that's just great. I go home and really try to carry that on.'

Student 4: 'A past teacher used to burden her pupils with her own difficulties: if she had a bad day, then so did her pupils, though I didn't realise that at the time. Though technically it was the best move to work with her – my technique improved tenfold.'

Effective one-to-one student–teacher relationships have been characterised as mutual, personally intimate and adventurous, and based fundamentally on trust.[3] It is perhaps not surprising then that students are likely to have quite different experiences with different teachers. The rapport that develops within each student–teacher pair is individual. One teacher's approach may work well with one student but not so well with another. The experience may depend on, among other things, the combination of personalities, the match between their expectations and aspirations, their approaches to learning, and psychological preferences in how they interact with one another.

This is not only the case in music but is also relevant to many one-to-one learning partnerships. Donald Schön explored the processes by which students acquired professional-level skills across a range of disciplines, including music. In a case study of a master architect and his students, there were considerable contrasts in the experiences of the different students. One student, for example, established a creative relationship with the master architect, learning at a remarkable pace, producing great work and feeling highly motivated. Another student was baffled and frustrated in the relationship, found that her efforts tended to be criticised, lost motivation, and struggled to progress. She was, however, able to thrive with another teacher.[4]

WHAT ARE INDIVIDUAL LESSONS FOR?

APPRENTICESHIP AND MENTORING

A key issue for anyone having individual lessons is to be clear about their purpose. Historically, the predominant way of thinking about individual lessons has been in terms of passing on craft and musical skills from a master to an apprentice.

The apprenticeship model is particularly powerful, in that it brings students into direct contact with a teacher who is an expert in their field. Students can absorb in minute detail what it is the teacher does, how they play, sing or compose, even when this cannot all be physically seen or described in words. Similarly, the teacher can experience a student's own efforts at close hand and give detailed feedback.[5]

Apprenticeship, however, is just one of several ways of thinking about individual lessons, and the last few years have seen considerable development of different perspectives. In particular a stronger focus on the student at the heart of learning has been identified, and on the significance of students articulating their own objectives and finding an individual voice.[6] In music, for example, the concept of a student–teacher relationship as a creative partnership underlines the importance of the student being active and creative in the learning process (rather than waiting to be filled with knowledge and skill by the teacher).[7]

The concept of mentoring being embedded within individual lessons also emphasises a focus on facilitating an individual's short-, medium- and long-term personal and professional development, with the process being driven by the mentee (student) rather than by the mentor (teacher).[8] Mentoring considers individuals in a broad context, and in essence aims to 'assist the learner to integrate as a fully functioning person within the society they inhabit'.[9] Mentoring within individual lessons supports a student in taking ownership of their learning, and enables them to focus on personal and professional development beyond the issues directly contained within the musical materials being studied.[10] This is perhaps particularly relevant now, because of the context of rapid change within the music industry, and the need for musicians to be flexible and to think outside the box, quite possibly beyond the immediate professional expertise of their individual teacher.[11]

DEMONSTRATION AND PROVIDING MUSICAL MODELS

Anyone wanting to be a practical musician has to develop practical craft skills. This is 'embodied knowledge', not something that can simply be learnt from a set of theories or facts presented in a book. Individual lessons tend, therefore, to be a way in which students interact directly with a professional practitioner, who is likely to demonstrate by playing or singing in lessons. A teacher may well therefore be asked to teach on a programme because of their exceptional expertise as a musician, rather than because of their proven skills as a teacher.

The degree to which teachers demonstrate musically in a lesson, either through playing the instrument or through singing, is a matter of personal style. Research has suggested that demonstrating (i.e. providing a musical model) is more effective than talking, or even mixing talking and demonstrating.[12] Some dangers, however, have been identified with copying musical models, for example the risk of the student becoming a copy of a particular artist or teacher and not establishing their own artistic voice.[13]

The advantages of demonstration are that, as a student, you can pick up all kinds of information aurally or through observing physical movements, rather than through listening to verbal instruction. Using musical models is also more common in some genres than others. In jazz, for example, having much less music notated than, for example, classical music, a student will have to work from the musical models all the time, typically learning to reproduce what others have done, and then starting to play around with the material, transposing, embellishing and then transforming it, as a personal language of expression evolves.

FEEDBACK

There is a lot of evidence that in fact teachers often spend a lot of time talking in lessons: a common pattern is that students tend to play in lessons and not say very much, while teachers tend to talk and not play very much.[14] This raises a critical issue about types of verbal interaction in lessons and what kind of feedback students get from them. It is important to understand what you find helpful in terms of feedback, and what is less effective.

Principles of good feedback that have been identified more widely in relation to higher education include:

- clarifying what good work/performance is
- facilitating the development of self-assessment and reflection
- delivering high-quality information to students about their learning and specific changes they can make in order to progress and improve work/performance
- encouraging dialogue around learning
- encouraging positive motivational beliefs and self-esteem.[15]

We know that comments such as 'that's lovely' or 'you're wonderful' may be a useful compliment at times, but they give no indication about what was particularly good and might be repeated. If nothing is identified that will give you the power to improve, this is likely to feel demotivating after a while. Similarly, negative feedback that gives you no clue about what or how to improve will almost certainly feel destructive. On the other hand, feedback that is specific about what is working well or less well, and how it might be improved, is likely to be constructive.

It is vital to understand how you respond to different kinds of feedback and how they affect your progress. In some cases, it may be possible to ask a teacher for particular kinds of feedback that you know will be beneficial.

EXERCISE 4.1: UNDERSTANDING HOW YOU RESPOND TO DIFFERENT KINDS OF FEEDBACK

How do each of the following kinds of feedback make you feel?
- That was fantastic. You have such a beautiful voice/instrument.
- My overall impression was that the performance was too static, lacking in flow. What would it be like if you took a faster tempo?
- That was unmusical. Try it again
- The crescendo in that passage helped to build up the musical tension of this section. How would the music be affected if you started even quieter?

In each case, how would you respond and what would you do next? To what extent would the feedback help to keep you motivated?

OPENING DOORS TO A PROFESSIONAL COMMUNITY

Through individual lessons, and a relationship built up over a period of several years, teachers may begin to introduce students to their professional networks, offer tips about getting started as a professional, or give them work. These wider dimensions of individual lessons can have a huge impact. A study in the UK found that in the cases where a teacher had a particularly good reputation, there was the feeling that becoming their student could increase the chances of success. One student reported:

> My current teacher…has a very strong reputation, and he has had a lot of successful students in the past. So obviously that also influences people in deciding to go to him…I guess that puts him in a little bit of a halo…[With him] I will be successful, perhaps he will spot something in me just as he spotted something in X person who has gone on to do this.[16]

The degree to which a teacher may introduce you into a professional community may be an important consideration for you. Note that when a teacher can offer a step up into the profession, the nature of the student–teacher relationship is likely to change, as it begins to extend into a relationship of professional colleagues. Some students, however, may also feel discriminated against, if their teacher gives such opportunities to others but not to them. It is therefore important to reflect on how much you are reliant on a teacher's help in this respect and how much you can build wider networks to assist with getting your career started.

GOAL-SETTING AND PLANNING

Learning in individual lessons is often focused around particular repertoire or technical development. In this context, concentration on detail and short-term goals is likely to dominate. Planning and reflecting on the work may also focus on immediate issues in hand. Research looking at classical musicians suggests that students' planning tends to relate to short- and medium-term performance goals (often relating to assessment requirements and/or performance engagements), with longer-term goals having lower priority.[17] A study of university-level students in the USA showed that these patterns were more prevalent with the more advanced students. Teachers indicated that it was important to have a long-range plan for students who were taking music as a minor part of their programme, but did not identify this as a priority for students who were taking music as a major part of their programme.[18]

A study of conservatoire musicians in the UK found that most students made occasional notes and directions in the copies of the music they were playing. A few kept a notebook in which they wrote details of new music to be found, recordings to hear, or particular ideas and exercises that teachers suggested. Very few kept reflective notes, for example about their individual practising or about inspiring comments and tips from masterclasses. In general, there was relatively little evidence of students planning or reflecting on their longer-term personal and artistic development as part of their individual tuition.[13]

At the same time, it is clear that considering and planning for longer-term artistic and personal development is vital. Indeed, it is both a feature of some individual lessons, and also something which many teachers wish to achieve.[19] Typically, the teaching approaches used to facilitate this kind of work will relate closely to a framework of mentoring. They will include reflective techniques to evaluate experience, form a vision for the future and plan key steps. They may also involve keeping a reflective journal over a period of time as a way of deepening self-awareness and understanding artistic, professional and personal identity. For more on setting goals, see Chapter 2.

EXERCISE 4.2: WHAT CAN YOUR TEACHER(S) HELP WITH?

Your personal needs from individual tuition will probably change over time. Different teachers have different things to offer. Your ideas will be affected by professional aspirations, previous experience and your stage of development. Choosing a teacher is extremely important (there is more on this later in this chapter). This exercise is designed to help identify what you are looking for from a teacher. Table 4.1 sets out a range of activities that might feature as a part of learning in individual lessons. Rate each of these on a scale according to your current needs:

- 1 for an essential priority
- 2 for definitely important
- 3 for having some relevance.

A word of caution: if you score each of these with a 1, you are unlikely to be satisfied by any one teacher. Be realistic and think about the different ways in which you can meet different needs. Remember as well that your priorities are likely to change over time.

TABLE 4.1: PRIORITISING NEEDS FROM INDIVIDUAL LESSONS

Activities in individual lessons	How important to you (1–3)?
Formulating and discussing short-term goals	
Formulating and discussing medium-term goals	
Formulating and discussing long-term goals, including discussing big questions such as 'Why are you a musician?', and considering possible professional pathways	
Considering what motivates you and how to strengthen and sustain intrinsic motivation	
Making professional contacts	
Developing effective personal and time management skills	
Enhancing health and well-being, including effective ways to manage injuries or prevent injuries	
Developing high-level practising skills	
Developing sight-reading skills	
Developing aural skills	
Developing performance skills and ways of preparing for performance	
Preparing for auditions and/or competitions	
Developing awareness of, and facility with, a broad range of musical styles	
Building knowledge and experience of particular repertoire	
Developing an individual artistic and professional voice	
Developing improvisation skills	
Developing composing skills	
Developing quality of sound	
Developing technical facility	

One thing that can really support the success of individual lessons is developing a shared understanding with a teacher about aims and objectives in the short, medium and long term. You may be able to do this together. However, you can also reflect and plan with support from friends, peers or mentors, and then share the goals you have identified with a teacher.

THE ONE-TO-ONE RELATIONSHIP

PERSONAL INTIMACY – A RELATIONSHIP BUILT ON TRUST AND MUTUAL RESPECT

The relationship between student and teacher is central to the impact of individual lessons. Evidence suggests that, in general, successful relationships are firmly based on trust and mutual respect. Establishing trust takes time, but this is what usually provides a student with the foundation to take risks in their development, have the confidence to move out of their comfort zone, and so reach new levels of achievement. As one student suggested:

> it takes a long time to actually trust the teacher...I would have thought it took the entire first year to trust my teacher, and then this year...I have been able to actually see the progress I have made, just because I have gone hell for leather into whatever he has said, and thought 'ok, well I will just do it and see what happens'.[16]

Teachers also tend to value the element of trust in the work they do with students, and emphasise the personal nature of the relationships that evolve, often drawing analogies with intimate relationships, such as those between parents and children, or between close friends, or even between a doctor and patient. Some examples are given in Case Study 4.2.

These analogies emphasise the sense of responsibility that teachers often feel, and throw up possible tensions between a personal and a professional relationship, or between authority and equality in the dynamics of learning.

CASE STUDY 4.2: TEACHER PERCEPTIONS OF THE STUDENT–TEACHER RELATIONSHIP

Teacher 1: 'It's a cross between parenting and friendship that makes the best relationship. I think parenting in as much as you shouldn't underestimate how much guidance they still need at this age…in terms of their personal lives… because you're the only person they see on a one-to-one [basis]…Just a little experience of life to be able to give a bit of advice…and friendship…because unless they feel that you're on their side, you can't give them what you need to give…I find that if I've made a good friend of them, then when I tell them that they've done well, or I can give them confidence, support them…I think they believe you…It's the balance of praise and criticism, to handle praise and criticism long term over three or four years, to have that balance.'

Teacher 2: 'It's a bit like going to the doctor's, isn't it? If you go to the doctor's and say, "Look, I've a terrible pain here in my neck here" or bad stomach… he's only doing what we are doing. He says, "Well I think it's so-and so. So get these pills from the chemist and come and see me next week." You go back the following week and he goes, "How did you go?" and you go, "It's still the same"…"Did you take the pills?"…"No." So he doesn't know if they would work or they didn't. If you took the pills and they don't work – you still have the same problem. Then he knows that that is the wrong thing.'

THE 'HALO' EFFECT AND BECOMING DEPENDENT ON A TEACHER

A downside of the intensity and intimacy of one-to-one student–teacher relationships is that they have the potential to create unhelpful dependency on both sides, for example resulting in reluctance to value other learning relationships and interactions as significant, and in tensions around responsibility for the success of a student.[20] Students' own musical interpretative skills and artistic voice may also be inhibited.[21]

Particularly in the earlier years of study, students may become reliant on their one-to-one teacher for advice on a range of issues not necessarily within the teacher's sphere of expertise. For example, they may turn to them for advice with health issues, rather than turning to health professionals with expert knowledge in this field.[22] Similarly, some one-to-one teachers may be tempted to provide all the answers for a student, about medical and personal – as well as musical – issues.[23]

One research study in the USA referred to a 'halo' effect, where students were unable to discriminate between the performing abilities of their various teachers, as they invested so much in the relationship.[18]

Another study in the UK revealed a student being awestruck by the success of the teacher, her musical achievements and perceived celebrity status. This student was in fact disempowered by the gap between herself and the teacher, and only began to find the confidence to believe in her own artistic voice when she started having lessons from another teacher as well:

> You obviously think that your teachers are fantastic…you worship them almost…you think, 'wow, I want your life and I want the way you play, I want everything', and you expect them to help you 100 per cent. Whereas, when you have got more than two teachers, you suddenly… make the decision of what you are taking to them…it takes a while for you to get the confidence to say 'no I am a person in my own right, and if I want to do "mf" here and "diminuendo" here, I can'.[13]

POWER DYNAMICS, ETHICAL AND SOCIAL BOUNDARIES

The dynamics of power and the boundaries to the relationship are rarely made explicit in individual lessons, particularly once a student is over 18. They are, however, worth considering, particularly when choosing a teacher (see also Preparation 4.1 later in this chapter). For example:

- Is what happens in lessons confidential?
- What are the ground rules around lessons being cancelled or postponed on either side?
- Is physical touch OK?
- Will you discuss personal issues?
- Will you socialise together outside lessons?

In practice, these issues are rarely negotiated openly, although this would be an essential requirement within other professional one-to-one relationships. Certainly the ways in which these ethical and social dimensions of the relationship operate can be hugely diverse.[13]

EXERCISE 4.3: REFLECTING ON YOUR OWN EXPERIENCES OF STUDENT–TEACHER RELATIONSHIPS

The images in Figure 4.1 illustrate a variety of possibilities with one-to-one relationships. Use these to reflect on your own experiences with a current or previous teacher, or to imagine the kind of relationship that you would like to have.

In each case think about:

- what the relationship feels like
- what sorts of behaviours the relationship produces
- how the relationship impacts on your development.

Figure 4.1:
Images of one-to-one relationships
Illustrations by Jamie Wignall

MAKING INDIVIDUAL LESSONS SUCCESSFUL

Learning in individual lessons is challenging. It requires dedication and emotional intelligence. This section sets out some key things to help you make the most of them.

EXERCISE 4.4: CHOOSING A TEACHER

The importance of choosing a teacher and finding a good match should never be underestimated.[24] A teacher's high reputation is of course important, but it does not necessarily mean that they will be the right person for you. Preparation 4.1 summarises questions to consider in choosing a teacher. Have your responses to Exercise 4.2 to hand, and see how these map against your answers to this exercise.

Where possible, have consultation lessons with several teachers, so that you can compare them. Observing a teacher is also extremely helpful and will give you a more objective view. If you are in a situation where you have no choice about your teacher, use this exercise to increase your understanding of how your teacher works and how you can most benefit from working with them.

PREPARATION 4.1: QUESTIONS TO CONSIDER IN CHOOSING A TEACHER

1. What does a teacher tend to focus on: aspects of technique, musicianship, certain types of repertoire, creativity, development of an individual voice, career development? How does this fit with your needs?

2. What kind of teaching methods does a teacher use: demonstration, detailed and scientific explanation, metaphors, questions? Which methods do you find most effective? What kind of feedback do they give and how constructive is it?

3. What expectations does a teacher have? Will they want you to follow a particular career path and how do you feel about this? How much do they focus on your longer-

term development? Do they have particular favourites or treat students differently in terms of the opportunities they offer?

4. What are a teacher's pupils like? Are they all very different as musicians, or all rather similar? How motivated do they seem? What do they enjoy most and least about their lessons? How much do they trust the teacher and how balanced a view do they have of them? How easy is it for any of them to change teacher if things do not go well?

5. What kind of rapport might you have with a teacher? How informal/formal might your interactions be and how would this suit you? How easy would it be to trust them? Would they be likely to breach confidentiality about you to other people? Does a teacher have any kind of reputation for entering into sexual relations with students?

6. How available is a teacher? How regular are the lessons they could give you? Where would these be and how long?

7. How much does a teacher ask you to give your own opinion, come up with your own ideas, solve your own problems?

8. Does a teacher ask you to record lessons? How much do they make notes for you or ask you to take notes? What kind of planning do they help you to do? How do they help you with what and how to practise?

9. What is a teacher's professional profile as a musician, and how does this align with your aspirations and goals? How will their profile affect your motivation? Will they be in a position to offer you work? If so, how will this affect you, for example spurring you on to work harder or making it difficult for you to be open about problems you are having?

10. What experience or qualification does this person have as a teacher, and how important is this at your stage of development? (Many individual teachers in music are not trained as teachers. This means that their repertoire of musical skills may be much stronger than their repertoire of teaching skills. As you become more sophisticated as a learner, the level of teaching skill will probably become less and less important to you. It may be more important in the earlier stages of development.)

11. Will you have one or more than one individual teacher? (This may make a difference to your choice. Having two teachers will encourage you to be more independent and to take greater responsibility for your own learning. You will have to plan your preparation more carefully and deal with differences of opinion between them.[25])

PREPARING FOR LESSONS

Preparation is a vital ingredient in making the most of individual lessons. This includes time spent practising, but it can also focus on other activities. These are summarised in Preparation 4.2.

PREPARATION 4.2: INDIVIDUAL LESSONS

1. Spend some time setting out your short-, medium- and long-term aims. Return to these regularly and update them.

2. Reflect on how you are learning and developing through your lessons. What strengths does your teacher have? How are you making the most of them?

3. Share experiences with your peers. How do you approach lessons? What strategies make your experience most effective? How can you adapt your approach to get more out of the lessons?

4. Work hard and develop your practising skills in the widest sense (see Chapter 3). Plan your work so that you can achieve the goals agreed with your teacher as far as possible.

5. Think about any questions that you have about what you are doing in lessons, for example questions about technical difficulties or musical ideas, questions about how to practise or what concerts/gigs to attend. This will help to avoid the habit of waiting to be told what to do.

6. Take responsibility for connecting the work in individual lessons to other aspects of your learning as a whole. Remember that your teacher may not be involved in other parts of the curriculum or have much knowledge of it. What skills or areas of music are you working on that might be useful for your teacher to know about? Are there particular things that your teacher could help you with in relation to these? Can your teacher help you to solve specific problems?

7. Be proactive in helping to shape your development. Look out for opportunities to perform, extra courses to go on, and relevant professional opportunities. Find repertoire or other things you want to study, so that you can bring these into the planning that you do with a teacher.

WORKING EFFECTIVELY IN LESSONS

There are many factors that may affect the success of individual lessons, and neither you nor your teacher can be completely in control of how things work out; they depend on the partnership. There are, however, a number of things that you can do that will help to make lessons a success. These are summarised in Preparation 4.3.

PREPARATION 4.3: WORKING EFFECTIVELY IN LESSONS

1. Discuss your aims and objectives with your teacher and agree some specific goals together for each few months of work. Have the courage to discuss focusing on areas of work that you have not covered previously.

2. Listen and watch carefully in lessons. So much of becoming a musician has to come through practical trial and error. Be open to absorbing what your teacher has to offer. Be brave, take risks and try things out, even if they feel strange to begin with. Treat lessons as a place to experiment and explore. This is a place where it should be fine to fail – a lesson does not always need to be a performance.

3. Find out what your teacher expects of you, not least in terms of how you approach your work in between lessons. Clarify at the end of a lesson exactly what you are going to work on for the next lesson and how you are going to do this. This will help you to be well prepared and to avoid misunderstandings.

4. Find ways to remember the key points from a lesson and reflect on them. Try recording your lessons, or making notes during or immediately after them. Ask for further explanation if anything is bothering you. Ask yourself questions about what you have learnt and how you can take this further in your own work.

5. Be professional in your attitude. Be on time for lessons and check that you have all materials needed with you. Contact your teacher as far in advance as possible, if you are not going to be able to attend a lesson. Whether or not you have a more social part to your relationship, be prepared to concentrate, work hard and have fun during a lesson, as this will make it more satisfying for both of you.

MANAGING DIFFICULTIES AND CHANGING TEACHERS

As individual lessons are such an intense experience, involving a personal relationship, it is not surprising that people do experience difficulties along the way. Most teachers acknowledge that they have difficulties with students of one kind or another. This is a normal part of the process. If you are struggling, you are not alone, and the first thing to remember is that usually many of the problems can be solved.

The key to managing difficulties with a teacher is to start communicating about the difficulties at an early stage. If you let them fester, they will tend to escalate and become harder to resolve. Talking to your teacher may be easier said than done, however. Acknowledging the difficulty may feel dangerous, as so much is invested in the relationship. It may be helpful to start by talking to someone else – a friend, mentor or programme leader – as this may enable you to gain a more objective perspective on the situation. However, it is also important to be proactive and to discuss issues with your teacher directly. If possible, identify steps that you can both take to improve the situation and refocus the activities.

In cases where difficulties cannot be resolved through discussion, most institutions will have formal processes for changing teacher. At this stage, it is vital to consult with relevant course leaders and senior staff, to ensure that you understand the procedures, your rights and the possible outcomes. It is also important to have a network of support. This might include previous teachers, peers, friends and family. Changing teachers as a result of difficulties in lessons is likely to be an emotionally charged experience, because of the personal nature of the student–teacher relationship.

It will probably also be important to begin a process of finding another teacher. Note, however, that it can be extremely damaging to the relationship with your current teacher if you have consultation lessons and find another teacher without discussing this with your current teacher or consulting with those responsible for your programme.

CHAPTER SUMMARY: MAKING THE MOST OF INDIVIDUAL LESSONS

Learning from others is crucial in becoming a musician – this can be through individual contact or in groups.

Teachers can provide demonstrations, give feedback and open doors to the professional community.

Having positive interpersonal relationships with teachers is important – these should be based on trust and mutual respect.

While learning from a teacher plays an important role in becoming a musician, it is crucial not to become dependent on the teacher, but to develop independence in learning.

To make the most of lessons, it is important to prepare for them and use the lesson time productively.

Where relationships with a teacher are interfering with learning, you need to seek advice on an appropriate course of action from senior staff within the institution.

FURTHER READING

Gaunt, H. (2010). 'One-to-one tuition in a conservatoire: The perceptions of instrumental and vocal students'. *Psychology of Music*, 38(2), 178–208. This paper sets out research findings that go into more detail about some of the key issues described in this chapter: particularly how one-to-one tuition may affect the ways in which students learn to think for themselves and plan their own professional development.

Goleman, D. (1996) *Emotional Intelligence: Why it can matter more than IQ*. London: Bantam Books. This is a classic book that highlights how much our emotional responses affect us and our interactions with others. It may be a particularly useful resource for those who experience a lot of one-to-one tuition, as the emotional dimensions of the student–teacher relationship in this context are clearly significant.

John-Steiner, V. (2000) *Creative Collaboration*. Oxford: Oxford University Press. The book contains examples of several different collaborations between eminent people. Most of these are not within music, but they provide a fascinating window on the dynamics involved between the collaborators and some of the processes they went through.

NOTES

1. Hewitt, A. (2004) 'Students' attributions of sources of influence on self-perception in solo performance in music'. *Research Studies in Music Education*, 22, 42–58.

2. Ramsden, P. (2003) *Learning to Teach in Higher Education*. London: Routledge Falmer.

3. Salmon, P. (1992) *Achieving a PhD: Ten students' experience*. London: Trentham Books.

4. Schön, D.A. (1987) *Educating the Reflective Practitioner*. San Francisco: Jossey-Bass Inc.

5. Gholson, S.A. (1998) 'Proximal positioning: A strategy of practice in violin pedagogy'. *Journal of Research in Music Education*, 46(4), 535–45.

6. Pratt, D.D. (1992) 'Conceptions of teaching'. *Adult Education Quarterly*, 42(4), 203–20.

7. Barrett, M.S. and Gromko, J.E. (2007) 'Provoking the muse: A case study of teaching and learning in music composition'. *Psychology of Music*, 35(2), 213–30.

8. Megginson, D. and Clutterbuck, D. (2009) *Techniques for Coaching and Mentoring*. London: Elsevier.

9. Garvey, R., Stokes, P. and Megginson, D. (2009) *Coaching and Mentoring: Theory and practice*. London: Sage, 21.

10. Gaunt, H. (2011) 'Understanding the one-to-one relationship in instrumental/vocal tuition in higher education: Comparing student and teacher perceptions'. *British Journal of Music Education*, 28(2), 159–80.

11. Renshaw, P. (2006) 'Lifelong Learning for Musicians: The place of mentoring'. Online. http://tinyurl.com/bv8yjtn (accessed 31 August 2011).

12. Rosenthal, R. (1984) 'The relative effects of guided model, model only, guide only and practice only treatments on the accuracy of advanced instrumentalists' musical performance'. *Journal of Research in Music Education*, 32(4), 265–73.

13. Gaunt, H. (2010) 'One-to-one tuition in a conservatoire: The perceptions of instrumental and vocal students'. *Psychology of Music*, 38(2), 178–208.

14. Hepler, L.E. (1986) 'The measurement of teacher-student interaction in private music lessons and its relationship to teacher field dependence/field independence'. PhD thesis, Cleveland, Case Western Reserve University.

15. Nicol, D. and Milligan, C. (2006) 'Rethinking technology-supported assessment practices in relation to the seven principles of good feedback practice'. In C. Bryan and K. Clegg (eds), *Innovative Assessment in Higher Education*. London: Routledge, 64–77.

16. Gaunt, H. (2006) 'Student and teacher perceptions of one-to-one instrumental and vocal tuition in a conservatoire'. PhD thesis, School of Lifelong Learning and International Development, Institute of Education, University of London, 195.

17. L'Hommidieu, R.L. (1992) 'The management of selected educational variables by master studio teachers in music performance'. PhD thesis, Evanston, IL: Northwestern University.

18. Abeles, H.F., Goffi, J. and Levasseur, H. (1992) 'The components of effective applied instruction'. *Quarterly Journal of Music Teaching and Learning*, 3(2), 17–23.

19. Gaunt, H. (2008) 'One-to-one tuition in a conservatoire: The perceptions of instrumental and vocal teachers'. *Psychology of Music*, 36(2), 215–45.

20. Jorgensen, H. (2000) 'Student learning in higher instrumental education: Who is responsible?' *British Journal of Music Education*, 17(1), 67–77.

21. Burwell, K. (2005) 'A degree of independence: Teachers' approaches to instrumental tuition in a university college'. *British Journal of Music Education*, 22(3), 199–215.

22. Williamon, A. and Thompson, S. (2006) 'Awareness and incidence of health problems among conservatoire students'. *Psychology of Music*, 34(4), 411–30.

23. Chesky, K. (2004) 'Health promotion in schools of music'. Proceedings of the Seminar of the Commission for the Education of the Professional Musician, International Society for Music Education. Barcelona, Escola Superior de Música de Catalunya, 29–34.

24. Presland, C. (2005) 'Conservatoire student and instrumental professor: The student perspective on a complex relationship'. *British Journal of Music Education*, 22(3), 237–48.

25. Haddon, E. (2011) 'Multiple teachers: Multiple gains?' *British Journal of Music Education*, 28(1), 69–85.

CHAPTER 5
IMPROVISING AND NURTURING YOUR CREATIVITY

INTRODUCTION

This chapter focuses on improvisation and how to nurture your creativity. It outlines:

- the processes involved in improvisation
- the skills that are needed
- how those skills can be developed
- how creativity develops
- how the individual can maximise opportunities to be creative.

Globalisation has had an impact on the way that we think about composition and improvisation. Music from around the world is now easily available, enabling the exploration of music and ways of working that are unfamiliar to those brought up in Western cultures. In many places, particularly where music is not notated, music-making is a social activity, the role of the individual as a composer is of less importance, and the division between improvisation and composition is blurred – as indeed it was in much early Western music and continues to be in jazz.

A wide range of activities involve improvisational elements. Young children improvise songs, while free improvisation can be used as a means of communication in music therapy, to develop self-esteem and a range of skills in those with special educational needs or mental health problems, and in collaborative work with disciplines outside the arts at the professional level. The common element in all improvisations is that creative decisions take place within the real time of the performance.

The term 'improvisation' covers a wide range of musical phenomena and incorporates a multiplicity of musical meanings. It may involve slight deviation of rhythm or articulation from what had been rehearsed, the relatively planned realisation of a piano continuo part, many kinds of free unplanned music, or variation in the interpretation of graphic scores. Broadly speaking, improvisation is the performance of music which is not written down. But the construct is not unitary. In the same way that what is creative is determined by societies, what is purported to be improvisation is also constructed. Some have viewed improvisation as a subset of composition.[1] But it can be viewed in many ways – as an exploratory means of composing, as a highly skilled performance which leads to the creation of an exactly specified product, or as a mode of free expression. It is a matter of opinion and practice.

An improvisatory stage may be part of the compositional process for some composers, whereas for others it may not. Composers and improvisers also work in different timescales. For the improviser the first idea must work. There is no opportunity to change it. Because of this, different processes will be adopted. With the exception of free improvisation, it is typically based around some predetermined structure, form, chord sequence or melody, where some aspect is left undetermined or unrealised. The quality of the improvisation lies in relation to its stylistic conventions, and in order to appreciate it the listener has to understand the genre. To improvise, musicians must have a knowledge base, acquired over time, through practice, which is idiomatic to a particular genre from which they generate novel routines in performance.

HISTORY OF IMPROVISATION

Historically, improvisation has been an important part of musical performance. Musical improvisation in Greece was common 2,000 years ago. The basis for those improvisations was 'nomos', an equivalent to standard melodies which every musician knew.[2] For centuries, improvisation was the branch of musical art which was thought to be of the highest importance.

Another early example was the art of descant, a free part sung with the existing fixed strand of plainsong. Between the twelfth and seventeenth centuries, much instrumental music was improvised, and the provision of the figured bass part played by the harpsichord player allowed and expected improvisation. The cadenza was also a quasi extemporary element. Up to the nineteenth century it was customary to leave the performer free to develop his or her own ideas in it. The great days of keyboard improvisation were the eighteenth and early nineteenth centuries. Bach, Mozart, and Beethoven were all great extemporisers, as were Liszt, Franck and Saint-Saëns. But with the onset of increasing technical demands on instrumentalists, and composers wishing cadenzas to be an integral part of the composition, there was a decline in the use of improvisation in the concert hall.

The twentieth century saw a revival of improvisation in Western music with the advent of jazz. Extemporisation occurred in breaks, which filled the gap between the end of one 8 or 16 bar section and another. The performance structure was shared by the musicians. This allowed interactive performance and improvisation. The improviser retained the rhythmic base of the song and its harmonic sequence but could discard the rest. Generally, the sequence of choruses was complemented only by an introduction, an end and one or more interludes. The first and last choruses were played in the original form while the intermediate choruses were reserved for improvisation. The art of improvisation continues to be practised in jazz, by the gypsy orchestras of Eastern Europe and by Indian musicians.

Improvisation is currently part of the national curriculum in music in the UK, so there is renewed interest in it in schools. Perhaps as a result of this there has been increasing use of free improvisation in a variety of educational and community projects. Free improvisation has the advantage that it does not require the acquisition of the rules of particular styles or genres. It allows musicians to express themselves freely, to be creative and to develop new ideas.

CASE STUDY 5.1: CLASSICAL IMPROVISATION

Andrew learnt to play the piano as a child and made quick progress, developing a reputation locally for his skill. His teacher was approached by the local church, which needed someone to play the organ during services. She suggested that Andrew might be interested and he agreed to try it. He found that he really enjoyed playing the organ and began to take additional lessons to develop his organ-playing skills. His interest in improvisation developed there and his teacher supported him in learning how to improvise on the organ.

Performing opportunities during his time at music conservatoire included working with a chamber orchestra and he found that he enjoyed working with other musicians. He realised that there would be more opportunities for this kind of work, if he extended his skills to include playing the harpsichord and reading from a figured bass. He acquired books of exercises, which he worked through, and took every opportunity to use his skills in ensemble work, also learning from listening extensively to recordings. His combination of instruments and skills ensured that he had many employment opportunities.

For young musicians starting out in the music profession, developing improvisational skills is crucial. Howard Goodall, an extremely successful composer, referring to the challenges he faced on leaving university in making his way in the music profession, stated in an interview at the 2009 Music for Youth Schools Prom:

> *After my school and college years of classical training I was ill-prepared,*
> *when I entered the profession as a freelance keyboard player, for the*

amount of improvisation that would be required of me. I had become too dependent on the dots on the page. My advice to anyone who wants to perform professionally is to learn how to improvise, to become less tied to the page and free up your musical mind!

Others have also begun to recognise the value of improvisational skills. In the USA, Robert Levin has revived the practice of improvising cadenzas in classical concertos. He suggests that what is of the greatest benefit to the performer is not the performance of the actual cadenza, but how the process increases understanding of the remainder of the work.

THE BENEFITS OF LEARNING TO IMPROVISE

While improvisation is valuable in its own right, the skills acquired through learning to improvise:

- enhance aural[3] and technical skills
- provide musicians with clearer comprehension of music performed with notation[4,5]
- can improve rhythmic accuracy in sight-reading.[6]

There are also personal and social benefits to developing improvisational skills within an ensemble. Learners who report anxiety regarding solo performance tend to find that playing in group improvisations, and making rhythmic embellishments of familiar tunes, helps to alleviate their concerns and gives them more opportunities to express themselves.[7] Where improvisation is free and does not require learning to play within a particular genre, there are opportunities for developing a range of creative skills.

EXERCISE 5.1: GETTING STARTED

What types of improvisation interest you? Can you build on your previous experiences to develop new skills? What types of improvisation are likely to be of most use to you in your future career? Is there a class that you could join to develop your skills? Are there improvisation groups which would allow you to become a member?

THE PROCESS OF IMPROVISATION

Improvisation requires the utilisation of complex abilities. A musical idea must be generated and developed. The sounds being produced must be understood and heard, and at the same time the player must decide what to do with the material and how to do it. The more experienced the player, the more sophisticated, ambitious and artistic the generated improvisation will be. For the expert improviser, knowing what sounds will be created before they are played is central. A mental image of the sound is created before it is played.

Much of what we know about improvisation is based on studies of improvisation within specific genres. We know little about the processes involved in free improvisation where there are no specific musical rules to be followed. Much improvisation is governed by rules. The rules limit the musician's creative choices. For instance in jazz, the rules take into consideration melody, harmony and rhythm. Within the framework of the rules, the musician must choose between several available alternatives. In Indian music, the composer is always composer-performer. What is learnt are the processes of making music. Ragas form the basis for ideas and are improvised upon.

The process of improvisation relies to a great extent on long-term memory and the simultaneous interaction of unconscious automatic processes with conscious cognitive processes.[8] To improvise effectively in a particular genre, the subconscious knowledge base processes need to be automated and submerged, so that the performer cannot access their own subconscious processes at the moment of creation. If the knowledge base is sufficiently internalised in long-term memory and automated through practice and performance experience, the resources used to generate surface melody are free to focus on developing an appropriate and coherent improvisation.[9]

In experienced players, ever more complex actions come under automatic or unconscious control. But in the early stages of learning to improvise, very simple processes using short-term memory can generate acceptable improvisations, although they may be somewhat mechanical. There are differences in the ways that instrumentalists face improvisation, depending on their level of expertise. An expert improviser will have the following knowledge and abilities:

- the skill to hear musical patterns internally as they are about to be played
- knowledge of the relevant musical structures
- the skill to manipulate an instrument or the voice to achieve musical intentions fluently

- knowledge of strategies for structuring an improvisation and the flexibility to change strategies if necessary
- knowledge of stylistic conventions for improvising in a given style
- the skill to transcend stylistic conventions to develop personal style.[10]

In reaching an expert level, the learner appears to develop through a series of six stages:[10]

- Stage 1 consists of exploration through play.
- Stage 2 is process-oriented, e.g. musical doodling without any overall coherence.
- Stage 3 is product-oriented, where some musical ideas are adopted into the playing.
- At Stage 4, improvisation becomes more fluid and there is more control over the technical aspects of performance.
- At Stage 5, improvisation is increasingly structured.
- At Stage 6, the learner demonstrates a developed style.

The improvisation becomes fluent and the appropriate musical style is adopted for the improvisation. So how are these skills acquired?

EXERCISE 5.2: PLANNING HOW TO DEVELOP YOUR IMPROVISATION SKILLS

For your chosen type of improvisation, plan how you can develop your skills. Explore whether there are any workshops that you can attend in your institution, or informal groups that you might join. Consider setting up an ensemble of your own. Keep a log of your activities and the extent to which your skills are developing.

THE DEVELOPMENT OF IMPROVISING SKILLS

Like all areas of expertise, becoming an expert improviser within a specific genre takes time and commitment.

Where improvisation is free, the issue for musicians is not learning new rules but being able to abandon previously learnt rules. Some musicians find this very difficult. Doing this within a group where ideas and sounds are developed through interaction with others is very effective, although it is possible for individuals to learn to improvise independently. The conceptual leap that is required to develop such skills is to be able to think in terms of sounds and musical communication, rather than melody, rhythm and harmony. Working in a group supports this transition.

CASE STUDY 5.2: A CLASSICAL PIANIST LEARNING JAZZ

There is one detailed account of how an already skilled classical pianist learnt to play jazz.[1]

First, he learnt the feel and make-up of typical left-hand jazz chords. He then learnt to combine these chords into sequences. At this stage he looked at his hands, visually monitoring what he was doing. Next he began to combine standard jazz melodies with their appropriate chord sequences. Particular formulas were then learnt, which gradually built up into a repertoire. In the third year of playing in this way, the formulas began to gel. He began to plan particular note effects. Sometimes these went wrong and he devised what he called a 'chromatic way', which enabled him to keep going. His learning then underwent change, when he observed a professional jazz player and realised that the process could be slower and more relaxed; that the notes for any particular sequence could be found under the hand; and that any note would work in a sequence and could be used to initiate an escape route. At the end of the period, he could play acceptable jazz breaks.

For him, the process was tedious, effortful and frustrating. He experienced difficulties in relation to acquiring knowledge bases from listening, and frustration with the technical constraints imposed by particular instruments which impacted on the improvised response, and with the relationship between spontaneously created material and improvised fillers. As his skills developed, he reported that conscious application of his internalised knowledge produced what he described as 'frantic' playing. To overcome this, he had to give up cognitive control and allow each hand to find the notes intuitively. This risk-taking led to more 'right' notes falling under his fingers, and his improvisation became more relaxed and sounded more like that of experienced players.

WORKING IN ENSEMBLES

To learn the rules of any particular improvisational genre takes time. The earlier that a learner engages with a relevant musical environment, the quicker skills will be acquired. The musical community needs to be used as an educational system, facilitating the acquisition of the repertoire, an appropriate musical vocabulary and the networks which enable further development.[12]

When learners are developing improvisation skills in particular genres, they benefit from becoming members of ensembles which demonstrate the practices that they are attempting to acquire. In this way, expertise develops through listening and copying the work of others. Then with increasing practice (often through individual work outside the group) they are able to attempt simple improvisations, gradually developing a distinctive personal style. Improvisation often requires interacting musically with others to develop the skills to anticipate and respond to one another's musical ideas.[13] In fact, the creative impetus for improvisation is interaction with fellow performers, the audience and the environment. These make each performance distinctive.[9]

CASE STUDY 5.3: ENGAGING IN FREE IMPROVISATION

Ben, a percussionist specialising in tuned instruments, joined a workshop on free improvisation while at college. He found that this provided a refreshing change from working from notation. He enjoyed it so much that he set up an ensemble, which focused on creative music-making using a variety of stimuli as ideas.

As the group worked together over time and developed their skills, they realised that there were opportunities for community work in schools and with other groups facilitating free improvisation around a theme. They developed marketing materials, began networking, and gradually built up work opportunities. They were well organised, and they behaved professionally, generated good ideas and produced excellent outcomes for participants. As a result, their reputation spread and this activity formed a substantial and very enjoyable part of their portfolio of work.

To work creatively within any musical genre requires the learner to acquire considerable knowledge of it. This knowledge can be acquired through listening, imitation, analysis and participating in making music with others more expert than themselves. In jazz, for instance, students can analyse selected performances of jazz musicians, particularly the melody, rhythm and harmony.[14] They can develop skills by ear, either through developing musical responses to particular patterns[15] or through memorising melodies, harmony, repertoire, counterpoint and other elements, and further develop them by taking musical risks.[16] They can use jazz texts or interactive computer programs[17] and join jazz groups. Whatever specific strategies are adopted, developing high levels of expertise takes time and effort. Similar processes are required whatever the genre: extensive aural immersion, semi-structured experimentation and, particularly important, active participation in the improvising genre.[12] Over time, this will enable internalisation of appropriate sounds to become possible.[18]

Free improvisation ensembles tend to be set up by individuals who have a shared vision of what they want to achieve, so it may be difficult to join an existing ensemble, although within institutions there may be opportunities to join specific classes that develop free improvisation skills.

APPROACHES TO LEARNING TO IMPROVISE

There are several approaches to learning to improvise. The approach adopted depends on the nature of the improvisation skills to be acquired. It can be approached through:

- real-time composition, where the learner works with a piece that they know well as a basis and attempts to vary, elaborate and embellish it
- the acquisition of patterns, models and procedures which will produce stylistically appropriate music, for instance using a figured base or a chord sequence as the basis for adding an improvised melody
- completing improvisational exercises which set tasks with specific constraints. This approach was pioneered by Jaques-Dalcroze,[19] who developed a series of improvisation exercises for piano. These include: composition-like problems in rhythm, melody, playing expressively and harmony; musical exercises; the imitation of a teacher; exercises in hand independence; notating improvisation just after performing it; and what can be described as an 'interrupt technique' (here the word 'hopp' is given by the teacher as a cue

for the student to perform a pre-set operation, such as transposition or change of tempo during performance)

- the presentation of many alternative versions of important musical themes, where the learner infers the ways in which the improvisation or variation has occurred. The learner copies the improvised solos, by repeated listening to recordings and, from this, extracts some general principles
- self-expression, where the performance develops in a free way and is driven by imagination and memory.

These approaches will not be successful unless the learner is familiar with the particular type of music within which the improvisation will take place. This may be related to the kind of chords and chord sequences which are used in that music, the idioms of the music, and the types of melodic material which are appropriate. So the first step is to engage with playing that music in a serious way. If the improvisation is to be within a particular musical genre, then that itself will impose constraints on the way that improvisation is learnt.

If improvisation is seen as a form of composition – or the learning of skills to enable the interpretation of the figured base – then specific exercises will be required. Texts are available which enable a structured progression in developing these skills, including the materials of Jaques-Dalcroze.[19]

If improvisation is seen as learning to improvise within a particular idiom (e.g. jazz), then the learner will need to listen to and imitate examples of such improvisation. This can be achieved through listening to recordings. Texts of jazz solos are also available commercially. Getting experience through joining an ensemble is also important.

If improvisation is seen as being within a self-expressive mode, then there are greater opportunities for creativity and the development of improvisation skills. While it is possible to develop free improvisation as a solo player, more usually it is within an ensemble. Experimentation is key to this. This may be undertaken with a range of stimuli. The stimuli may be a musical idea, a phrase or motif, literary (e.g. a poem) or related to moods and emotions. Over time, with repeated sessions, skills develop. What is crucial in learning to improvise, as in any other musical skill, is practice.

CASE STUDY 5.4: LEARNING TO IMPROVISE IN JAZZ

Emily plays the clarinet and her ensemble experiences were largely orchestral, although she also played in wind bands. The youth orchestra that she played in decided to perform *Pictures at an Exhibition* by Mussorgsky, which has a part for saxophone. She undertook to learn to play that part.

She found that she enjoyed playing the saxophone and joined a big band to develop her skills. Hearing others improvise in the band, she decided that she wanted to learn how to do so herself.

She adopted more than one approach. She bought a book, which included all the jazz standards and example improvisations, and learnt to play them from memory. She also acquired a lot of recordings, which she listened to extensively to develop more ideas and to enable her to more easily 'feel' the rhythms and style. She also tried to copy some of the improvisations from the recordings by ear. This was very difficult initially, but she found that while she couldn't copy them exactly, she could get a sense of their shape, which helped her to develop her own ideas.

Broadening her skills in this way gave her more work opportunities and also considerably enhanced her musical skills.

EVALUATING IMPROVISATION

Developing self-evaluation skills in relation to improvisation is important. The evaluation of improvisation is similar in many ways to that of composition. It needs to take account of the particular genre within which the improvisation is being developed. Within that framework it should then consider issues relating to:

- the appropriateness of the style
- the development of ideas
- the use of different sound textures
- melodic, rhythmic, harmonic, dynamic and expressive qualities
- the extent to which the improvisation is structured
- originality and imagination
- effectiveness.

Recording improvisations, and listening to and critiquing them, is a valuable way of assessing progress. Ensembles can also use material derived in this way for marketing purposes.

EXERCISE 5.3: EVALUATING YOUR IMPROVISATION

Make recordings of your improvisational activities. Listen to them critically to see how you might be able to improve. Consider in detail where you need to do more work. Draw up a plan with specific goals – and dates when your goals will be reached.

CREATIVITY

Music is both a creative and a performing art. Improvisation and composition require creativity. Performing requires creativity for the development of interpretation, but also requires of those involved in it the attainment of very high levels of technical, cognitive, expressive and communication skills.

The increasing use of advanced recording techniques means that technical perfection can be assured in a recorded product. As a result, performers are increasingly expected to demonstrate perfection in live performance. Some would argue that this has been at the expense of the development of creativity in performance.

Creativity is not a unitary concept. It can be considered from a number of different perspectives. We can think of it in relation to: its products; the processes involved in it; the individuals who contribute to it; and environments which may be conducive to it.[20] These issues will be considered in depth in relation to composition in Chapter 6.

We can also consider creativity as operating at a number of different levels. For instance, in music we might want to argue that the highest level of creativity is composition. This is because it is permanent (in a way that improvisation is not) and also because it is original in its conception. Arranging and improvising might be at a lower level: arranging because, although it is permanent, the material is derived from elsewhere; improvisation because of its lack of permanence. However, we may draw on examples from the great masters in music and put forward an argument that the themes and variations they wrote, based on the original ideas of others, or indeed arrangements that they made of others' works, are more creative than the original compositions.

On the one hand, performing might be seen as at a low level of creativity because, although the performer is being creative in developing interpretation and communicating it to an audience, the major creation of the work has been undertaken by the composer. The interpretation is also temporary. On the other hand, one could argue that nowadays, making use of recording technology, improvisations and performances are as permanent as compositions. We might argue equally that because of their spontaneity, performing and improvising demonstrate higher levels of creativity.

What is clear is that any discussion of levels of creativity depends on value judgements that societies, and influential groups within them, have formed about the nature of any particular products of musicianship.

EXERCISE 5.4: IDENTIFYING BARRIERS TO DEVELOPING CREATIVE SKILLS

Think carefully about how often you engage in new musical activities. Are you open to new ideas? Are your musical experiences rather narrow? Would there be any benefit in considering embarking on some new activities or pushing the boundaries of what you are already doing? Have you considered participating in some cross-arts activities? What opportunities are there for you to enhance your musical creativity? What, if anything, is stopping you pursuing them?

PROMOTING YOUR CREATIVITY

Any major creative breakthrough, in any field, takes time, commitment, extensive knowledge and expertise on the part of the creator. The traditional guidance for how to become creatively gifted stresses specialisation (see Tips and Reminders 5.1), reflecting the considerable length of time that it takes to develop the highest levels of expertise. While in many ways this constitutes sound advice, the fast-changing nature of life in the twenty-first century means that there is a need to be open to new areas of work. It is important to achieve a balance between specialisation and being able to exploit new opportunities.

TIPS AND REMINDERS 5.1: HOW TO GROW UP CREATIVELY GIFTED[21]

1. Don't be afraid to 'fall in love with' something and pursue it with intensity. (You will do best what you like to do most.)

2. Know, understand, take pride in, practise, develop, use, exploit and enjoy your greatest strengths.

3. Learn to free yourself from the expectations of others and to walk away from the games they try to impose on you.

4. Free yourself to play your own game in such a way as to make good use of your gifts.

5. Find a great teacher or mentor, who will help you.

6. Don't waste a lot of expensive, unproductive energy trying to be well rounded. (Don't try to do everything; do what you can do well and what you love.)

7. Learn the skills of interdependence. (Learn to depend on one another, giving freely of your greatest strengths and most intense loves.)

CHAPTER SUMMARY: IMPROVISING AND NURTURING YOUR CREATIVITY

Innovation is a crucial element of modern economies.

New ideas are constantly needed to generate new products and address the problems faced by increasingly globalised and technological societies.

The term 'improvisation' covers a wide range of musical phenomena.

Historically, improvisation has been a valued skill. It remains so in many cultures and is returning to popularity in the constant demand for new ideas.

There are musical, personal and social benefits in learning to improvise.

Learning to improvise takes time and effort.

Joining or creating an ensemble is particularly valuable in learning to improvise.

There are a variety of ways to learn to improvise; the most appropriate or effective depends on the genre.

It is important to maintain a balance between focusing on one specific area of work and being able to respond to new opportunities.

FURTHER READING

There are a range of practical books which provide structured exercises in learning to improvise in a range of genres and on a range of instruments. To develop your skills, consult your teacher or colleagues about what is the best resource for your instrument, level of expertise and genre.

NOTES

1. Paynter, J. (1992) *Sound and Structure*. Cambridge: Cambridge University Press.

2. Reese, G. (1941) *Music in the Middle Ages*. New York: Norton.

3. Wilson, J. (1971) 'The effects of group improvisation on the musical growth of selected high school instrumentalists'. Doctoral dissertation, New York University. *Dissertation Abstracts International*, 31(7), 3589A.

4. Azzara, C.D. (1992) 'The effect of audiation-based improvisation techniques on the music achievement of elementary instrumental music students'. Doctoral dissertation, Eastman School of Music, University of Rochester. *Dissertation Absracts International*, 53(4), 1088A.

5. McPherson, G. (1993) 'Evaluating improvisational ability of high school instrumentalists'. *Bulletin of the Council for Research in Music Education*, 119, 11–20.

6. Montano, D.R. (1983) 'The effect of improvising in given rhythms on piano students' sight reading rhythmic accuracy achievement'. Doctoral dissertation, University of Missouri-Kansas City. *Dissertation Abstracts International*, 44(6), 1720A.

7. Leavell, B. (1997) 'Making the change: Middle school band students' perspectives on the learning of musical-technical skills in jazz performance'. Doctoral dissertation, University of North Texas. *Dissertation Abstracts International*, 57(7), 2931A.

8. Pressing, J. (1988) 'Improvisation, methods and models'. In J.A Sloboda (ed.), *Generative Processes in Music: The psychology of performance, improvisation and composition*. Oxford: Clarendon Press.

9. Johnson-Laird, P.N. (1988) 'Reasoning, imagining and creating'. *Bulletin for the Council for Research in Music Education*, 95, 71–87.

10. Kratus, J. (1991) 'Growing with improvisation'. *Music Educators Journal*, 78(4), 35–40.

11. Sudnow, D. (1978) *Ways of the Hand: The organisation of improvised conduct*. London: Routledge and Kegan Paul.

12. Berliner, P. (1994) *Thinking in Jazz: The infinite art of improvisation*. Chicago: University of Chicago Press.

13. Monson, I. (1992) *Saying Something: Jazz improvisation and interaction*. Chicago: University of Chicago Press.

14. Moorman, D. (1985) 'An analytic study of jazz improvisation with suggestions for performance'. Doctoral dissertation, New York University. *Dissertation Abstracts International*, 45(7), 2023A.

15. Bash, L. (1984) 'The effectiveness of three instructional methods on the acquisition of jazz improvisation skills'. Doctoral dissertation, State University of New York at Buffalo. *Dissertation Abstracts International*, 44(7), 2079A.

16. Azzara, C.D. (1999) 'An aural approach to improvisation'. *Music Educators Journal*, 86(3), 21–5.

17. Fern, J. (1996) 'The effectiveness of a computer-based courseware program for teaching jazz improvisation'. Unpublished doctoral dissertation, University of Southern California. *Dissertation Abstracts International*, 57(1), 144A.

18. Gordon, E.E. (1993) *Learning Sequences in Music: Skills, contents, and patterns. A music learning theory*. Chicago: GIA Publications.

19. Jaques-Dalcroze, E. (1921/1976) *Rhythm, Music and Education*. New York: B. Blom.

20. Sternberg, R.J. (ed.) (1988) *The Nature of Creativity*. Cambridge: Cambridge University Press.

21. Torrance, E.P. (1983) 'The importance of falling in love with "something" '. *Creative Child and Adult Quarterly*, 8, 72–8.

CHAPTER 6
COMPOSING

INTRODUCTION

This chapter sets out issues relating to composition. It considers:
- the traditional view of composition and how this has changed in recent years
- the processes of composing and how these can be developed
- issues relating to the assessment of compositions.

Historically, in the Western musical tradition, the composer has been viewed as someone with considerable talent, who creates unique works of art. Composition was taught from models derived from the accepted masters. Students learnt the rules, such as how to embellish melodies, how to harmonise. At undergraduate level, students were taught to write pastiche in a variety of styles, classical sonata form, fugue, and so on. At school, examinations consisted of traditional exercises in harmony and counterpoint, which enabled assessment to be based on technical requirements, such as avoiding certain consecutive intervals and choosing appropriate cadences. Creativity itself was not central to assessment. There was a preoccupation with rules and with emulating the masters, for instance Bach, Mozart and Haydn. Exercises required the addition of another phrase or the completion of harmonisation. Composing in different styles led those wishing to become professional composers to acquire a wide range of skills. From this disciplined and rigorous training they gradually developed their own styles. This made it impossible for those who had not had a rigorous musical training to compose formally.

In the twentieth century, classical composers have explored a much wider range of sounds in their compositions. Technology is now available which has made composition at a very high level possible for those who do not have highly developed technical skills on an instrument. Electronic keyboards have made it possible to replicate a range of sounds easily and cheaply, and computer technology has made notating composition a much simpler process. Composition now constitutes part of the music national curriculum in the UK and is assessed in relation to criteria that are sensitive to creative elements. These circumstances, in combination, have opened up the possibility of composition for all. The use of music in advertisements, television, films and the theatre supporting other creative outputs has also increased the opportunities available for composers beyond those where music is at the forefront.

THE CHARACTERISTICS OF COMPOSERS

Historically, we have tended to think of the genius of particular composers as if their creative skills were a facet of their personality and other characteristics. However, attempts to identify the personality characteristics of great composers across a range of genres have proved difficult, as they are very different from each other.

What they do have in common is the length of time that they have spent developing high levels of musical expertise, their extensive knowledge of music, and their dedication and commitment to what they do. Study of the greatest composers has shown that they tended to have begun composing when they were very young, made their first contributions to the repertoire at a very young age and continued to be prolific in their writing throughout their lives.[1] Similar commitment has been identified in creative individuals across a range of fields.

Although it has proved difficult to identify common personality characteristics, creative individuals tend to:

- be willing to take intellectual risks
- be open to new experiences and growth
- have positive responses to novelty
- be curious
- question norms and assumptions
- resist entrenched modes of thought
- be flexible and skilled in making decisions
- be independent in their judgement
- have a preference for creating new structures, rather than using existing ones
- be alert to novelty and gaps in knowledge
- have a tendency to use existing knowledge as a base for new ideas
- be imaginative.[2]

They are strongly motivated and demonstrate:

- perseverance
- driving absorption
- discipline and commitment to work

- a focus on the task in hand
- a high degree of self-organisation
- an ability to find order out of chaos.[2]

The individual's upbringing may contribute to the development of this pattern of motivation, independence and drive. For instance, a number of renowned composers are first-born children. Other experiences which may contribute towards the development of the creative individual are the loss of one or both parents in childhood, unusual living situations, and being reared in an enriching and stimulating home environment.

One underlying theme that has been suggested is one of the creative individual as being in conflict, with tensions between self-criticism and self-confidence, social withdrawal and social integration. On the one hand, creative individuals appear to avoid interpersonal contact and resist societal demands, while on the other hand they desire attention, praise, recognition and support. It may be the internal tension between the characteristics of the individual and their surroundings which acts as the spur to their creativity.[2]

DEVELOPING A CREATIVE ENVIRONMENT

Everyone is influenced by the environment within which they find themselves. Our behaviour is determined not only by our own characteristics but also by the environment. For an individual to engage in musical composition, they must have the opportunity to become involved in music, to experiment with ideas, and to have them accepted and performed. An environment which provides appropriate resources and stimulation is essential. Environments which are overcritical may inhibit creativity in the short term; however, as considerable determination is required to succeed as a composer, overcoming opposition and practical difficulties may serve to increase motivation in the long term.

Some historical periods may be more conducive to creativity than others, for instance some movements in the arts (e.g. Impressionism) have led to surges of activity, and warfare often leads to an outpouring of creativity.

For composers there also appear to be clear effects of role models.[1] If there are outstanding composers, the young will emulate them. Those embarking on a career as a composer tend to compose works that conform to the standards of the day. As they progress, their work changes and develops and their individual style emerges. As this occurs, they change what is accepted as the standard of the day.

EXERCISE 6.1: MAKING USE OF COMPOSITION

How might being able to compose support your development as a musician? In what ways might it contribute to your future career plans? Even if it is unlikely to form a major part of your future career, are there ways in which composition could make a contribution? Could it be useful for teaching or creating musical ensembles with unusual combinations of instruments?

THE PROCESS OF COMPOSITION

There is general agreement that any highly creative process takes time, although the length of time taken will vary between individuals, and will depend on the nature of the task. The actual processes involved in composition depend on the particular genre within which the individual is working. Composing a major, lengthy, classical piece of music will take a long time and will require inspiration and much thought. The composer may make use of a range of resources to support the process and many problems might be encountered along the way. Composing a short advertising jingle of less than one minute in length is clearly a challenge of a different order, although the composer will need to draw on a similar range of skills.

There is some debate about the processes involved in creativity in general. One approach suggests that there are two stages: an initial inspiration, which seems to depend on unconscious processes; and then an execution stage, which depends on conscious, cognitive work. Others propose four stages (see Table 6.1).

Not everyone believes that composition proceeds in stages. For them, creative problem-solving is a process where individual sub-elements are gathered into a whole structure. Restructuring, or the flash of illumination, occurs when the problem-solver or creator sees an unexpected solution to the problem. This process may occur many times during a single composition, particularly where the work is long and complex. Ideas for such a work evolve over significant periods of time, often with many goals and sub-goals and false starts and dead ends. Trial and error searches take place through a variety of possibilities.[3]

TABLE 6.1: THE FOUR STAGES OF CREATIVITY

Stage	Wallas (1926)[4]	Ross (1980)[5]
1	Preparation – gathering of relevant information	Initiating – beginning of the creative impulse, tactile explorations, doodling, playing, chance and accidents
2	Incubation – time to mull over the problem	Acquainting – becoming conversant with sound, practice, invention, further tactile motoric experience, playing around with ideas
3	Illumination – derivation of a solution	Controlling – mastery of basic skills and techniques to manipulate the medium, manipulating, constraints and limitations
4	Verification – formalisation and adaptation of the solution	Structuring – gathering into a comprehensible whole, relatedness, rescanning, reviewing, building blocks

Whatever the nature of the composition, the composer needs to have knowledge of the particular musical rules and grammars that apply within the genre within which she or he is working.[3] If that knowledge is secure, the composition process typically involves the emergence of an initial idea, which is then developed. The idea then forms the basis for the composition, with a period of intense work to produce the entire, structured composition. Throughout the process there will be continuous monitoring and evaluation or progress.

The processes by which famous composers of the past have worked indicate considerable variability. Some committed to paper what was in their head, making no changes afterwards; others adopted a more problem-solving approach, working on particular sections in isolation. A recent study of a professional composer working on a fugue[6] showed that:

- more constraints emerged as the process proceeded
- some elements were temporarily ignored during the process
- some plans or actions were delayed until their implementation became necessary
- there was continual movement backwards and forwards, as ideas developed and were implemented.

Another composer had a clear mental picture of the composition from the outset. This acted as a loose framework throughout the process. Problems were identified and solved as composition proceeded. Moments of creative insight supported this process. Some problems and their solutions overlapped in real time. There were no clear boundaries between the various stages. For each problem arising, solutions themselves were developed, implemented or deferred. Overall, it was an extremely complex process.[7]

Broadly, the processes of composition are similar whatever the nature of the work. Even children's spontaneous creativity in developing playground songs suggests a deliberate process of innovation, reorganisation of ideas, elaboration and condensation.[8] In long, complex compositions, different elements of the composition may be at different stages and greater creative problems will be faced. The importance of having some concept of the nature of the finished product cannot be overstated. This may be determined by the nature of the commission and genre. For instance, an advertising jingle will be short and must relate to the product it supports; film music has to reflect the theme of the film and the sequence of events in it; popular music has typical structures and harmonic and melodic norms. These all act to constrain the nature of the composition.

Skills in composition develop in the same way that expertise develops in learning to play an instrument – through active engagement in composing. Once expertise is attained, the composer:

- takes a more holistic view of the whole composition and maintains this conceptually, while working on arising problems
- chunks information into larger units
- holds the focus of attention on the task in hand
- looks forwards and backwards through the music at the same time
- considers the detail of the task within the structured whole.[9,10]

Despite the more automated processes available to those with expert skills, there is one key similarity with those who do not have expert skills: the process is always supported by the constraints imposed. These may be the professional composer's commission, the expectations of the genre in terms of structure and form, or the instructions given by teachers. These always provide the framework for the process. Composing without such a framework is very difficult. Equally, if the requirements are too restricted, it is very difficult for the composer to develop new ideas.[11]

DEVELOPING IDEAS

Ideas for compositions can emerge from a wide variety of sources, including:

- poems
- stories
- works of art
- places
- life events
- emotions
- existing music
- particular musical techniques, e.g. drones, ostinato
- composition adopting particular forms, e.g. rondo
- compositions using particular pitch configurations, e.g. major, minor.

The sounds of particular instruments or sounds created electronically, technologically or from naturally available materials can also inspire composition. In beginning to develop your compositional skills, you need to take account of your interests and preferences for particular types of music and the particular musical skills that you already have and build on these.

MONITORING PROGRESS AND OUTCOMES

The most creative composers set goals, negotiate the relationship between global and detailed plans, experiment and are very critical of their work. However, this criticism is constructive as they strive to constantly improve what they are doing. Monitoring of progress and critical evaluation of the developing product are crucial to being creative.

While self-criticism is crucial, it can also be helpful to seek comments from others, as they can offer a fresh perspective. Constructive feedback from others provides pointers for enhancing future compositions and can act as inspiration. Providing informational feedback sensitively does not discourage creativity. Friends and colleagues are usually willing to offer support and to provide such feedback. Some people find that composition can be a joint enterprise, although one may take a more dominant role in any particular piece (see Case Study 6.1).

CASE STUDY 6.1: COMPOSING IN PARTNERSHIP

John Lennon and Paul McCartney of The Beatles jointly wrote and published in the region of 180 songs between 1962 and 1969. Both of them wrote words and music, although often one of them undertook most of the work. They developed many of their musical skills by learning and copying the songs of their idols: the Everly Brothers, Elvis Presley and Buddy Holly.

Although they often wrote independently, songs typically had at least some input from both of them. One might outline an idea or a section and then the other would finish it or improve it. Sometimes ideas for songs that each had worked on independently would be combined to create a new song. A common practice was for one to add the middle eight or bridge to the other's verse and chorus. John Lennon described the process as 'writing eyeball to eyeball' and 'playing into each other's noses'. The success of the working relationship seemed to depend on competitiveness and mutual inspiration. Latterly, songs tended to be written independently, with less input from the other.

In an interview for *Playboy* in 1980, Lennon said of the partnership: 'He provided a lightness, an optimism, while I would always go for the sadness, the discords, the bluesy notes. There was a period when I thought I didn't write melodies, that Paul wrote those and I just wrote straight, shouting rock 'n' roll. But, of course, when I think of some of my own songs – *In My Life*, or some of the early stuff, *This Boy* – I was writing melody with the best of them.'

ASSESSING COMPOSITIONS

Assessing the quality of composition is particularly difficult. How would you go about doing it? You might ask whether the work was original, or whether it would stand the test of time. You might ask to what extent it might influence the work of future composers. Or you might judge it in terms of its commercial success, or the extent to which you enjoyed it. Clearly, the assessed quality of any composition depends on the particular criteria being adopted, the timescale over which it is being evaluated and the culture within which it is embedded. We are all aware that the works of some composers are denigrated or neglected during their lifetime only to become renowned later, and that some composers may be revered by a small group of experts but are criticised or ignored by the general public.

CASE STUDY 6.2: BECOMING A PROFESSIONAL COMPOSER

Howard Goodall is one the most prolific, well-recognised and award-winning composers of our time. His compositions include choral music, stage musicals, and film and TV scores, and he is well known as a TV and radio broadcaster and as an ambassador for singing.

He grew up in Rutland and Oxfordshire, became a chorister at New College, Oxford, aged 8, then attended Stowe School, where he played the organ, and Lord Williams's School, Thame, where he composed, sang and played in bands. He completed his degree in music at Oxford, where he met Richard Curtis and Rowan Atkinson, with whom he then worked on Rowan's live stage shows and revues, *Not the Nine O' Clock News*, *Blackadder* and many other subsequent projects.

In an interview for the 2009 Music for Youth Schools Prom he was asked how he managed to bridge the gap between classical and popular music with ease. He responded: 'In my experience, people with long-ish careers in music tend to develop a flexible attitude to the work they do. I don't know in fact if it has ever really been possible to make a living as a composer by sticking to just one style or genre. Bach, Mozart, Prokofiev – most of the composers we recognise from the past did a wide variety of jobs in music and composed all types of music for all sorts of occasions and clients too, so in that respect the twenty-first century's not that much different.'

Goodall believes that there are some important qualities that all young musicians need to have if they are to have a chance of 'pursuing their dream'. 'First, you need to be patient. Very few musical careers happen overnight. Second, you need to be able to work collaboratively with other people, not be precious and moody, not act like a prima donna, not behave like you are the only one with the solution to a given problem. Third, you need to be open to new possibilities, even if at first they don't seem like an obvious fit with your aspirations. Fourth, you need to be able to work jolly hard, long hours, with very little reward, for years, before you become financially stable. And working hard in this context doesn't mean the kind of slog associated with glamorous photo and video shoots, recording sessions or tours. I mean doing things you don't want to do, things that are onerous, boring, repetitive or unglamorous. It is in the undertaking of tasks you didn't want to do at first that you learn the most, similarly it is from bad reviews, poor audience response and unexpected setbacks that you begin to understand your weaknesses and your potential, not from your successes.'

Derived from Howard Goodall's website (www.howardgoodall.co.uk), accessed 7 January 2011.

EXERCISE 6.2: GETTING STARTED

Taking account of your interests and musical skills, develop a compositional task. Ensure that you have sufficient constraints and that the task is manageable. Give yourself a deadline for completion. Consider whether it will be notated or whether you will record it. Be realistic about the instruments, materials or technology that you use, so that it can be performed. Seek feedback from friends when the work is near completion. Try to find an opportunity to perform the piece.

Given the above, it does not come as any surprise that there has long been debate as to whether there is any value in undertaking assessment of composition, or indeed, whether it is possible to provide objective evaluation, a perspective legitimised by the frequent disagreements among professional music critics. Assessment of composition, improvisation and performance is subjective and depends on the assessor's personal preferences and their level of expertise.[12] Composition is normally assessed through its performance, which creates the problem of differentiating between the performance and the composition. There are also issues relating to the genre in which assessment takes place, as each has its own stylistic conventions. Expertise in one area of music does not necessarily transfer to others, so it may be difficult for someone who is classically trained to assess other types of composition.

While there are no simple solutions for assessing musical outcomes, the composer has to make decisions constantly about their progress and success. Having a clear idea of what is intended is the chief way in which this can be done. How compositions will be judged by others in the long or short term is very difficult to predict, although success within one's lifetime is apparent by the number of commissions received and the ability to make a living by composing. Composers have to establish for themselves the criteria by which they will judge their success.

CASE STUDY 6.3: A COMMITMENT TO MUSIC AS ART

Michael Tippett produced a large body of work, including five operas, three large-scale choral works, four symphonies, five string quartets, four piano sonatas, as well as concertos and concertante works, song cycles and incidental music.

In his childhood he showed an early aptitude for music and enjoyed home theatricals and singing in the church choir. Although he learnt piano and harmony at secondary school, his early composing skills were self-taught, with Tippett acquiring and learning from Stanford's *Musical Composition*.

Despite limited musical knowledge, he was accepted at the Royal College of Music and, while there, he took advantage of the opportunities to access the wide range of music on offer in London. His composition tuition at the RCM was traditional, with study of the masters and their use of musical form and syntax. He also developed knowledge of the orchestra and conducting. Although his formal employment on leaving the RCM was as a music teacher, he continued to compose. Following a concert in 1930 consisting solely of his works, and despite a favourable reception by the press, he felt that he still lacked technique, so he arranged further study on sixteenth-century polyphony, where he learnt to write fugues in the style of Bach.

His career took a long time to develop and public recognition was slow. Despite this, he was committed to his work and demonstrated an ongoing commitment to learning and openness to a wide range of influences, including sixteenth-century church music and madrigals; Purcell, Bach, Handel, Beethoven, Stravinsky, Sibelius, Hindemith and Bartók; and styles from folk music, blues, and jazz-rock to Balinese gamelan music. In later life he refused to allow commissions for concertos and other works for specific artists to divert him from his own agenda.

Tippett only began notating compositions when he had a clear concept of the structure and character of the piece and usually composed immediately onto the full score. Despite the complexity of much of his work, he remained focused on the musical impact. In response to a young composer who was disappointed that his own mathematically complex work sounded boring when played, Tippett responded: 'Just use your ears, love'.

ARRANGING

Learning to make arrangements is a very useful skill. It enables musicians to adapt music that they would like to play for their own instrument, and to adapt music to play with others when the combination of instruments is not conventional.

Arranging can be very simple, for example transposing melodies for different instruments, or very complex, for example making sophisticated elaborations on a theme. The principles involved in learning to arrange are similar to those of composition, and skills will be enhanced the more frequently they are used. For some people, learning to make arrangements can be a useful way to develop compositional skills.

EXERCISE 6.3: MAKING AN ARRANGEMENT

Select a piece of music that you like and which is not for your instrument. Make an arrangement of it that you can play on your instrument. You may feel it necessary to have an accompaniment. Record your arrangement. Listen to the recording critically. Can you improve the arrangement? When you are satisfied with this, try to find an opportunity to perform it or play your recording to others. Ask for feedback. Use the feedback to make further improvements. Using what you have learnt from this exercise, make an arrangement of the same piece for a small group ensemble that you play with regularly.

CHAPTER SUMMARY: COMPOSING

Learning to compose and arrange can be useful for all musicians.

Composition requires the application of a wide range of musical skills, the specific nature of which depends on the particular musical genre.

The composition process depends on having:
- a clear conception of what is required
- a constrained framework within which to work
- the capacity to monitor progress and to be self-critical.

Assessing the quality of compositions is problematic and individuals must define their own success criteria.

FURTHER READING

There are a number of very practical books which support the development of composition for those who have not had musical training. They tend to be written for those playing specific instruments, for instance guitar or keyboard. Other texts are available on writing within particular genres.

NOTES

1. Simonton, D.K. (1997) 'Products, persons and periods'. In D.J. Hargreaves and A.C. North (eds), *The Social Psychology of Music*. Oxford: Oxford University Press.

2. Sternberg, R.J. (ed.) (1988) *The Nature of Creativity*. Cambridge: Cambridge University Press.

3. Newell, A. and Simon, H.A. (1972) *Human Problem Solving*. Englewood Cliffs, NJ: Prentice Hall.

4. Wallas, G. (1926) *The Art of Thought*. London: Watts.

5. Ross, M. (1980) *The Arts and Personal Growth*. London: Pergamon Press.

6. Reitman, W.R. (1965) *Cognition and Thought*. New York: Wiley.

7. Collins, D. (2005) 'A synthesis process model of creative thinking in composition'. *Psychology of Music*, 33(2), 193–216.

8. Marsh, K. (1995) 'Children's singing games: Composition in the playground?' *Research Studies in Music Education*, 4, 2–11.

9. Davidson, L. and Welsh, P. (1988) 'From collections to structure: The developmental path of tonal thinking'. In J.A. Sloboda (ed.), *Generative Processes in Music: The psychology of performance, improvisation and composition*. Oxford: Oxford University Press, 260–85.

10. Younker, B.A. and Smith, W.H. (1996) 'Comparing and modelling musical thought processes of expert and novice composers'. *Bulletin of the Council for Research in Music Education*, 128, 25–35.

11. Folkestad, G. (2004) 'A meta-analytic approach to qualitative studies in music education: A new model applied to creativity and composition'. In J. Tafuri (ed.), *Research for Music Education: The 20th Seminar of the ISME Research Commission*, Las Palmas, Spain, 4–10 July 2004.

12. Hickey, M. (2001) 'An application of Amabile's consensual assessment technique for rating the creativity of children's musical compositions'. *Journal of Research in Music Education*, 49, 234–44.

CHAPTER 7
GETTING INVOLVED IN WIDER LEARNING ACTIVITIES

INTRODUCTION

This chapter considers the ways in which being involved in a wide range of musical activities can be of benefit to developing a musical career, including:

- playing in an ensemble
- listening to a wide variety of music
- attending concerts
- participating in masterclasses
- taking opportunities to interact with other musicians
- teaching.

These activities all contribute to the development of a wide range of musical skills.

The development of electronic media in the latter part of the twentieth century revolutionised access to, and use of, music in people's everyday lives, making it possible to listen to music at the push of a button through the radio or television, or by playing video and sound recordings and downloading from the internet. The introduction of iPods has also made it possible for individuals to organise their personalised selection of music. Alongside this increased access to music, globalisation has led to interest in music from around the world and the desire to preserve folk traditions, while increasing commercialisation has led to the constant need for new musical products.

For musicians, these changes represent enormous opportunities, providing that they are willing to continue learning and adapting throughout their lives. A wide range of hybrid musical ensembles are already developing, with interesting combinations of instruments, digital technology and multimedia. At Stanford University, for example, a mobile phone orchestra (MoPhO) has been established, which invites involvement at multiple levels. In addition to performing, MoPhO ensemble members are engaged in designing components of the instruments (such as wearable speakers), as well as planning interactions between musicians and instruments, and composing and improvising.[1]

EXERCISE 7.1: DEVELOPING NEW AREAS OF WORK

Make a list of the different musical activities that you have participated in. Do they follow a particular pattern? Are there other areas of work that it would be useful for you to develop or that you are interested in? Are there opportunities to access these locally? Background Briefing 7.1 provides some information that may help you to explore opportunities.

BACKGROUND BRIEFING 7.1: MUSICAL ACTIVITIES IN THE UK

- British Choirs on the Net (www.choirs.org.uk/) currently includes 2,700 choirs that have a website or are contactable by email.
- UK Amateur Orchestras (www.amateurorchestras.org.uk/) provides information about a range of amateur orchestras, bands and other groups in the UK by area. Some 739 are listed in England, 54 in Scotland, 12 in Wales, and 4 in Northern Ireland.
- There are over 3,000 maintained secondary schools in England (over 3 million pupils), about 370 in Scotland, over 200 in Wales, and over 200 in Northern Ireland.
- There are over 17,000 primary schools in England (over 4 million pupils), over 2,000 in Scotland, about 1,500 in Wales, and over 800 in Northern Ireland.
- There are over 2,000 independent schools in the UK, teaching about 7 per cent of pupils.
- Over 1.15 million children are learning to play a musical instrument in the UK at any one time.
- In 2008, over 250,000 children in the UK entered for Associated Board of the Royal Schools of Music examinations.

These new types of ensembles, and these new approaches, challenge accepted conventions and offer opportunities for improvisation and creativity. It is now possible for virtual ensemble performances to take place in real time (synchronously) or even to be put together when participants contribute at different times (asynchronously). For instance, virtual choirs and orchestras have been set up, where prospective members submit videos of themselves playing for audition. Individual performances of the various parts are then selected, edited and mixed to provide a final performance. Considerable technical – as well as musical – skills are required to set up this kind of enterprise. It is possible for musicians to play together online in synchronous mode, but the technology is not as yet sufficiently advanced to overcome issues relating to time delays. Over time, this difficulty is likely to be overcome.

Musical learning of any kind involves becoming part of a community of practice, which has its own culture and characteristics. Formal training is usually embedded within one such community. Exploring the work of other musical communities provides valuable opportunities for developing ideas, acquiring new skills and enhancing motivation. Informal learning, which occurs through working with other musicians and through self-tuition, provides a suitable vehicle for engaging with other communities of practice and adapting existing skills to meet new challenges. For those embarking on a portfolio career, engagement in informal learning can be particularly valuable as a means of extending opportunities.

FORMAL AND INFORMAL LEARNING

There are many different routes into the music profession. Those followed depend to a great extent on musical genre, although formal institutional training is now on offer in many genres, including jazz, folk, popular music and musical theatre.

For non-classical musicians, informal or non-formal learning or self- or family-tuition is common. For instance, popular musicians often develop their skills through listening to recordings, copying what they hear, practising until they can reproduce the material accurately, and ultimately developing sufficient skills to be able to compose their own songs. Learning to play by ear in this way is common among musicians outside the Western classical genre. While musicians learning in this way may not participate in formal lessons, they frequently seek or receive advice and guidance from those with more experience within or outside the group they are working with.

The distinction between formal and informal learning is not clear-cut; whatever genre they are involved in, musicians learn informally as well as formally. For instance, a Western classical musician having formal tuition at a conservatoire will also listen to recordings, attend concerts and masterclasses, learn from those experiences and may copy what they have heard. In relation to self-instruction, the boundaries are even less clear. If a learner uses a manual with the support of audio or audio-visual materials, should this self-instruction be considered to be formal, even though the actual learning environment might be informal? Is self-instruction only informal if the learner is learning to play by ear through copying the performance of another musician?

To some extent these distinctions are irrelevant. As discussed in Chapter 2, learning is a natural process for human beings. We learn all the time in a wide range of different ways, using different resources. Whatever the musical genre or form of learning, professional musicians become part of a community of practice, moving – as their expertise develops – from its periphery to a more central position. For instance, when playing in a jazz group, the learner will initially learn from listening to more experienced players and practising improvisation in solitary practice. She or he will gradually be given opportunities for short solo breaks, and over time, if these are perceived as successful, will be given more frequent opportunities. Gradually, credibility within the group will be acknowledged and the individual's role as a member confirmed.

EXERCISE 7.2: THE BENEFITS OF PLAYING IN ENSEMBLES

What benefits have you gained from playing in ensembles? Did different types of ensemble activity have different benefits? If so, what were they? Are there other types of ensembles which you might form or join that would develop your skills further?

LISTENING

Listening is central to all musical activity. Whenever we engage with music, whether as performers, composers or audience, we are listening. As we listen to music, we also appraise and respond to it. As we saw in Chapter 2, humans are born equipped with the necessary neural and physical structures to perceive and respond to music.

Listening is key to developing musical understanding. Repeated listening to a piece of music changes a listener's perceptions, leading to a greater understanding of the structure of the music and how the themes within it are related. The more familiar we are with a piece of music, the more we like and value it, although overfamiliarity may lead to boredom or even dislike.[2] The speed with which familiarity leads to boredom seems to be related to the complexity of the music, i.e. the degree of variability or uncertainty. A moderate level of complexity elicits the most positive response. The effect of exposure to music, repetition, training or practice is to lower the perceived complexity. These changes seem to develop cyclically as music is listened to more than once.

Appraisal and evaluation of music occur simultaneously with listening. The musician has to constantly appraise their work and that of colleagues. This process guides future planning and learning activity. The process of appraising involves making comparisons (implicit or explicit) with already acquired internal representations of music. These may be specific, of the same piece of music; generalised to particular types or styles of music; or generalised to particular features of performance, for example intonation or tone quality. The principle of comparison is central. Without comparison with some already-held conception, appraisal cannot occur. It is in this context that musicians should take every opportunity to listen to as much music as possible.

Live performance provides not only listening opportunities but also authentic musical experiences which enrich learning more generally. A particular advantage of live performance and video recordings of musical performance is that the movements of the performer can be seen. These are important in communicating musical meaning.[3] New technology, particularly the World Wide Web, has increased the opportunities for observing the performances of musicians from around the world. Masterclasses are particularly valuable, as they provide opportunities for not only observing the performance of other young musicians but also drawing on the advice given to them by teachers. Masterclasses can also provide opportunities for enhancing skills in relation to particular genres and styles of playing[4] (see Tips and Reminders 7.1).

TIPS AND REMINDERS 7.1: LEARNING FROM MASTERCLASSES

Learning as a performer

- Make sure that you are well prepared for the performance.
- Listen to and observe what is being communicated to you by the 'master'.
- Try to make the changes suggested, but don't be afraid to put your own point of view if you disagree.
- Immediately after the masterclass make some notes, so that you can refer to them later.
- If the masterclass has been recorded, take the opportunity to listen to it later and critically evaluate your own performance and the comments made.

Learning as a member of the audience

- Carefully, observe and listen to the initial performance, taking account of its strengths and weaknesses. How might you have done things differently? What feedback would you give to the performer?
- Listen to the comments made by the 'master'. Do you agree with them?
- Are there any useful technical, musical or communication ideas that you can use in your own practice or performance?
- Make a note of anything that strikes you as particularly interesting or surprising.

PARTICIPATING IN ENSEMBLES

Ensembles can take many forms and vary in size, make-up and level of formality. The benefits are similar in many respects, but small-group participation offers more opportunities for solo work and developing organisational skills. The kind of benefits that might be expected are outlined in Key Point Summary 7.1.

KEY POINT SUMMARY 7.1: BENEFITS OF WORKING IN ENSEMBLES

Musical skills

Ensemble participation:

- deepens musical knowledge
- enhances musical understanding
- enhances listening skills
- enhances technical skills
- provides opportunities for learning new repertoire
- provides performance opportunities
- provides the opportunity for trying out new musical ideas (small ensembles).

Social benefits

Ensemble participation:

- provides the satisfaction of making an active contribution to a group
- supports a strong sense of belonging
- facilitates making friends with like-minded people
- provides opportunities to enhance social skills.

Personal skills

Ensemble participation enhances:

- self-discipline
- concentration
- musical identity
- self-confidence
- a sense of achievement
- responsibility
- teamworking skills.

Organisational skills

Small-group ensemble participation enhances opportunities to gain experience in:

- booking rooms
- timetabling rehearsals
- selecting repertoire
- creating a website
- developing marketing materials
- getting and negotiating bookings.

SKILLS OF WORKING IN SMALL GROUPS

Working in small groups without the supervision of a teacher can help to stimulate creative ideas and to establish a group that has employment potential. It can also provide an opportunity to develop teamworking skills through rehearsals.

There is no single best strategy for rehearsing repertoire.[5] Individual ensembles find their own best ways of working. Typically, there are four main activities:

- initiating (coming up with ideas)
- performing (playing)
- orienting (steering the direction of work)
- assisted learning (helping each other to learn).[6]

In preparing for specific performances, it is a good idea to have a plan of the material to be covered across a series of rehearsals, with time for extra sessions should they be needed.[7]

For groups that are going to work together over long periods of time, trust and respect are crucial for the group to function effectively.[8] For long-term success, rehearsals have to be underpinned by strong social frameworks, as frequently there are disagreements about musical content and how the group is co-ordinated.[8,9] Where groups cannot work well together, much time is spent in attempting to resolve interpersonal difficulties and there is less time to devote to the music. There can be advantages of working with friends, because the relationship itself does not have to be worked on and effort can be focused on the task.[10] Key Point Summary 7.2 sets out the skills required for working with others.

CASE STUDY 7.1: EXAMPLE OF ADVANTAGES OF GETTING INVOLVED IN AN ENSEMBLE

Anna was a pianist, who had spent her time prior to attending conservatoire largely practising and working alone as a soloist. She continued to hold aspirations of being able to become an international soloist, but while at the conservatoire she wanted to increase her social networks and explore other opportunities for making music.

She formed a trio with a violinist and cellist. This provided her with opportunities for exploring a wider repertoire of music (including arrangements that they made of popular music) and developing a greater understanding of the works of particular composers. She also made new friends and increased her opportunities for performing.

KEY POINT SUMMARY 7.2: SKILLS REQUIRED FOR WORKING WITH OTHERS

In working in ensembles, a number of skills are required. These may be utilised by any group member at any time. The skills include:

- listening
- explaining
- demonstrating
- leading
- communicating
- questioning
- challenging
- critiquing
- facilitating
- encouraging
- supporting
- negotiating
- organising.

These skills, once acquired, will transfer to other group-working situations.

OPPORTUNITIES WITHIN COMMUNITY MUSIC

Community musicians come from a wide variety of backgrounds, offering expertise across all genres. What they have in common is that they are involved in collaborative, high-quality music-making in a wide range of community settings, including schools, music centres, community centres and places of worship, offering opportunities for everyone to engage with music-making.

In addition to their musical expertise, community musicians require high-level interpersonal and teamworking skills, and a willingness to develop understanding of the social and musical cultures within which they are working. They also need to acquire administrative skills and knowledge of the ways that the various organisations with which they work operate. While they do not need a teaching qualification, they do need to be able to lead and facilitate musical activities. For this reason they are sometimes referred to as 'music leaders'. In addition to individual musicians, a wide range of musical ensembles, including major symphony orchestras, are involved in community work.

The aims of community music vary, depending on the particular context. They may: be educational; be related to the personal development of participants; involve community development; be therapeutic; or have other social objectives.[11] Community music workshops usually have an emphasis on creativity and aim to involve all participants in being able to express themselves spontaneously and in co-operating with each other.[12] Community musicians facilitate this.

Skills as a facilitator can be acquired in a range of ways. Many higher education institutions now engage in community music education outreach work, where young musicians work in schools. The process of actively facilitating music-making can be enhanced by observing those with existing expertise and participating in such projects. There are also many opportunities for developing skills through short- and medium-term courses. A number of institutions also offer formally accredited programmes or modules at foundation, undergraduate and postgraduate levels. Those with a portfolio career across all musical genres are likely to participate in community music during their career and need to develop skills relating to this (leadership, facilitation, teaching, interpersonal, administrative).

CASE STUDY 7.2: A CREATIVE COMMUNITY PROJECT IN A PRIMARY SCHOOL

The Making Waves project at Gallions Mount Primary School was delivered by Trinity College of Music (now Trinity Laban) through Raising the Roof (Trinity's music education programme for schools in Greenwich and Lewisham).

The project aimed 'to enthuse, inform and encourage children and adults alike in developing confidence in composition, to support structuring and shaping original work for sharing and performing'.

The whole school took part, using an overarching theme of water. Five Trinity music leaders went into the school to structure the work appropriately for different classes. A total of three INSET sessions were delivered, and eight planning meetings with teachers, 50 workshop sessions and 16 performances to other classes and teachers in the school took place.

While the school engages in a lot of singing and some instrumental work, support was needed in delivering the music national curriculum, as none of the teachers was a music expert. In particular, staff needed support with organising music in (open-plan) classrooms and knowing how to manage composition. The central theme of water was convenient and unifying, because of the possibilities it represented throughout the curriculum, e.g. in science, geography.

Each class worked with a musician to create and perform an original piece of music, based on the central theme of water. Younger pupils worked with stories they knew, creating a musical accompaniment to the telling of the story or writing poems that, with the help of the music leader, were set to music. At nursery level, the learning was in terms of the music curriculum and more widely in terms of social skills and giving pupils confidence with communication. Teachers observed that some pupils found it easier to sing something than to say it, and described one pupil who found it difficult to express himself when talking, as he could not sequence words properly, but who could do this when singing.

Adapted from Duncan, Katrina, 'Cross-curricular Creative Projects.
Online. www.anewdirection.org.uk/file_download.aspx?id=7203
(accessed 23 April 2012).
Reprinted with permission from A New Direction.

TEACHING AND DIRECTING

While teaching is sometimes viewed as a less prestigious alternative to performing, it has a range of benefits in addition to providing a source of income. One benefit is that explaining to others deepens and reinforces one's own learning. It can enhance understanding of technical skills and facilitate the undertaking of a critical appraisal of exactly how particular musical sounds are created, which in turn can enhance the teacher's skills. If instruments related to one's own instrument are taught or coached, it can increase understanding of those instruments and may even encourage the development of a limited ability to play them.

Coaching and directing ensembles enhances the skills of people management, while conducting demands score-reading and provides opportunities for developing conducting techniques.

There are many opportunities for developing teaching skills as elements of undergraduate and postgraduate programmes in addition to workshops and short courses.

TRANSFER OF LEARNING

Transfer of expert musical skills to other types of music and genres may be easy or difficult, depending on how similar the skill requirements are. The greatest challenge is acquiring representational knowledge of a new tonal system, as the tonality of the culture in which one grows up is acquired like language and becomes automated very early on in life.

Musicians also acquire high levels of automatisation of reading or aural skills early in their careers. They may come to rely on either of these to the exclusion of the other. This can be remedied, but requires considerable effort. For instance, if a popular musician has only learnt to play by ear and never worked from notation, a substantial amount of work will be required to learn to read music. But if they do not acquire reading skills, this may preclude them from certain types or work. Similarly, a musician who has learnt to play from notation may find it difficult to learn to play by ear. Issues are not limited to those relating to the reading of notation. Written notation cannot indicate all of the information required to perform certain types of music. It provides only a near representation. To develop versatility, musicians need to gain experience with as many types of music as possible. A classically trained musician may experience no difficulties in providing backing to a pop group, providing that notation is supplied, but playing in a big band where rhythms are interpreted in particular ways may prove problematic, as may playing folk music. Gaining as much experience early on in a variety of genres increases opportunities for developing different work streams.

CASE STUDY 7.3: A CREATIVE COMMUNITY MUSIC PROJECT IN A YOUNG OFFENDERS' INSTITUTION

The Good Vibrations Gamelan in Prison project is a music programme for young offenders between the ages of 15 and 25. The gamelan music ensemble lends itself well to encouraging group interaction and the development of social skills.

The aim of the project was to help prisoners to acquire the social skills to help them find employment after their release from prison, since research shows that if you can get and keep a job when you get out of prison, you are less likely to reoffend. Unlike most prisoner education schemes, Good Vibrations is run in an 'out of classroom' manner, making it more accessible to young offenders who find the classroom environment too stressful. The project was integrated into the prison's own educational and rehabilitation activities. Sessions were co-ordinated with the prison educational staff.

The programme had record attendance levels, with stories of difficult inmates taking to the gamelan classes and in some cases becoming central to the project. One participant on suicide watch was particularly violent at the start of the project. As classes continued, he settled down and displayed excellent concentration skills. He later commented: 'The music makes me relax. I enjoyed being in the team. The highlight was the play-through at the end, because I had learnt something and I felt good doing it.'

Many participants, including staff, benefited from a new cultural experience. Many may not have otherwise experienced such diversity.

Youth Music (2008) (http://dev1.youthmusic.org.uk/case_studies/ Good_vibrations_gamelan_in_prison.html), accessed 4 January 2010.

The speed with which new instrumental skills can be acquired also depends on the degree of similarity with the original instrument. Violinists may find playing the viola relatively easy, although reading notation from a different clef may prove problematic. Learning instruments from the same family is likely to be easier than those from a different family and may be worthwhile in terms of teaching, even if performing on them is not feasible.

There are frequently opportunities in schools for creative project work with children and young people. Some examples are provided in Case Studies 7.2 and 7.3. In addition, a range of world musics have gained in popularity and are in demand, for instance, gamelan, African drumming, samba. If skills are acquired on a wide range of instruments, the more employment opportunities will become available.

ACQUIRING NEW SKILLS

There are a number of ways in which musical experiences can be expanded. If it is a question of understanding how to perform in different musical genres, listening to recordings and attending live performances will assist in learning new aural representations, which can then be emulated. Further knowledge can be acquired through joining existing amateur musical groups, where skills can be developed in a non-professional environment. Another alternative is to form a group with colleagues who may have more experience in particular fields.

Technology also has a useful role in acquiring new musical skills. Asynchronous communication in relation to learning new skills can include email, while synchronous communication might make use of Skype and MSN Messenger. Materials for tuition are available for download, and this can provide an easy way to acquire some basic skills on another instrument. Various packages are available for this. Virtual learning environments are also being developed, which will enable learners to communicate online with peers, teachers, facilitators and other experts. This will enable learners to choose to work individually or collaboratively, with or without a teacher. Demonstrations are also available, providing examples of how to acquire a range of technical skills. There are already some examples of these activities, particularly in the popular music genre,[13] and a number of websites which offer such opportunities. Lessons freely available on the internet, particularly on YouTube, contain excellent demonstrations of how to play a wide range of instruments in a variety of musical genres, catering for learners with a range of different levels of expertise.

Available technological resources for learning include:

- published materials in a wider variety of genres
- tutors accompanied by recordings
- videos, CD-ROMs and DVDs
- web-specific learning tools, which include notation and MIDI files
- online tuition

- play-along sites
- YouTube videos
- wiki sites
- tuition through Skype
- internet interactive group lessons.[14]

EXERCISE 7.3: EXTENDING YOUR MUSICAL INTERESTS

What other genres might you be interested in exploring? What other instruments might you be interested in learning? Make a list. Use the World Wide Web to explore how you might go about developing these additional interests.

CHAPTER SUMMARY: GETTING INVOLVED IN WIDER LEARNING ACTIVITIES

The development of electronic media in the latter part of the twentieth century revolutionised access to, and the use of, music in people's everyday lives.

These changes represent enormous opportunities for musicians, providing that they are willing to continue learning and adapting throughout their lives.

New skills can be acquired through informal or formal learning in a variety of different ways.

It is easier to acquire new skills if they are close to existing skills.

Participating in ensembles is a very effective way to acquire and enhance skills.

FURTHER READING

Creech, A. (2010) 'The role of music leaders and community musicians'. In S. Hallam and A. Creech (eds), *Music Education in the 21st Century in the UK: Achievements, analysis and aspirations*. London: Institute of Education, University of London. This chapter provides information about the role and activities undertaken by those operating as community musicians in the UK. It provides examples of projects and the nature of training.

USEFUL WEBSITES

MusicLeader: www.musicleader.net

Sound Sense: www.soundsense.org

NOTES

1. 'From pocket to stage, music in the key of iPhone'. Online. www.nytimes.com/2009/12/05/technology/05orchestra.html (accessed 19 February 2010).

2. North, A.C. and Hargreaves, D.J. (1997) 'Experimental aesthetics and everyday music listening'. In D.J. Hargreaves and A.C. North (eds), *The Social Psychology of Music*. Oxford: Oxford University Press.

3. Davidson, J.W. (1993) 'Visual perception of performance manner in the movement of solo musicians'. *Psychology of Music*, 21(2), 103–13.

4. Creech, A., Gaunt, H., Hallam, S. and Robertson, L. (2009) 'Conservatoire students' perceptions of master classes'. *British Journal of Music Education*, 26(3), 315–32.

5. Davidson, J. and King, E.C. (2004) 'Strategies for ensemble practice'. In A. Williamon (ed.), *Musical Excellence*. Oxford: Oxford University Press, 105–22.

6. Berg, M.H. (2000) 'Thinking for yourself: The social construction of chamber music experience'. In R.R. Rideout and S.J. Paul (eds), *On the Sociology of Music: Vol 2. Papers from the Music Education Symposium at the University of Oklahoma*. Amherst: University of Massachusetts Press, 91–112.

7. Goodman, E. (2000) 'Analysing the ensemble in music rehearsal and performance: The nature and effects of interaction in cello-piano duos'. Unpublished doctoral dissertation, University of London.

8. Young, V.M. and Coleman, A.M. (1979) 'Some psychological processes in string quartets'. *Psychology of Music*, 7, 12–16.

9. Murningham, J.K. and Conlan, D.E. (1991) 'The dynamics of intense work groups: A study of British string quartets'. *Administrative Science Quarterly*, 36, 165–86.

10. Hallam, S., Creech, A. and McQueen, H. (2010) *Musical Futures: A case study investigation: Interim report December 2010*. London: Institute of Education, University of London.

11. Mullen, P. (2002) *We Don't Teach, We Explore: Aspects of community music delivery*. Online. www.worldmusiccentre.com/uploads/cma/mullenteachexplore.PDF (accessed 27 December 2010).

12. Higgins, L. (2008) 'The creative music workshop: Event, facilitation, gift'. *International Journal of Music Education*, 26(4), 326–38.

13. Koh, L. (2010) 'Beatboxing as lived curriculum: Implications for the Singapore music classroom'. Paper presented at C-DIME 10. Sydney Conservatorium of Music, 11–13 January 2010.

14. Waldron, J. and Vleben, K. (2008) 'The medium is the message: Cyberspace, community, and music learning in the Irish traditional music virtual community'. *Journal of Music, Technology and Education*, 1(2 and 3), 99–111.

CHAPTER 8
HEALTH AND WELL-BEING

INTRODUCTION

This chapter explains the importance of health and well-being for musicians. It:

- provides an overview of the particular issues that musicians face in relation to health and well-being
- outlines a range of ways to promote health and well-being and to avoid difficulties
- offers strategies and further resources for anyone suffering from injury or psychological stress.

INTRODUCTION

What do health and well-being mean for musicians? Essentially they cover a complex set of issues that relate both to the specific physical and psychological demands of music, and to more general aspects of managing professional life, personal development and work–life balance.

The interrelationship between physical and psychological dimensions is particularly important in any practical music-making that requires fine-tuned motor control. There are profound interconnections between posture, quality of movement, breathing, concentration, listening and interpersonal awareness, creativity, presence in performance, and responding to internal and external feedback.

Important dimensions of health and well-being for musicians include:

- physical fitness in order to provide stamina for long hours of rehearsing or travelling, and to manage stress
- detailed motor control and flexibility to play, even when this involves a lot of repetitive movement
- protecting hearing and managing exposure to excessive sound volumes
- supporting the creative process in a professional context, including managing creative block
- managing performance anxiety productively

- establishing and maintaining work–life balance, particularly when self-employed and/or when required to travel or undertake anti-social hours of work.

THE RISE IN INJURY AND STRESS-RELATED PROBLEMS

For anyone young, successful and in the peak of health, a proactive approach to health and well-being may feel like a low priority. Furthermore, until fairly recently, health and well-being tended to be something of a taboo subject in many areas of professional music. However, as instances of physical injury and psychological stress have grown dramatically in the last 30 years, the subject has gained a much higher profile.[1] Research has shown that the majority of performing musicians have suffered from musculoskeletal or other medical conditions as a result of their work. A study of 2,212 musicians in 1988 found that 76 per cent of participants had experienced a serious medical condition that affected their playing.[2] A survey of orchestral musicians across the world in 2000 found that 56 per cent of them had experienced pain while playing within the period of a year, and that 34 per cent experienced pain regularly, once a week or more.[3] The causes of injury have been attributed to factors such as the stresses of the lifestyle, too much practice, the demands of particularly difficult repertoire, and adapting to a new instrument. Many of these problems, however, are preventable. They require musicians to be physically, mentally and emotionally fit.[4]

Performance science has long been established in sport, and is now growing rapidly in the performing arts, particularly in dance and in music. This means that a significant research base is steadily being developed, which can underpin pedagogy and improve practice. The science of the voice in particular has received detailed attention, and the impact has been a major cultural shift in understanding how the voice works and how singing can most effectively be taught.[5] Health and well-being are also now part of many education and training programmes oriented towards performing. In addition, the number of national and international organisations dedicated to supporting the music industry is increasing. In the UK these include:

- awareness promotion and advice through the Musicians' Union[6]
- the British Association for Performing Arts Medicine (BAPAM)[7]
- the Musicians Benevolent Fund[8]
- the Healthy Orchestra Charter.[9]

A critical thing to recognise is that health and well-being for the professional musician are deeply personal, relating to the particular demands of the field of work, individual needs and preferences. Some people find they benefit from focusing on general fitness and take up aerobic exercise, cycling, running, tennis or going to the gym. Others are inclined to explore things that are more explicitly body–mind oriented, such as yoga, Pilates, T'ai Chi or Alexander Technique. Meditation of all kinds is popular with musicians, and there are a range of techniques dedicated to assisting with performance anxiety, such as biofeedback and neurofeedback,[10] and mental skills training.[11]

What is essential is that this aspect of being a musician is not ignored. Each person needs to discover how best to embed health and well-being within their own practice.

PHYSICAL FITNESS

Physical fitness is about tuning the body to maintain flexibility and co-ordination, stamina and an appropriate level of strength to cope with daily life and the particular demands of a field of work.[12] Physical fitness can also improve concentration, mental agility and willpower, and help to combat stress. It depends on three things: nutrition, exercise and sleep.

A healthy diet is central to everyone's well-being. Musicians are no different, but there can be particular challenges associated with an irregular work pattern, being on tour and eating late at night. These situations can make it difficult to establish a healthy routine, and can easily lead to the consumption of too much junk food. Performers may be prone to post-performance bingeing and alcohol/drug consumption as part of the winding-down process after the adrenalin highs.

NUTRITION

Detailed nutrition advice is changing all the time but is readily available. Following basic guidelines about eating a balanced diet with plenty of fresh foods, fruit and vegetables is as important for musicians as anyone else. A wealth of information is provided, for example, by the British Nutrition Foundation.[13] For musicians, particular strategies for coping with being a performer ('performing' here refers to a wide range of work, including lecturing, running workshops and recording sessions, as well as gigs and concerts) include:

- keeping well hydrated – drinking plenty of water and other liquids that do not contain caffeine or alcohol

- avoiding lots of caffeine, and particularly caffeine for several hours before performing, as this can increase adrenalin levels
- avoiding lots of alcohol, and any alcohol before performing
- avoiding eating a heavy meal before performing, particularly one which is rich in carbohydrates, as carbohydrates tend to slow the body down
- eating particular foods to boost energy levels depending on the length of the performance and energy required – fast-release foods such as bananas can be useful shortly before or in the intervals of a performance; slow-release foods such as nuts can help to sustain energy over a period of time.

LIVING ON A BUDGET AND PREPARING HEALTHY FOOD

Many student musicians, and indeed professionals, live on a fairly meagre budget. This can bring with it all sorts of challenges and can be a source of stress. Eating healthily, for example, may be problematic, particularly when you have to be away from home and find that fast food is cheaper than more nutritious options. You can, of course, eat healthily in these situations, but planning is essential. This may not be the most exciting thing to have to do, but once it becomes a habit, it makes a big difference to sustaining health, and can save money in the end.

For those who do not feel they can cook, or only have access to limited cooking facilities, there are many resources available online, including easy recipes, fast recipes, recipes that require no cooking or perhaps one pot or a microwave, and introductions to the most basic culinary skills. Examples include:

- Beyond Baked Beans (www.beyondbakedbeans.com/): blog-based and includes a 'Healthy eating on a budget' section and one for beginners
- Student Cooking TV (www.studentcooking.tv/)
- Student Recipes (www.studentrecipes.com/)
- BBC Food (www.bbc.co.uk/food/recipes/): has 13,000 recipes and a 'Quick and easy' search option.

Remember as well that cooking in itself can be a stress-busting activity!

TAKING PHYSICAL EXERCISE

It is now widely understood that increased physical exercise helps to reduce the risk of heart attacks, strokes, high blood pressure, obesity, cancer, musculoskeletal problems and osteoporosis.

There are also particular benefits for some musicians. A study of student instrumentalists in the UK found that their self-reported physical activity levels were below the national recommendations for most students. However, once introduced to the benefits of exercise and how to build exercise into a pre-performance preparation routine, many reported significant benefits, not least in their experience of performance anxiety and reduced dependency on alcohol or drugs.[12]

A difficulty for musicians can be that, as a talented musician, at school they took less physical exercise (even to the extent of missing all games lessons), in order to create time to pursue music. The consequence is reduced experience and awareness of how exercise benefits general fitness and the particular business of being a musician. It can also mean that structural imbalances are set up from the particular posture and movements necessary for playing a specific instrument. These imbalances may not be immediately obvious at a young age, but may cause problems later with increased hours of music-making and a natural ageing process.

TIPS AND REMINDERS 8.1: STRATEGIES FOR INCREASING PHYSICAL EXERCISE

Choose physical exercise which you find enjoyable and that can be integrated into your lifestyle.

Exercise with a friend or group of enthusiasts – this helps to sustain motivation and challenge.

Begin a new programme of physical exercise slowly, and build up intensity and length of sessions. Make use of relevant advice and literature that will help to guide this process.

Build exercise into your existing schedule, for example using cycling as a mode of transport.

Warm up and warm down before and after exercise – this helps to avoid injury.

Monitor how increased physical exercise impacts on your experience as a musician in terms of enjoyment, stamina, physical ease, stress levels.

Increasing physical fitness is usually an excellent way of supporting development as a musician. Practical strategies are suggested in Tips and Reminders 8.1. Before taking up any exercise, however, it is important to consider risks associated with the activity relating to existing health issues, the activity itself, and the relationship of the activity to the physical demands of musical activity. If in any doubt, medical advice should always be sought.

SLEEP

Quantity and quality of sleep are critical to health and well-being for everyone. A study investigating the sleep patterns of managers in business and their impact found that, on average, they slept for less than seven hours per night, and that this decreased further as they became more senior. Eighty per cent of them woke up at least once a night and took on average 15 minutes to go back to sleep (for chief executives this was 30 minutes). Some 72 per cent of them reported that they found it difficult to concentrate on tasks because of a lack of sleep. This study built on extensive research, which has demonstrated that while not all behaviour is affected by poor sleep (for example logical, deductive and critical reasoning skills), a number of skills are highly susceptible, including several particularly important ones for musicians:

- comprehending and coping with a rapidly changing environment
- multi-tasking
- communication skills
- decision-making involving complex and creative ideas.[14,15]

Musicians often find that they cannot maintain a regular sleep pattern, given professional commitments. This can exacerbate problems with sleep, which clearly can affect the quality of work, and can contribute to long-term burnout. There are plenty of strategies, however, to help establish sufficient high-quality sleep. These include:

- keeping to a regular bedtime and waking time whenever possible
- avoiding alcohol, caffeine or heavy food in the three or four hours before going to bed
- regular physical exercise, although not immediately before going to bed
- blocking out light and noise
- keeping the room well ventilated and at an appropriate temperature

- taking up relaxation exercises, such as breathing used in yoga, meditation or mindfulness.

MIND AND BODY FOR MUSICIANS

Musicians make great demands on themselves in both mind and body, and the two interact in subtle ways. This is true at the most general level of finding a healthy work–life balance. It is also true at the most detailed level of particular practices, for example in optimising the biochemical environment for the vocal folds as a singer, or in enabling the creative process of writing a piece of music.

BREATHING

The way we breathe is a strong indicator of how we are, both mentally and physically. The most natural form of breathing is demonstrated by young babies who, when resting, tend to breathe regularly and deeply with easy movement of the abdominal muscles making the tummy rise and fall. There is little tension observable in their shoulders, chest or neck.

Breathing, however, is greatly affected by physical and psychological experiences. Postural tension or injuries, for example, can constrict lung volume or the elasticity of exhalation and inhalation. Similarly, anxiety or psychological trauma are likely to inhibit breathing, in particular through muscles tightening up and so reducing range of movement. This is symptomatic of our natural reflex: when someone suddenly senses extreme danger, they tend to tense up and breathe much faster and more shallowly than normal.

Usually, once the source of anxiety has passed, breathing returns to its natural resting state. When, however, something particularly traumatic is experienced, or when lower levels of anxiety are felt persistently over time, breathing may remain tense and shallow. Most adults find in fact that their habitual patterns of breathing are constricted compared with those of a baby. Musicians, particularly those who perform a lot, find themselves experiencing regular performance anxiety, and this may well exacerbate those habits. With breathing, then, a vicious circle is set up. This can be physically uncomfortable, emotionally upsetting, and can also mean that performers become disconnected from their musically expressive selves.

Although breathing is an automatic function, it can also be regulated through voluntary control. It is possible to learn new habits. Developing an ability to breathe deeply and easily with a soft expansion and contraction of the abdominal girdle undoubtedly helps to maintain health and well-being. It is the foundation of a number of techniques, such as yoga and Chi Gong, and can be a useful tool in managing performance anxiety.

EXERCISE 8.1: DEVELOPING FLEXIBILITY AND DEPTH IN YOUR BREATHING

Changing your breathing patterns to the point where they become automatic and available to you when under stress takes practice. The following exercise will give you a taste of how breathing affects you.

1. Lie on your side, one arm under your head and the other arm in front of you resting on the floor. Have your knees drawn up a little, as in the recovery position.

2. Breathe normally and notice how you feel – notice any tensions in your body and any sensations of anxiety.

3. Breathe out as far as you can (more than normally), drawing in your tummy and tensing your abdominal muscles so that your belly button moves towards your spine.

4. When you have exhaled as far as possible, deliberately release all your abdominal muscles so that your tummy softens and moves outwards. You should find that this makes you breathe without thinking about it.

5. Repeat steps 3 and 4 for a few minutes. You can try varying the speed of step 3, as this may help to release tensions. If you feel at all lightheaded, slow the speed down. With each inhalation, imagine the breath going deeper into your body. You can also try putting one hand on your tummy or your waist to monitor the movements. You should find that you experience greater and more flexible movement as you go through the exercise.

6. Notice the changes in how you feel physically and psychologically. You may well find that you feel less tense, and pain may reduce or disappear. You may also feel calmer and more alert, with the pace of your thoughts slowing down.

Further suggestions for developing healthy breathing are given in the 'Further reading' section at the end of this chapter.

POSTURE AND THE FIT WITH AN INSTRUMENT

The nature of a specialised field in music is that it often involves repetition of specific physical movements. This usually means that people become accustomed to taking up particular postures, and can become moulded by them. For example an academic may spend a lot of time sitting down and looking at books, scores or writing. In time, they may begin to slump forwards when sitting, the spine curving more than usual, and their shoulders drooping as a result of leaning forward and straining to see small print. Flexibility may also be lost, as the body becomes more and more familiar with some positions and less practised with others.

These issues are important for all musicians, and particularly for those who play instruments that rely on fine-tuned movements. Everyone will be affected to some degree. There are, however, things which can be done to minimise the consequences. The most important things to consider are:

- warming up muscles before playing – flexibility exercises get muscles, tendons and joints moving, and improve elasticity
- cooling down after playing – stretching exercises help to release tension after playing, eliminate waste products from muscular effort and so reduce the risk of injury.[16]

Many instruments naturally suit some body shapes better than others. For example it is usually thought to be an advantage for keyboard players to have quite large hands, as this facilitates playing chords spread over more than an octave. Someone with a very long neck may experience trouble holding a violin or viola under their chin without tensing up one side of their neck. Someone with long legs may have difficulty sitting comfortably with the cello, as their knees end up being too high in relation to their hips, and this creates unwanted tension in the support for the torso. Someone with very short arms may have problems fully extending the slide of a trombone. In all these cases, if a player simply tries to adapt their own position around the instrument, they will almost certainly run into difficulties.

Increasingly, however, things can be done to adapt the instrument to fit the player's physique better. For example, an extended shoulder rest will mean that the violinist can maintain the full length of their neck. It is well worth researching the different solutions available and experimenting with them. While teachers may be expert in assessing how a particular piece of equipment supports a player, they may not always be aware of the newest solutions available. You can seek knowledge and advice most usefully through organisations dedicated to musicians' health, such as those mentioned earlier in the chapter. Equipment is usually most easily accessed through specialist instrument retailers, organisations or interest groups.

VOCAL HEALTH

Singers carry their instrument with them all the time. There is much less opportunity for singers to adapt the shape and size of their instrument to suit their taste, and any changes that occur around the vocal chords almost certainly impact on their ability to sing. Vocal health, therefore, is a vital issue for all singers. It involves a complex range of psycho-physical issues including, for example, hydration, postural issues, tiredness and stress. These issues go beyond the scope of this book. Suffice to say, the sooner singers engage with them, the better.[17]

STRAIN INJURIES

Strain injuries are common. They can be caused either by over-use of particular movements or by the misuse of particular parts of the body. They can have a profound psychological effect, even though very often they can be treated effectively over a period of time.

Extensive repetition of movements with insufficient recovery periods can result in inflammation from the loading of joints and soft tissues, or in muscle fatigue.[18] The risks of a strain injury are increased by poor posture, static posture and muscular hypertension, particularly when parts of the body are twisted or used in ways that are quite different from the body's neutral position. Indications of strain injuries include sharp pains or dull ache, numbness, tingling, or reduced field of movement or ability to grip.

You can do a great deal to prevent such injuries through self-awareness and a proactive approach to prevention. Strategies include:

- being aware of the particular physical demands of musical activity and the kinds of strain injury that may arise
- making a balanced posture a priority and avoiding hypertension, particularly in performance situations (note that breathing has a vital part to play in this)
- warming up and warming down before and after playing an instrument, singing or performing, to ensure that muscles work at an optimal level and recover after use

- taking regular breaks every half hour or so, particularly during long periods of intensive work
- improving physical use and posture through, for example, Alexander Technique, yoga or Feldenkrais (see Table 8.1 for more details).

Anyone experiencing discomfort or pain while playing should immediately seek the advice of specialist health professionals. Injuries tend to heal much more quickly if they are attended to at an early stage, and different kinds of injury often require different approaches to treatment. One brass player reported:

> I had some embouchure problems. I went to my GP and to BAPAM: they referred me to an ENT [ear, nose and throat] consultant and a muscle specialist. Also I went to my old professor and asked him to look at me play, and he said my technique's fine, there's something physiological. I didn't delay. As soon as I realised it was getting to me and I needed to deal with it, I talked to doctors, charities, my old professor, and musicians I could trust. I did have a few dark teatimes of the soul thinking, '…it's over, what am I going to do?'. I was catastrophising but it does go through your mind. Also I wrote down all the things I do in my life that might have contributed to something going on…With musicians and injury, time is of the essence: you can't wait six months for an appointment. BAPAM will give you a free hour's consultation with a GP who is often a musician, and they understand that things can be emotional as well as physiological.

Increasingly, musicians are realising the need to talk openly and to seek support if they begin to experience problems. Nevertheless, this can feel extremely difficult, not least when this may appear to threaten a professional livelihood, their career trajectory or their personal and professional identity. Case Study 8.1 clearly demonstrates the psychological challenge of injury over a period of years, but also indicates how the experience has ultimately strengthened motivation, self-understanding and the ability to create a satisfying career.

CASE STUDY 8.1: THE PSYCHOLOGICAL IMPACT OF INJURY

'At the age of 15, while studying piano at...school, I began to suffer from playing-related pain in my right wrist. Through a combination of ignorance (I knew nothing about the danger of injuries), denial (as I now see with hindsight), fear (of failing and disappointing those around me), and an emotional need not to feel excluded and rejected or to lose a means of expressing myself, I carried on playing and the injury became progressively more serious.

'There then followed multiple periods of rest and recommencements of playing, but it was not until I was taken to see an osteopath a couple of years later, and began to reassess my approach to piano playing around the same time, that my injury began to feel more under control.

'I have been lucky enough to forge a successful and happy career, and to perform and teach regularly, but the physical scar tissue will probably always remain, meaning that I always have to be mindful of the possibility of a recurrence of my injury with an unusually heavy playing load.

'Living with this injury has been one of the most significant, psychologically challenging periods of my life. I certainly recognise the emotions of denial, depression, loneliness, loss of identity, self-confidence and self-esteem, anger and anxiety which appear in the [research] literature... Long-term, however, the most powerful elements to arise from this experience psychologically have been positive; these benefits include a better understanding of my body and of piano-playing technique and, I hope, the capacity to pass this on to my students; a real awareness of my love of playing the piano; an ability to appreciate each performance for what it is, and not where it might lead; and a broadening of my career to encompass many varied and enjoyable experiences.'

THE CONNECTION BETWEEN HEALTH AND WELL-BEING AND THE APPROACH TO LEARNING

Studying music is a multi-layered experience and one that has no limits. Musicians tend to go on learning throughout their lives – music is a passion. It is easy to become obsessive about studying. The specialised nature of many areas of music means that it is easy to be narrow in the field of focus and also narrow in terms of approaches to learning. In all cases it is important to make sure that the body and mind do not become rigidly set in particular learning patterns, not least as these may lead to injury or burnout.

A healthy approach to learning may well require a degree of inventiveness to find diverse ways of pursuing one thing. For example, in the case of learning a piece of notated music, this would mean varying practice strategies, including reading and singing from a score, practising silently and visualising the movements, as well as varying strategies when actually playing. As one student suggested, if you are doing eight hours alone in a practice room and your brain is understimulated by continually repeating the same thing, you go a bit mad! This student developed an approach of exploring composition alongside playing. She followed Schoenberg's ideas about improving aural skills through composing, and found that this reduced her need for practice time on her instrument. Having some time off studying is also essential, as this allows the body and mind to recharge. This is as true for music as for any profession.

A number of particular approaches to learning music have focused on mind–body connections and the development of focused but easy concentration – or 'flow'. Many musicians have found that these approaches have given them significant insights into their practice and have enabled them to break through to a new level in their work.[19]

STRESS, RELAXATION AND RECREATION

The classic symptoms of stress from study or work becoming too intense include:

- anxiety
- anger
- depression
- loss of motivation/decreased enjoyment of music
- food cravings/loss of appetite
- difficulty sleeping
- feeling tired
- difficulty concentrating
- physical pains or dizziness
- feeling restless or sweating more than usual
- breathlessness.

It is easy not to recognise that symptoms are being caused by stress, particularly in their early stages, and when following a busy schedule. This makes it all the more important to be proactive in creating a healthy lifestyle. Regular exercise, balanced sleep and a healthy diet, for example, all play an important part in combating stress.

Recreation and relaxation provide an opportunity to refresh mind and body, and to reflect. This is an easy thing to say, and not always so easy to put into practice. Many musicians, driven by their passion, the need to prove themselves and the opportunity to earn, want to say yes to everything. It is not always so easy to see what the implications will be for the quality of the work and for health and well-being. One performance student suggested:

> I find it very difficult to say no to things, but you have to say no sometimes even if you'd like to do them. It's good to do things for free to make contacts, but sometimes you can't afford to any more, you have so many demands on your time. When snowed under, I tend to do a head down thing and not get too emotionally attached to projects, just do it professionally and try not to let it get to me if things go wrong. I've had to develop this strategy – I wasn't used to it when I came.

Learning when to say no is an important professional skill, and is discussed further in Chapter 11.

Many musicians also find that practising specific techniques dedicated to holistic well-being and/or finding support from health professionals is essential in maintaining a successful career. Examples are given in Table 8.1.

TABLE 8.1: AN OVERVIEW OF PRACTICES USED BY MUSICIANS TO ENHANCE HEALTH AND WELL-BEING

Alexander Technique	The Alexander Technique focuses on developing skilful 'use of the self'. This can include aspects of posture, physical movement, breathing, self-awareness, direction of attention, how we approach learning, and how our reactions may change when we face more or less demanding situations.
	Musicians frequently turn to the Alexander Technique either to avoid, or to deal with, physical problems related to performing and also aspects of performance anxiety. Instruction is often available for students at conservatoires. The UK body for Alexander Technique is the Society of Teachers of the Alexander Technique: www.stat.org.uk
BodyMapping	BodyMapping is a practical approach to developing awareness and understanding of our individual physical structure and how it works. It derives from work by Barbara and Bill Conable that drew on the Alexander Technique and a detailed understanding of anatomy. A central premise is that enhanced understanding of this kind provides us with greater choice in terms of posture and movement.

BodyMapping courses are usually delivered by Andover Educators™, a not-for-profit organisation of music educators committed to saving, securing and enhancing musical careers by providing accurate information about the body in movement. Many BodyMapping teachers are based in the US: www.bodymap.org. There are, however, some opportunities to explore this work elsewhere.

(Note that the term 'BodyMapping' has been appropriated by various different ventures, some of them with little connection to musicians' well-being.)

Counselling and psychotherapy	Counselling and psychotherapy aim to assist people in overcoming psychological challenges that they may have, including performance anxiety, depression or a phobia. They can also be used where someone simply wants to gain insight into their own personality and how they relate to others.
	Psychotherapy uses talking (and, in some disciplines, practical activities) in the context of a relationship with a therapist, to effect personal change and development. Psychotherapists generally work within one of a number of theoretical approaches, though combining elements from these is quite common:
	• Behavioural and cognitive approaches (including cognitive behavioural therapy or CBT) emphasise the importance of actions and thoughts, rather than their causes.
	• Psychoanalytic and psychodynamic approaches are interested in the causes and meanings of thoughts and behaviours for the individual, and relate them to past experiences and theories of the unconscious mind.
	• Humanistic approaches (e.g. existential and Gestalt therapies) are concerned with self-fulfilment and the construction of meaning in one's life, and emphasise the role of the individual's free will in achieving these.
	Integrative therapies draw on aspects of more than one tradition. Cognitive analytic therapy (CAT) and schema therapy are examples of this.
	Counsellors are trained to listen to people's problems sympathetically and help them to address negative emotions and ideas. They do not necessarily do this within one of the frameworks above, although some do. There is considerable overlap between the skills and approaches of counsellors and psychotherapists.
	There are no legal restrictions on who can offer services as a counsellor or psychotherapist in the UK, so it is wise to check that a practitioner is registered with one of the following bodies:
	• British Association for Counselling and Psychotherapy (BACP) (mainly counsellors)
	• British Association for Behavioural and Cognitive Psychotherapies

- The United Kingdom Council for Psychotherapy (mainly psychoanalytic practitioners)
- British Psychoanalytic Council
- British Association of Psychotherapists.

If you think you may have a specific difficulty such as depression, you can raise it with your GP, who may refer you to a clinical psychologist or a psychiatrist, if you wish. Clinical and counselling psychologists must by law be registered with the Health Professions Council.

Feldenkrais	The Feldenkrais Method is described as a form of 'somatic education' that may be used to assist recovery from muscular strains and injuries or postural issues. It seeks to train the body (the neuro-muscular system) in order to offer greater ease and co-ordination of movement. As clients build increased awareness of their movements and how they feel, so they learn to change them if they wish. The nature of the work is relatively gentle physically. Feldenkrais also uses a process of 'functional integration', where the practitioner guides the clients' movements with their hands so as to increase awareness of how they are performed. Feldenkrais may be taught in groups or one-to-one. The professional organisation for Feldenkrais in the UK is the Feldenkrais Guild UK: www.feldenkrais.co.uk
Mentoring and coaching	A mentor or coach supports a client in identifying, prioritising and achieving specific goals. Mentors/coaches may draw on diverse methods and approaches, including psychological ones, but they are not therapists. Their work is directed towards future goals. They may be specialised in a particular field, such as relationships or specific professional skills, or they may look more holistically at personal goals. Further information may be obtained from the European Mentoring and Coaching Council: www.emccouncil.org
Mindfulness	The essence of mindfulness is directing your awareness to the present moment, without passing judgement. This can be practised through meditative exercises, such as mindfulness of breathing, where you pay attention to your breath for a period of time, allowing other thoughts to pass by. Mindfulness meditation has been practised for centuries in the Buddhist tradition, but classes can increasingly be found without any religious orientation. There is good evidence for the efficacy of mindfulness techniques in treating psychological problems such as stress, anxiety and depression, as well as enhancing well-being and concentration in people without specific disorders. Mindfulness has been integrated with other psychological approaches in therapies such as mindfulness-based stress reduction (MSBR) and mindfulness-based cognitive therapy (MBCT). More information can be found at: www.bemindful.co.uk

Osteopathy and cranial osteopathy	Osteopathy is based on the principle that the well-being of an individual depends on the skeleton, muscles, ligaments and connective tissues functioning smoothly together. The aim of osteopathy is to bring the body to a state of balance, where possible without the use of drugs or surgery. Osteopaths will use touch, physical manipulation, stretching and massage to increase the mobility of joints, to relieve muscle tension, to enhance the blood and nerve supply to tissues, and to help the body's own healing mechanisms. They may also provide advice on posture and exercise to aid recovery, promote health and prevent symptoms recurring.[20] By law, osteopaths in the UK must be registered with the General Osteopathic Council in order to practise: www.osteopathy.org.uk
	Cranial osteopathy is a refined and subtle type of osteopathic treatment that encourages the release of stresses and tensions throughout the body, including the head. It works through tiny movements perceived in the plates of the skull, which have an independent rhythm or 'primary respiratory movement', and can be influenced, for example, to enhance the flow of cerebrospinal fluid to the peripheral nerves. It is a gentle approach, with less direct manipulation of limbs than other forms of osteopathy, and may be used in a wide range of conditions for people of all ages, from birth to old age.[21] The Sutherland Society is the largest UK organisation for cranial osteopaths: www.cranial.org.uk
	There is mixed evidence for efficacy of osteopathy, for example in treating lower back pain, and small risks may be associated with certain chiropractic and osteopathic manoeuvres. In some quarters, the fundamental premises of cranial osteopathy and its health benefits are contested.
Physiotherapy	Physiotherapy, often referred to as 'physio', uses physical methods, such as massage, manipulation, heat, electricity and remedial exercise, to promote healing and well-being. Physiotherapy treatments are often used to help restore a person's range of movement after injury or illness.
	For some conditions, your GP can refer you for NHS physiotherapy, and in some areas it is possible to access a physio direct on the NHS. BAPAM may also be able to help, and maintains a list of practitioners. You can access physiotherapists privately, but make sure you find one who is registered with the Chartered Society of Physiotherapy (www.csp.org.uk) or the Health Professions Council (www.hpc-uk.org).
Pilates	Pilates is an exercise method that places emphasis on 'core strength' for developing control over movement. It is practised to improve posture, flexibility, body awareness and a sense of mental and physical well-being. Some classes use large apparatus ('studio classes'), while others concentrate on 'mat work'. Group classes are common, though individual lessons are also possible. Classes are offered at varying levels of experience and ability.
	The Pilates Foundation maintains a register of practitioners: www.pilatesfoundation.com

T'ai Chi

T'ai Chi developed as a martial art, although some modern forms dispense with the reference to combat altogether. The underlying theory derives from the idea in traditional Chinese medicine of balancing 'Chi' or internal energy.

There are many forms of T'ai Chi, some involving contact and some emphasising slowly performed movements and meditative aspects. This reflects the varying interests of modern-day practitioners in T'ai Chi as a martial art, a sport or a technique for promoting well-being. There is some evidence from modern scientific testing that T'ai Chi can help mental and physical well-being, but it is important to check what the emphasis of a particular class is before enrolling.

The Tai Chi Union for Great Britain is the largest collective of independent T'ai Chi instructors in the British Isles: www.taichiunion. com

Trager®

The Trager® practitioner uses gentle manipulation of a client's limbs with the intention of increasing relaxation and suppleness and releasing muscular tension. Trager® can be effective in treating particular injuries, may be helpful in addressing long-term issues of tension, and should promote a sense of physical and mental well-being. A Trager® practitioner may also suggest daily actions ('mentastics') that the client can perform to regain and develop the state achieved in the session of 'tablework'.

Trager® practitioners are certified by Trager® International. The UK organisation is: www.trager.co.uk

Yoga

Yoga refers to a range of physical and mental disciplines that emerged centuries ago in India. As practised most commonly in the UK, it consists of adopting and moving between specified postures (asanas), sometimes in co-ordination with the breath. People practise yoga for many reasons, including physical flexibility, improved body movement and mental well-being. There is some scientific evidence that it is beneficial for certain medical conditions, including back pain and depression, and that it may be of value in increasing the quality of life in a number of situations.

There are various forms on offer:

- Ashtanga yoga is based on eight principles: restraint, observance, posture, breath control, sense withdrawal, concentration, meditative absorption, and 'enstasy' (meaning 'standing inside of').
- Hatha yoga, one of the most common forms currently practised, focuses on posture and breath control.
- Iyengar yoga makes use of apparatus.
- Bikram yoga is quite vigorous and takes place in a heated room.

It is certainly worth checking the approach and emphasis of a class before signing up. Several organisations exist in the UK that can provide further information and details of instructors. The largest is the British Wheel of Yoga: www.bwy.org.uk

PERFORMANCE ANXIETY

Just about every musician experiences performance anxiety to some degree. Sensations associated with this include:

- physical tension, often in the chest, shoulders and neck
- faster, shallower breathing than normal
- difficulty in breathing deeply
- butterflies in the stomach
- racing thoughts and difficulty with concentrating on the task in hand
- negative thoughts about being about to make mistakes or fail, make a fool of oneself, or be judged not good enough
- sweating and clammy hands
- feeling too hot or too cold
- desire to go to the toilet.

Performance anxiety is often perceived in a negative light, something that inhibits achievement and puts musicians under terrible pressure. However, it is also widely understood that performance can be lifted onto a new level by performance anxiety, or rather the excitement that adrenalin brings. This is an essential ingredient in making the difference between mundane and exceptional performance. It is now widely recognised that adrenalin arousal will enhance performance up to a certain level. When it increases above this level, it starts to have a negative effect. This explains, perhaps, what is meant when musicians talk about performance anxiety being like excitement but without the breath.

Most musicians will experience rushes of adrenalin, particularly in the lead-up to important performances. There are big differences, however, in the degree to which musicians experience it as exciting or as anxiety-provoking. In some instances, musicians can find performance anxiety to be so acute that it is crippling. This is still not always openly discussed in professional music arenas, perhaps because it is likely to be associated with a fear of failure and loss of a professional career. Many things can, however, be done to help manage anxiety, and a number of associations offer information and access to further advice and support.

Dealing effectively with preparation for performance and performance anxiety usually involves numerous factors, and many of these are considered in Chapter 3. The techniques for holistic well-being outlined in Table 8.1 can also be useful. There are some chemical interventions that are quite commonly used by musicians to combat performance anxiety, or indeed to manage post-performance highs, although these are not necessarily advisable, particularly in the long term. They work in different ways and may well have side-effects. They are summarised in Table 8.2.

TABLE 8.2: DRUG TREATMENTS USED TO MANAGE PERFORMANCE ANXIETY

Technique	Features
Beta blockers	Prescription drugs, these are sometimes used to manage extreme experience of anxiety. Beta blockers work by reducing the physical symptoms of anxiety, by blocking the transmission of certain nerve impulses that are particularly stimulated by adrenaline. Typically they will reduce heart rate when anxiety sets in. They do not alter thought processes. Side-effects, however, may be experienced, such as tiredness and depression, cold hands and feet. These tend to inhibit speed of reactions in performance.
Alcohol and recreational drugs	Alcohol and recreational drugs have been widely used by musicians as they can reduce experience of performance anxiety, and/or can help musicians to enjoy and come down from a post-performance high or numb the feeling of a post-performance low. The social life of musicians, particularly when on tour, often revolves around alcohol and it can be difficult to avoid drinking too much. Alcohol and drugs do, however, usually impair performance considerably, and they do nothing to address the underlying causes of anxiety.

NOISE AND HEARING

Quality of hearing is a vital part of musicianship. Permanent damage can be caused by exposure to loud sounds. The risk of this happening depends on both the volume level and the length of exposure to it. The louder the sound and the longer the exposure, the greater the likelihood of damage being done. There is no cure if the inner ear hair cells, an essential part of hearing, become damaged. Twenty years ago, musicians hardly ever discussed hearing loss. There is now greater awareness of this issue. An example is given in Case Study 8.2.

CASE STUDY 8.2: A DJ NOW USING CUSTOM-MADE EARPLUGS

'If you're a DJ or a muso and you're reading this and thinking "maybe it's time I got some earplugs...," hold that thought and listen: there is *no* "maybe" about it. I cannot stress to you how important it is to protect your ears, they are your living, and they are under almost daily barrage. I've been on tour...and played gigs so big the monitoring is 30,000 watts of sound, but if you're thinking "I only play little gigs," it's often those...little sound systems...that will cause the most damage...I'd get tinnitus *so* badly after every gig, that I couldn't sleep, and I'd be ill as a result. My immune system was shot through and I was a mess.

'Since getting...[ear]plugs, I carry them *everywhere* and use them at big gigs, little gigs, parties, anywhere with a sound system. Now I sleep, I'm healthy and my ears aren't getting any worse despite my job.'[22]

Unfortunately, nearly all musicians find themselves exposed to excessive sound levels at certain times. Situations where damage can occur include:

- practising in a small room
- performing in, or attending, gigs which are amplified
- rehearsing and performing with an orchestra or another large ensemble
- playing a particularly loud instrument, such as drums/percussion
- listening to music through headphones, particularly when there is a lot of background noise, for example on a train.

Musicians need to learn to monitor personal sound exposure and take appropriate action. This is particularly important for younger people, as hearing damage often goes unnoticed in the early stages. A person is only likely to become aware of the problem years later. Signs of damage are: not being able to hear properly for several hours after being in a very noisy environment; or a ringing sensation in the ears. Many education and training programmes will offer screening and, for example, earplugs at reduced rates.

In many countries there is legislation about acceptable levels of sound and length of exposure for anyone while at work. There are also likely to be a number of organisations dedicated to helping musicians through, for example, providing hearing tests, access to custom-made earplugs and advice on managing particular situations where sound levels are problematic. In the

UK, for example, support can be found through the British Association for Performing Arts Medicine (BAPAM), the Musicians' Hearing Services, and the Musicians' Union.[23]

National regulations may set levels of exposure, whereby employers and venues are required to provide protection of different kinds, maintenance of relevant equipment and training in the protection of hearing. Sound levels are likely to be measured in terms of average noise levels (dB(A)) and a peak level (dB(C)). Facts about sound levels are shown in Table 8.3.

TABLE 8.3: FACTS ABOUT SOUND LEVELS[24,25]

	Exposure levels (Decibels)
Typical sound level reached by a rock band	125 dB(A)
Typical sound level reached by an orchestra	94 dB(A)
Daily or weekly exposure level where legislation in the UK requires employers to make suitable hearing protection available	80 dB(A) or 135 dB(C)
Daily or weekly exposure level where legislation in the UK requires hearing protection to be used	85 dB(A) or 137 dB(C)
Daily or weekly exposure level which must not be exceeded, taking account of reduction provided by hearing protection, according to UK legislation	87 dB(A) or 140 dB(C)

There are also a number of strategies that can be used to reduce exposure. These include:

- wearing custom-made earplugs (where possible) in a noisy environment
- requesting acoustic shields (screens which absorb sound coming from behind them) if playing in an ensemble/band
- using a wireless in-ear monitor, which delivers the monitor mix directly to the ear at a volume that can be personally controlled
- practising with a mute when in a small room
- taking regular breaks when in a noisy environment.

EYESIGHT

Musicians who spend a lot of time reading music, particularly if they are working in places where lighting is poor, or if they are sharing a music stand with someone else and distance from the notation is not ideal, will find that their eyesight is put under strain. As with hearing, it can be easy to miss the fact that your eyesight is beginning to deteriorate, and it is highly recommended, therefore, that all musicians have regular eye tests, where the specific demands of your working situations are also considered.

It may also be possible to improve your working environment, for example by asking for a stronger bulb for a music stand in a pit, or even acquiring your own portable focused light. Issues to do with lights and positioning of stands can, however, be a source of real tension between musicians, or between musicians and management of a venue, and so need to be dealt with sensitively. Advice can be sought from the Musicians' Union, for example, or from an eye specialist.

CARRYING HEAVY INSTRUMENTS

Carrying heavy equipment around is an inevitable part of the job for quite a few musicians. It can have a profound effect on muscle tension, posture and injury. Education and training programmes should all offer health and safety training that demonstrates the most effective ways to lift and carry particular equipment. Advice can also be sought through organisations dedicated to musicians' health and specialist instrument retailers, organisations or interest groups. Increasingly, lightweight cases and specially adapted trolleys are available for instruments.

MANAGING LONG, IRREGULAR OR ANTI-SOCIAL HOURS OF WORK AND EXTENSIVE TRAVEL

The variety of a diary that changes all the time, the excitement of travelling, meeting new people, the buzz of working with others and of performing are all things that musicians tend to love about their work. Equally, these aspects of being a musician can be stressful. They can lead to sleep deprivation, unhealthy eating habits, or a tendency to rely on caffeine, alcohol or drugs. They also make issues of personal organisation or time management particularly important and challenging.

Some musicians find that their priorities as professionals change over time. A freelance career of performing, touring and recording may be ideal for someone with few other commitments. It is much harder to sustain a lot of touring in a situation where there are family commitments, and particularly children to care for. Some artists have felt they had to sacrifice either family or work. Many others have managed to combine both successfully through making some compromises.

Each person has to balance the attractions and stresses of working in music, and how best to pace themselves. It is important to be aware of the issues and to be practical about the realities of different kinds of work in music. When you are preparing for a career in music, it is useful to note the importance of being able to use skills in different contexts, as this quality may well enable you to make the transitions you want along your career path. See Chapter 9 for more on the practical implications of career choices.

CHAPTER SUMMARY: HEALTH AND WELL-BEING

To perform well, musicians need to be physically fit, to eat healthily and to get sufficient high-quality sleep.

Practising, rehearsing and performing can lead to physical injury and stress.

There is a risk of over-exposure to excess noise – knowledge of strategies for protecting hearing is important.

Musicians need to develop strategies for maintaining health and well-being.

The nature of these strategies may vary for different musicians.

FURTHER READING

Green, B. and Gallwey, W.T. (1987) *The Inner Game of Music*. London: Pan. This book is a favourite with many musicians, and focuses on developing a healthy overall approach to learning and to performance. It takes its inspiration from Gallwey's earlier book *The Inner Game of Tennis* (Pan Books, 1986), and explores the interrelationships between physical and mental processes in the practical skill of playing an instrument.

Rodenburg, P. (2007). *Presence: How to use positive energy for success in every situation*. London: Michael Joseph. Written by a specialist in voice and acting, the book sets out a practical method for achieving integrated mental and physical balance as a performer, and enabling expression that is neither forced nor withdrawn.

Rosset i Llobet, J. and Odam, G. (2007) *The Musician's Body: A maintenance manual for peak performance*. Aldershot: Guildhall School of Music & Drama and Ashgate. Designed specifically for musicians, the book offers a practical guide to, for example, warming-up and warming-down exercises, and explains fundamental aspects of anatomy and physiology.

Williamon, A. (ed.) (2004) *Musical Excellence: Strategies and techniques to enhance performance*. Oxford: Oxford University Press. The book provides a comprehensive exploration of recent pioneering initiatives into enhancing performance and managing aspects of performance anxiety and the physical stresses of being a performer. It includes chapters on practice strategies, fitness, Alexander Technique and mental skills training.

Williams, M. and Penman, D. (2011) *Mindfulness: A practical guide to finding peace in a frantic world*. London: Piatkus. This is a practical guide to developing mindfulness techniques, increasingly used by professional musicians. It comes with a CD of guided meditations.

Wills, G. and Cooper, C.L. (1988) *Pressure Sensitive: Popular musicians under stress*. London: Sage. This offers some powerful facts and figures about the impact of stress on musicians, and includes interesting insights from individuals.

NOTES

1. Wills, G. and Cooper, C.L. (1988) *Pressure Sensitive: Popular musicians under stress*. London: Sage.

2. Fishbein, M., Middlestadt, S.E., Ottati, V., Strauss, S. and Ellis, A. (1988) 'Medical problems among ICSOM musicians: Overview of a national survey.' *Medical Problems of Performing Artists*, 3: 1–8.

3. James, I.M. (2000) 'Survey of orchestras'. In R. Tubiana and P.C. Amadio (eds), *Medical Problems of the Instrumentalist Musician*. London: Martin Dunitz, 195–201.

4. Wynn Parry, K. (2004) 'Managing the physical demands of musical performance'. In A. Williamon (ed.), *Musical Excellence: Strategies and techniques to enhance performance*. Oxford: Oxford University Press, 41–60.

5. Online. www.british-voice-association.com (accessed 20 January 2011).

6. Online. www.musiciansunion.org.uk (accessed 15 January 2011).

7. Online. www.bapam.org.uk (accessed 15 January 2011).

8. Online. www.helpmusicians.org.uk (accessed 3 February 2011).

9. Online. www.abo.org.uk/Information/Healthy-Orchestra (accessed 3 February 2011).

10. Gruzelier, J.H. and Egner, T. (2004) 'Physiological self-regulation: Biofeedback and neurofeedback'. In A. Williamon (ed.), *Musical Excellence: Strategies and techniques to enhance performance*. Oxford: Oxford University Press, 197–219.

11. Connolly, C. and Williamon, A. (2004) 'Mental skills training'. In A. Williamon (ed.), *Musical Excellence: Strategies and techniques to enhance performance*. Oxford: Oxford University Press, 221–245.

12. Taylor, A.H. and Wasley, D. (2004) 'Physical fitness'. In A. Williamon (ed.), *Musical Excellence: Strategies and techniques to enhance performance*. Oxford: Oxford University Press, 163–78.

13. Online. www.nutrition.org.uk (accessed 15 January 2011).

14. Culpin, V. and Whelan, A. (2009) 'The wake-up call for sleepy managers'. *The Ashridge Journal*, 360: 27–30.

15. Online. http://tinyurl.com/cczd44r (accessed 15 January 2011).

16. Rosset i Llobet, J. and Odam, G. (2007) *The Musician's Body: A maintenance manual for peak performance*. Aldershot: Ashgate, 92–6.

17. See, for example, Chapman, J.L. (2006) *Singing and Teaching Singing: A holistic approach to classical voice*. Oxford: Plural Publishing.

18. Online. www.rsi.org.uk (accessed 15 January 2011).

19. Green, B. and Gallwey, W.T. (1987) *The Inner Game of Music*. London: Pan.

20. Adapted from the website of the General Osteopathic Council. Online. www.osteopathy. org.uk (accessed 5 April 2011).

21. Adapted from the website of the Sutherland Society. Online. www.cranial.org.uk (accessed 5 April 2011).

22. Online. www.musicianshearingservices.co.uk/mhs_testimonials.asp (accessed 16 January 2011).

23. Online. www.musicianshearingservices.co.uk (accessed 15 January 2011).

24. Online. www.legislation.gov.uk/uksi/2005/1643/regulation/4/made (accessed 15 January 2011).

25. Online. www.musiciansunion.org.uk (accessed 15 January 2011).

CHAPTER 9
CAREER OPTIONS

INTRODUCTION

This chapter provides an overview of professional work in music. It:
- sets out the different areas of work available and the skills they require
- indicates different ways in which employment works in music, and how portfolio careers may be put together
- offers practical exercises to help you consider your professional potential and possible career paths.

Chapter 1 began to illustrate the wealth of opportunities that professional music offers. This included traditional fields, such as music teaching, songwriting and composing, artist management, orchestral playing, producing for radio or television, performing as a soloist or with small ensembles, or sound recording. Chapter 1 also indicated that, although the extent of such work in some cases is diminishing, new possibilities are also opening up, and musicians with imaginative and entrepreneurial attitudes are creating niche areas of work for themselves that had not been thought of a few years ago. This chapter focuses in more detail on different kinds of careers and work in music, the key skills they require and the kinds of work patterns they involve.

THE PORTFOLIO MUSICIAN

Increasingly, professional musicians are multi-skilled and work in several different parts of the industry. Thirty years ago, most musicians tended to work in one particular field. Since then, the concept of the 'portfolio' musician – a musician who takes on several different kinds of work and is usually self-employed – has emerged and become well established.[1,2]

On the one hand, portfolio careers have lots of benefits: they offer variety and flexibility to devise and direct projects; they can help to develop new skills and may well be exciting and fast-paced. This can be extremely rewarding. On the other hand, a portfolio career can have downsides: for example, it can feel as if the overall workload is overwhelming or that it is only possible to engage in each project superficially. Case Study 9.1 sets out some examples of different musicians' perspectives on their portfolio careers.

CASE STUDY 9.1: MUSICIANS' PERSPECTIVES ON THEIR PORTFOLIO CAREERS

Drummer and teacher

'My teaching affords me the chance to do loads of different projects. I was in an Aerosmith tribute band, which was great for three weeks, then you're just playing the same things all the time. My best mate played in *Miss Saigon* for two years, *Rocky Horror Show* for a year and a half. I would have come very close to madness – I get bored so quickly. He was disappointed I was doing so much teaching but – apart from the fact I love it – it affords me the opportunity to play what I want to play. I just recorded a concept album with my punk band; often the most interesting stuff doesn't make much money. You can't do that if you're committed to a touring schedule. There'll be a crossroads – that came for most of my friends in their mid- to late-twenties. Do I continue playing music and doing what I want to do, and that means a portfolio career and not knowing where the next pay cheque's coming from and working hard at working hard, or do I play the guitar in my bedroom and get an office job? I'm not a person who could not engage with music every day.'

Orchestral player, soloist and entrepreneur

'I do a lot of other things [besides being in an orchestra]. I play solos, concertos a lot, and one helps with the other...I've never spent my life just wanting to do one thing. And I continually ebb and flow in different directions, because I have other interests from playing cello anyway...I do a lot of building. I have a hotel as well...I didn't build the structure, but designed the way it runs.'

An instrumentalist, one year after finishing a Masters programme

'I am doing a huge mixture of teaching, playing and workshop leading...I'm teaching about 25 hours per week...for a couple of different music services, and I do some private teaching as well...The teaching for the music services is a mix of one-to-one, small groups and whole-class situations...and I teach oboe, piano, recorder and ocarina...ocarina for 5-year–olds, which is really fun...I play in a wind quintet...a contemporary music ensemble...and a trio we set up for educational purposes...I've kept a foot in the amateur loop, so that I get as much orchestral playing as possible.'

Producer, writer/composer and drummer/ percussionist

'I work as a producer, writer/composer and perform as a drummer/percussionist. I also run my own music production company and studio in East London and teach on a Masters programme in the Netherlands. The ability to associate, collaborate and create with a wide range of people from different musical cultures is so rewarding. I love the frequent change in working environment, meeting people and seeing new countries. Every day there is a new and bold experience that feeds my personal, cognitive and emotional growth. There is a certain "adrenaline" and excitement, which comes from placing yourself within ever-changing work environments and working roles. One of the biggest challenges is time management, being able to assess which "job" should be prioritised over another and allocating the right space within life for personal development. Another challenge is in being able to engage with the emotions, artistic identity and personalities of a number of different people at the same time. It is demanding to make sure that there is sufficient personal engagement at all times and a sense of informality, without ever losing sight of the bigger aim of producing or performing music.'

A creative performer, musical director and teacher

'I need the combination of roles – self-expression through performance and creation of new work (musical director for large dance/music production, including sourcing musicians, advising on musical production, some compositional input, and liaising with technical team; also developing own practice as a collaborative instrumentalist and creating own work using live electronics), while also the "giving" involved in tutoring (managing and steering a programme in a conservatoire with special emphasis on devising and tutoring creative cross-arts projects, together with supervising individual students). The "professional" work is absolutely relevant to what it is I teach, so having current creative projects to relate to in teaching makes a strong dynamic. Teaching also gives me a powerful framework for analysing and evaluating my own creative work. Time management, though, is difficult, and sustaining energy – how can I sustain family life?! The Programme Leader role means I am mostly working alongside people with full-time jobs, so it always feels like I don't have the same capacity to fulfil the job as these folks do. There are long periods where I don't play my instrument, and my own creative project always takes a couple of days to pick up where I last left off – frustrating.'

As careers in music become increasingly diverse – and tend towards portfolio work – so it becomes even more important to have a clear and realistic sense of one's musical and professional abilities and to reflect on how best to develop a career. How can you realise your personal and professional aspirations in the real world? How can you ensure that your work feels like a rich and diverse expression of your abilities rather than a series of disconnected fragments? The next part of this chapter provides some tools to assist with this.

MAPPING OUT CAREER OPTIONS

'Every musician must have artistic skills, must have something to tell others through music, must have the ability to convince a listener, musically. There are many ways in which a performer of an instrument, for instance, can show artistic skills, and we should appreciate artistic diversity. But we should not accept artistic short cuts or impressive instrumental or vocal surfaces without anything beneath. Artistic skills in the real sense are reflected through such characteristics as musical refinement, originality and reflection.'[3]

Making decisions about which areas of music to pursue should be informed by three things:

- the skills you have as a musician (and how much you may be able to develop existing abilities through further study or continuing professional development)
- you and your audiences: the things that motivate and interest you, the contexts in which you can use your abilities
- practical considerations about work patterns and lifestyle.

MUSICAL SKILLS

Musical skills are, of course, essential for just about any career in music, but vary greatly in terms of the level of different aspects of musicianship required. Components to consider include:

- having a good ear – skills in aural perception
- understanding harmony and musical structure

- knowledge of, and skills relating to, musical style, repertoire and performance practices
- creative and improvisation skills
- collaborative skills
- facility with an instrument/voice/notational language.

More detail on these is given in Chapter 2.

YOU AND YOUR AUDIENCES

When thinking about career options, return to your fundamental motivation – what matters to you about music. (If you have not already done so, take a look at Exercise 1.3 in Chapter 1). It is important to consider your work in relation to a fundamental set of relationships between yourself, music and your audiences (see Figure 9.1). 'Audiences' here are taken in the broadest sense: they might be audiences for concerts/gigs, recordings and books; equally they might be students or clients, for example when teaching, running workshops or running an agency.

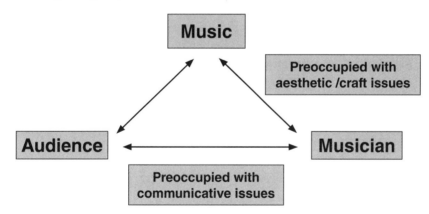

Figure 9.1
Relationships between musician, music and audiences

Some people will find that they are thoroughly engaged with their art, less so with their audience. For others, work is more driven by the relationship with audiences, and the music itself takes more of a back seat. The balance of these relationships often changes for individuals over time and in different contexts. However, failing to pay attention to one of the relationships can be problematic. For example, performers who are completely immersed in their music but have no thought for their audiences may create disconnected performances that leave audiences underwhelmed. Equally, workshop leaders who are predominantly occupied with social and interpersonal dynamics may lose connection to their own voice and an artistic agenda.

There are no perfect ways to balance these relationships, and every musician has to find their way. Some useful questions to consider are:

- Who are your audiences and what do you know about them?
- How could you learn more about your audiences?
- What feedback would be useful from your audiences? What kinds of interaction or creative dialogue with them might be helpful?

For more on communication with audiences in the context of performance, see Chapter 3.

It is important to remember that the idea of audiences for music who passively consume what is offered to them is very much changing. Active participation in music – an audience directly engaged in moulding the product, or an experience characterised by two-way exchange rather than one-way performance or transmission – is increasingly the norm. For examples of innovative work in this respect, see Case Study 1.3 in Chapter 1.

PRACTICAL CONSIDERATIONS

Career options are often affected by practical issues, such as the demands of touring, flexibility with working hours, the degree to which a stable income is needed, and the extent of responsibilities in caring for family members. Some case studies of the impact of such practicalities are given in Case Study 9.2. These sorts of issues are rarely discussed formally within programmes, and it can be easy to overlook them, particularly in the early stages of a career.

Think about the following questions:

- Where do you want to work (in one location, several places, touring around the world)?
- How much time do you want to spend working, and how do you feel about regular or irregular or antisocial hours of work?

CASE STUDY 9.2: THE IMPACT OF PRACTICAL ISSUES ON CAREER CHOICE

Performer and music therapist

'I'll hold at what I'm doing because I love this...Yes, I could earn more money, but actually I wouldn't be any happier. I'm 40 and I'm still saying, 'Ooh, can I pay my mortgage?'. But that's alright, I can get by. That's the risk, of not getting by...Also, I haven't had children. The life of a female musician isn't particularly easy and I've only got the meagre amount of success that I have because I haven't had to take the time out to bring up a child. You can't take career breaks as a musician – once you're out of the loop, you're out of the loop. I bought a house in Kent and everyone thought I'd migrated to Mars! I've potentially risked normality, a family, my marriage – that didn't work because he was a musician and out constantly. I was a musician and out constantly.'

Performer and teacher

'I went abroad for a year, to Cologne. You're taking yourself off the circuit, but when I got back I was still young enough to do the audition circuit anyway... Having a baby is a risk – you feel that people's attitudes towards you might change. I've put a lot of work in, generating work for after the baby has come. And the things I do regularly, I've explained that I'll still come and how I'll manage to do that.'

- To what extent are you keen to travel on a regular basis and internationally?
- How important to you is job security?
- Do you prefer working for others, working collaboratively as equal partners, or being self-driven and self-determining in your work?
- Do you have, or are you likely to have, dependants? How do these responsibilities impact on your professional life and need for income?
- How do you cope with repetition or with new challenges every day?
- Do you prefer working on lots of short projects or do you prefer longer-term projects?

EXERCISE 9.1: USING SWOT ANALYSIS TO CONSIDER CAREER OPTIONS

In order to integrate the considerations outlined above within the context of the real world and its professional opportunities, try using a SWOT analysis. SWOT stands for Strengths, Weaknesses, Opportunities and Threats. It is a process much used in business and provides a framework for assessing career choices or developmental ideas. It requires you to focus on a particular type of work or idea, and to analyse it in terms of your abilities and aspirations as well as its practical feasibility and future potential.[4] The grid below provides further detail about features of each part of the SWOT analysis. These should help to stimulate your thinking as you consider a particular career pathway or project.

It may well be useful to choose two or three possible career options and to do SWOT analyses for each. (The rest of this chapter provides an overview of different kinds of work in music, if you want some ideas.) If possible, share this process with a friend or mentor, who can support and challenge your thinking where needed. Compare outcomes for different options, decide which combination seems most appropriate, and identify specific steps that you want to take to pursue such work.

Strengths	Weaknesses
• Strong match with existing skills, experience, professional standing/reputation	• Weak match with existing skills, experience, professional standing/reputation
• Provides an exciting but manageable challenge. Boosts motivation	• Relies on skills, knowledge or experience in which known to be vulnerable
• Distinctive, unique, innovative within the field	• Is not exciting, saps motivation
• Does not require major new investment in terms of skill development, finance, etc.	• Replicates lots of existing work with a risk of market saturation
• Taps into a clear gap in the market. Provides high quality and value for money	• Deadlines and pressures to develop new skills, financial resources, products, etc., are too great
• Offers a stepping stone to further work	• Distracts from core professional activity
• Facilitates work–life balance	
Opportunities	**Threats**
• Builds new skills and professional adaptability	• Destabilises existing professional profile – danger of losing credibility
• Diversifies portfolio and rekindles motivation	• New skills, knowledge, experience required are not achieved
• Generates income	• Reduces income
• Enables desired lifestyle changes	• Required support may not materialise
• Strengthens professional visibility and influence	• Insufficient market demand, not sustainable
• Pioneers innovative professional directions	• Jeopardises work–life balance
• Establishes significant partnerships	• Destroys significant partnerships

AREAS OF WORK IN MUSIC

The different areas of work in music outlined in the rest of this chapter fall into ten categories:

1. Arts management (see pages 184-88)
2. Music education and creative learning (see pages 189-93)
3. Composing (see pages 194-97)
4. Performing (including conducting) (see pages 198-213)
5. Instrument building and maintenance (see pages 214-16)
6. Sound production (see pages 217-18)
7. Music therapy (see page 219)
8. Music publishing and libraries (see pages 220-22)
9. Research (see pages 223-24)
10. Broadcasting and journalism (see pages 225-26).

There are tables below that give information about each one. The information provides a description of the work, skills and qualifications required, and the kind of employment offered.

1. ARTS MANAGEMENT

Arts management ranges from programming and festival direction to artist representation, orchestral fixing and event management. Many professionals in this sector will have specialist knowledge/experience as a musician, and will combine this with strong administrative and leadership skills.

TABLE 9.1: CAREERS IN ARTS MANAGEMENT

Management roles for festivals, arts venues, orchestras, record companies or local authorities		
Description	**Skills/qualifications required**	**Employment type**
Senior positions such as general manager (GM) or chief executive officer (CEO) focus on setting the strategic direction, artistic vision and financial planning of an organisation. This will often involve identifying the distinctive aspects of the organisation, developing international connections, long-term planning and positioning the organisation in relation to competitors.

Less senior positions concentrate on day-to-day management of the organisation's activities. They may hold overall responsibility for an area within the organisation, such as marketing (overseeing a team that can include audience development, press, public relations (PR), external relations, website management), artistic planning, touring, finance, development (sponsorship and fund-raising), outreach/education (often in collaboration with marketing or audience development), IT or human resources. They may therefore entail more | This field requires passion for music, flexibility, vision and imagination, creativity, attention to detail, adaptability, good humour, willingness to work long and sometimes unsocial hours, and IT skills.

For senior positions, being able to articulate artistic and strategic vision is vital, along with considerable experience in the sector at a lower level of management. Sophisticated leadership skills, including facilitating a team and responding to fast-changing situations, are also essential.

For most management positions, experience and sometimes qualifications in a particular area, such as marketing or accounting, will be required. Almost everyone in this field will be a graduate. A music degree may be useful, but a qualification in another area combined with significant detailed understanding of how the music sector works may be equally appropriate. | Contracts are predominantly full-time and either permanent or for a fixed term. There are some part-time opportunities, particularly in smaller organisations, and some fixed-term contracts, for example to cover maternity leave.

Short-term contracts can be a powerful way of gaining experience. Part-time positions will suit those who wish to combine arts management with further study or another area of work, such as composing, teaching, conducting, instrument building and repair, journalism or sound recording.

Internships and work placements (anything from a few weeks to a full year) can be a good way to gain experience and skills, but are usually unpaid. Each opportunity should be carefully considered, weighing up the balance of experience gained for no salary with consequent employability and career potential. |

specific technical expertise than is required in the most senior posts, where leadership is central.

For example, in an orchestra, the orchestra manager undertakes day-to-day line management for the orchestral players, including scheduling, appraisals, first-stop discipline, and working with the CEO/GM on contractual negotiation.

An assistant orchestra manager will often be responsible for fixing freelance and other players. Other posts overseen by an orchestral manager may include a librarian and assistant librarian(s), a stage manager (also responsible for transportation of instruments, including the heavy instruments), and a concert manager (responsible for concert management and creating the schedules for players).

For initial posts in this field, such as an administrative assistant, duties may be fairly mundane (e.g. photocopying, filing, basic tasks of project management), but this kind of job does provide an opportunity to find out how an organisation works and which specific areas are attractive and offer further potential.

In the early stages of a career it is common to engage in a variety of different activities, especially in smaller organisations where most people have to cover many different roles. For example, in an orchestra you might find concert management, librarianship, artist liaison and marketing all in one job. The smaller the organisation, the wider the set of tasks likely to be required – and you need to be able to learn fast on the job.

Familiarity with as many elements as possible that comprise arts management is invaluable, either to help decide which area you might specialise in as your career progresses (and those you want never to have to do!) or to provide breadth of experience in preparation for taking on a leadership role.

Many starting-grade positions are filled by interns who have previously done an unpaid work placement.

A private income is helpful if you are to obtain unpaid experience, as well as an understanding that salaries in the arts are not high. Finding a mentor, and a wider support network (such as through Young People in the Arts: www.ypia.co.uk) can be extremely helpful.

Freelance project manager		
Description	**Skills/qualifications required**	**Employment type**
Project management encompasses any aspect of the management of an arts project – from conception of an idea, through fundraising and bid-making, setting up partnerships, recruitment of staff and participants, marketing and PR, delivery, monitoring, reporting and evaluating. Projects can vary in profile and size, from one-off, small-scale events to projects spanning several years.	High levels of skills in planning, time and resource management are essential. This includes being able to solve problems and troubleshoot, think quickly and flexibly, and be open-minded. Interpersonal skills are vital in enabling effective communication with all parties, including artists, management and audiences. Common sense and the ability to think logically, take initiative and anticipate what could go wrong are equally important. Previous experience as a project manager (PM) in an organisation is very useful, along with significant understanding of how the music sector works. There are many opportunities to gain experience through internships and work experience. Most PMs are graduates and many will have a postgraduate qualification in the arts or arts administration. Specific qualifications in project management, such as Prince 2, are often recommended, although these are not arts-specific.	PMs tend to be self-employed, and the duration of each contract depends on the project, ranging between a few weeks to several years. Successful PMs will often be running several simultaneous projects. Musicians who want to run their own projects need to have many project management skills anyway. This kind of work is quite often therefore combined successfully with, for example, teaching, composing and/or performing.

Event promoter		
Description	**Skills/qualifications required**	**Employment type**
An event promoter is responsible for promoting (as well as sometimes organising) an event or tour, including fixing contracts with venues, and making arrangements for advertising and ticketing. The promoter will estimate the cost of the tour and suggest the appropriate ticket price to the artist/agent, bearing in mind factors such as the genre of music, geographic area, size of venue, date and artists' profile. The promoter takes most of the financial risk of an event being unsuccessful, as the artist tends to receive a guaranteed fee and the venue receives a minimum rental fee.	A promoter will often have prior experience in project management within music. Knowledge and skills in marketing are essential, along with excellent negotiating skills. Detailed knowledge of particular genres of music and geographic areas and types of venue is also vital. Many promoters therefore develop this work as a result of being a performing musician and having already done some project management or 'fixing'.	Promoters are nearly all self-employed. Some work full-time in this field. There are also plenty who make this part of a portfolio career, and continue, for example, to perform.

Artists' agents and diary management services		
Description	**Skills/qualifications required**	**Employment type**
Artists' agents seek engagements for the artists on their books and negotiate terms with promoters. They manage artists' diaries, arrange travel and accommodation. They may also be involved in programming decisions and in helping artists to plan their own development, for example through the addition of new material to their repertoire.	Detailed knowledge of the music industry is required, in particular of the sectors relevant to the artists on their books, including knowledge of the pricing levels in different markets around the world. Agents will have established strong relationships with promoters in different countries, and must have strong communication skills together with an entrepreneurial flair.	An agent usually runs their own small business, funded by charging a proportion of artists' income from a tour, typically between 10 per cent and 20 per cent. Successful agents will have several full-time or part-time employees who look after particular artists. Most agents do this work full-time, and those employed by larger agents tend to be on full-time permanent or fixed-term contracts.

Larger artist management agencies employ assistants, each of whom will tend to focus on a specific sub-group of the artists. A first job in such an agency will tend to involve servicing particular artists: booking travel and hotels, organising the logistics of touring schedules, drawing up contracts, etc. Diary management services manage the organisation of professional engagements for large numbers of freelance musicians. Such engagements include, for example, orchestral concerts, gigs, West End shows and film sessions. A diary service makes it easy for fixers to find the musicians they need for particular events, and enables musicians to give a quick answer about their availability. Working for a diary management service involves communicating with artists and fixers and meticulously scheduling artists' professional diaries.	People working for a diary management service need to have excellent organisational skills and attention to detail, and the ability to communicate (particularly by phone, SMS and email) with a wide range of musicians and arts managers.	Work with diary management services may be part-time or full-time, permanent or fixed-term. Many people go on from this kind of work to management roles in arts organisations such as orchestras or arts venues.

2. MUSIC EDUCATION AND CREATIVE LEARNING

Music education has a huge and diverse workforce, including private instrumental teachers, animateurs, workshop leaders and school teachers, many of whom combine part-time activity in this area with other fields of work.

TABLE 9.2: CAREERS IN MUSIC EDUCATION

Workshop leader/animateur		
Description	**Skills/qualifications required**	**Employment type**
Workshops are widely used to give groups of people practical experience of participating in music. They may be used to provide basic instrumental tuition (e.g. as through the Wider Opportunities scheme in the UK), or equally to engage participants in creating their own music and building on their existing instrumental and vocal skills. A workshop leader may be: • a regular visitor in a school, helping to deliver the national curriculum in music through approaches that are otherwise not available • leading education and outreach projects in any kind of social or cultural setting (including preschools, schools, youth centres, after-school groups, young offenders institutions, prisons, third age groups,	Creative music workshop leaders are skilled musicians with strong communication skills, and the ability both to access their own creativity and to enable others' creativity in the process of creating new work to which all workshop participants have contributed. They tend to be strong composers, arrangers and performers as well as having the ability to collaborate with a range of people of all ages, abilities, social position and cultural or artistic background. A good ear is needed, along with the ability to work quickly in order to capture ideas from the participants, identify the potential within the material, and then bring their own musical knowledge, training and sensibility into the equation to shape and structure the material into a cohesive and artistically satisfying whole. A workshop leader also needs to perform several tasks simultaneously or in	Most work is offered through short-term contracts, and the musicians will be self-employed. It is possible to make contact with potential employers by sending a CV together with audio-visual evidence of past work and a meeting request. Agents do not operate in this field. Workshop leaders often take their first steps in schools. Once they have acquired more experience, they may be hired by arts organisations to deliver outreach or education projects. Delivering training for other musicians or music students is usually undertaken by well-established workshop leaders. Few musicians are workshop leaders/animateurs exclusively; most combine this work with other jobs such as teaching, performing, composing, conducting or arts management.

special needs groups, hospitals, or whole family ensembles) for organisations such as orchestras, cultural centres, music venues, music colleges, opera companies or chamber groups
- running an ongoing ensemble in the community
- delivering training in creative approaches to music-making for professional musiciansand/orstudents in higher education.

rapid succession: performing, teaching, composing, arranging, conducting, collaborating, keeping the participants engaged and adapting to new ideas coming from participants.

A few, usually postgraduate, programmes are available. Shorter continuing professional development courses are also offered, focusing on specific aspects of, or contexts for, workshop leadership.

Many musicians develop these skills by shadowing experienced workshop leaders, volunteering or assisting with projects.

Many will perform regularly in various ensembles, both creating original work and being members of existing chamber groups. Cross-arts collaborations are common, resulting in installations and curated events.

Instrumental/vocal teacher for a music service, school or higher education institution

Description	Skills/qualifications required	Employment type
Teachers in schools, music services, universities and conservatoires provide music lessons (instrumental, vocal, composition and/or theory) that may include one-to-one tuition, small-group teaching, whole-class teaching, coaching small ensembles and conducting large ensembles and/or orchestras, including taking them on tours. This work may also require considerable travelling between schools or centres, particularly in rural areas. A head of department or senior manager in a music service organises the activities of the service and manages staff and their schedules as well as doing some teaching themselves.	Teachers need to be skilled players of the instrument being taught (or of a closely related one). It is quite common for people to be asked to teach instruments other than their principal instrument for students in the earlier stages of learning. Keyboard skills are a great benefit for accompanying pupils and demonstrating harmony. Conducting skills are necessary for large ensemble directing. All teachers need to have a passion for enabling others to learn, a passion to continue learning themselves, excellent interpersonal skills, and the flexibility to respond to the needs of different students and to work	Employment types vary from full-time to hourly-paid contracts. Some schools (especially independent schools) may engage instrumental teachers directly. Others engage them through the local music service. In some contexts, rates of pay will change according to the level of teaching qualification and experience acquired. In the UK, applicants to work in schools or for a music service will usually be subject to Criminal Records Bureau (CRB) vetting. This process often takes several weeks and can delay the start of employment.

| | creatively in different social contexts and learning environments. Teachers will usually have a degree in music. When working in a conservatoire environment, an instrumental teacher will almost certainly be a leading exponent of their discipline. Those who take on a senior management position, e.g. in a music service, will have several years' experience as a teacher and will also have good IT, artistic and educational planning and administrative skills. | |

Private studio teacher

Description	Skills/qualifications required	Employment type
Independent teachers provide music lessons (instrumental and/or theory) in their own home or in pupils' homes or other premises. They often work with a wide range of people – children and adults of different ages and levels of ability and with different motivations to learn. Teachers may have connections with local schools or community centres, but often operate as an isolated business. Teachers of this kind may also become well-respected individuals within their local community.	This area of work is unregulated: no qualifications are officially necessary, and anyone can in fact choose to set themselves up as a teacher. In practice, teachers need to be skilled players of the instrument being taught (or in a closely related one). They also need high-level teaching skills and a passion for enabling others to learn, a passion to continue learning themselves, excellent interpersonal skills, and the flexibility to respond to the needs of different students and to work creatively in different situations. Many musicians start teaching while still studying themselves, and learn on the job and informally through contact with peers and mentors.	Independent teachers are self-employed and typically charge fees per lesson, sometimes payable a term in advance. Fee levels vary according to local demand and the perceived excellence of the teacher. There may be some flexibility with scheduling this work around other commitments. This makes it a popular choice for those pursuing a career that includes performing, but the degree of flexibility does depend on client expectations. Some websites (such as www.thetutorpages.com) can be useful as a way of recruiting pupils.

	Various organisations, such as the Associated Board of the Royal Schools of Music (ABRSM), Trinity Guildhall and the Incorporated Society of Musicians (ISM) in the UK, offer professional development opportunities for teachers that can help to build skills, enhance professional credibility and facilitate networking.	

Classroom teacher

Description	Skills/qualifications required	Employment type
Classroom teachers teach aspects of music in the national curriculum, including GCSE and A-level courses. They may also run bands and after-school activities.	Qualified Teacher Status (usually through a degree and Postgraduate Certificate in Education (PGCE)) is usually necessary to teach in state schools and desirable for teachers in the independent sector. In a secondary school your degree would normally be in the subject you teach. Primary school teachers may become music co-ordinators but teach the full range of subjects. Teachers require an understanding of a very broad range of musical genres, and almost certainly understanding of music technology. It is a great advantage to be able to play the piano well enough to accompany choirs and instrumentalists and to demonstrate points of harmony.	Full-time and part-time contracts. There are also some opportunities to do 'supply' teaching on short-term contracts. Applicants for a classroom teaching post would normally be subject to a CRB check.

Examining and adjudicating		
Description	**Skills/qualifications required**	**Employment type**
Examining and adjudicating covers a variety of contexts, including formal music exams for independent bodies (for example the ABRSM in the UK), local and national music competitions and festivals. Musicians engaged in this field will sometimes work individually and sometimes as a member of a panel. The work may involve examining candidates of all ages, and is likely to include prep tests, grade exams from Grade 1 to Grade 8, and Diplomas up to Masters level. Examinations and competitions/festivals exist for performers, music directors and teachers, choirs and chamber music groups. Musical genres covered include classical music, jazz and popular music. An examiner may also be involved in training and moderating other examiners, mentoring teachers, lecturing, consultancy work, and setting and revising all aspects of syllabuses. Musicians working for an examination board may be asked to examine abroad as well as at home, and for up to six weeks at a time. Work for more experienced examiners will include training examiners and working in quality control, moderating colleagues.	A strong musical education, with supporting qualifications, is vital, together with a high level of professional achievement in your own discipline, such as a strong personal profile in teaching, performing and publishing. Some teaching experience is also essential, at least at the levels of the students being examined or adjudicated. In addition, examiners and adjudicators must be able to write quickly, legibly, concisely and objectively, to frame feedback constructively, and to work calmly under pressure. Strong interpersonal skills are extremely helpful in these contexts, and being open to professional development is important. Examiners require competent piano skills, so that they can undertake the required aural tests.	Remuneration compares favourably with orchestral playing, and examining is a growth industry. Examining and adjudicating are not usually designed to be a full-time career. Contracts are freelance and the work is very flexible. This makes the field an ideal part of a portfolio career. Examination boards tend to require examiners to travel widely, including abroad in some instances, and to commit to having at least a week to offer in each examining session. Applicants for foreign tours will need to commit to a timetable several years in advance.

3. COMPOSING

Careers in composing cover a wide range of possibilities and musical genres – from commercial commissions for film and TV, to jingles, ring tones, music for games and composing in the field of art music.

TABLE 9.3: CAREERS IN COMPOSING

Composing in the field of art music		
Description	**Skills/qualifications required**	**Employment type**
Composers may be involved in writing music, rehearsing and performing music, talking about music, teaching, outreach, broadcasting, academic research, collaborative work, and work in music technology. They may compose for choirs, choruses, chamber music groups, ensembles, orchestras, chamber opera groups, opera houses. They may work in dance, ballet or film, may do multimedia work, and may compose for electro-acoustic technology.	Art music composition requires a thorough knowledge of all aspects of music, both practical and theoretical. Training in an instrument, and preferably also in singing, is very important, as is training in music technology. A detailed knowledge of the history of musical composition and its techniques is needed, plus high-level training in aural skills, such as pitch, chord and rhythm dictation. Training in instrumentation (the workings of all standard musical instruments) and orchestration (how to combine those instruments into successful musical textures) is essential. It is important to have practical experience of performing music yourself, both singly, in groups, or in orchestras, etc. Training in conducting is also very useful in getting your music played. Training in handling outreach workshops can also be very useful. International composition competitions, music colleges, universities and international summer schools offer	In the initial stages, you may be lucky enough to obtain a place on one of the several schemes in the UK for young composers run by ensembles or orchestras. Apart from that, your initial work will usually be with friends from music college or university, or in music technology studios. The focus is likely to be on music for solo instruments and voices, duos, trios, quartets and 6–14 piece ensembles. Commissions for full orchestras, aside from workshop miniatures, are rarer and usually come only after you have built up a reputation as an experienced and fluent composer. A general agreement with a prestigious music publisher can be a huge advantage in providing consistent promotion of your work. Publishers are the preferred points of contact for professionals or organisations wanting to commission art music. Such contracts are, however, becoming increasingly rare. Publishers own the copyright to your music, and in return for promoting

courses in musical composition, and often have long-standing close relations with the best performers, etc.

It is very important to be completely committed to this area, as initially it brings unpredictable rewards and can involve demanding work both intellectually and manually. Obtaining a high-level music degree or equivalent qualification is essential. Many now go on to do doctoral study, both due to interest in the research involved and due to the fact that many jobs require such a qualification (or its equivalent in high-level professional experience, which is increasingly rarely obtained before late middle age, if at all). Fluent and easy communication skills, and a ready ability to work in collaborative situations with people from other arts and the wider world, is very important. An ability to work in outreach is often useful. Familiarity with various communication media and skill in using them is a great help in getting your music known. Above all, you need the confidence and professional fluency to work in any situation, including high-stress ones, and to produce, often at great speed and at short notice, the most imaginative music of which you are capable.

it, they take 50 per cent of the resulting performing royalties.

Some composers now have agents, but this is a relatively new area of development and can be controversial. Agents who have worked only with performers can mishandle the promotion of composers, as it requires a different, often more subtle, approach to organisations.

Many composers promote their work through their own website. Ensuring that information is accurate and up to date, and avoiding exaggeration are essential aspects of producing an effective composer website. (More information about websites is given in Chapter 10.)

Many composers support their work through related work, such as arranging, copying, editing, and teaching composition. Quite a few have posts in higher education.

The ability to teach composition is very useful; if you are successful at this, it can be a very simulating and exciting complement to the activity of composing, though some find it too demanding for comfort. Conducting can complement composition very helpfully, both in giving you practical experience of the realities of music-making, and in getting your own music performed. If you have high-level performing ability on any instrument, you should try to explore how that can usefully be brought to bear both in securing an income and in putting across your own music to the world. Teaching other aspects of music, and engaging in outreach workshops, may be involved.

Ability to work in film is also very useful, though be warned: contrary to widespread supposition, employment in film or television music is in fact much harder to come by than work in the art music field. Most of the work in this field is done on spec, and therefore completely unpaid, in the hope of it leading to future work. (While this does happen also in art music composition, it is much more frequent in film and television music, and for far longer.) Lucrative work in film and television is, in practice, restricted to a very select few and it can prove impossible to break into this world.

Composing for the theatre and commercial sectors (including jingles, songwriting and arranging)

Description	Skills/qualifications required	Employment type
Despite the decline in conventional sales outlets for commercial music, numerous new opportunities for the entrepreneur are regularly opening up. These include: • licensing self-produced tracks to media production companies • individual commissions for specific media projects (TV shows, films, corporate films, commercials, etc.)	Qualifications have rarely been a prerequisite to working in commercial music, but the essential skills that can be learnt in good training institutions are indispensable. These include: • excellence in a specific composition/production area • understanding and general ability across a range of compositional styles and music production	Normally a 'composer producer' will work on a series of freelance contracts and also pitch finished tracks for licensing opportunities. In all but the larger production companies, most clients expect broadcast quality 'end product' for a single, fixed fee and one point of contact. Composers in this field tend, therefore, also to be their own publisher, promoter, agent, etc. Some more established composers will have agents. The nature

- songwriting publishing agreements
- production of broadcast-ready tracks for library companies
- self-generated projects.

In the early stages of a career you will probably do more speculative compositional work in order to build up a portfolio. Some of this may be done on pilot projects or demos. At a more experienced stage, a composer may be trusted with bigger projects, and may have more choice and influence on the style of work they do.

- the ability to 'produce to a brief'.

Composers in this field also require passion and tenacity, a willingness to learn and adapt, excellent organisational skills, the ability to meet deadlines, ingenuity and resourcefulness to meet the fast-changing fashions and diverse personalities in the field, and determination to succeed. They will often have to produce music very quickly, and will also need some knowledge about copyright and the business aspects of music.

One of the best ways to enter the industry is to take on an assistant role – often for very poor pay – as a way of refining skills and learning from those already in the industry. Many musicians may spend the initial years of their career working at a tangent to their main aspirations in order to gain experience. Many successful songwriters, for example, have started their career working in the administration of publishing companies, while refining their composing skills out of office hours.

of contracts varies considerably. Often little or no money is paid up front, but is earned through royalties and scale of music usage.

Many composers will combine working in a related field, particularly in the earlier stages of a career. This may include performing, teaching or music administration.

4. PERFORMING (INCLUDING CONDUCTING)

While a few performers have salaried posts, for example in an opera company or orchestra, many more are self-employed, sometimes with an agent or manager, and pursue a diverse portfolio career.

TABLE 9.4: CAREERS IN PERFORMING AND CONDUCTING

Classical music – orchestras		
Description	**Skills/qualifications required**	**Employment type**
Working in an orchestra will focus on live performance and may well also include recording sessions and a range of outreach, education and development work. The variety of work depends on the type of orchestra. For example, 97 per cent of the members of the London Symphony Orchestra are involved in their Discovery Programme, whereas in other orchestras education and outreach is often undertaken by a smaller proportion of players. National and international touring is also a regular feature of many (but not all) orchestras. Opera orchestras inevitably cover less repertoire than a symphony orchestra, and some orchestras tend to focus on particular areas of repertoire (for example the BBC Symphony Orchestra plays a lot of contemporary pieces). These factors make individual orchestras quite distinctive and may well affect which players are best suited to them.	Excellent instrumental, musical and ensemble skills are the first essentials, along with the ability to work with different conductors. Sight-reading skills are also vital, particularly in orchestras that cover a lot of repertoire quickly or focus on contemporary repertoire. An ability to get on with other musicians and fit into the orchestra's culture is also critical – musicians look carefully for someone whom they feel will be a good colleague all round. Entry is almost always via a highly competitive audition/series of auditions, and then through undertaking a 'trial', playing with the orchestra for a period of time. Rehearsal times vary between orchestras, but in the UK, orchestral musicians have a reputation for being excellent sight-readers, and there is often very little rehearsal time, particularly on standard repertoire. Being familiar with this repertoire is a huge advantage.	Some orchestras offer full-time and permanent contracts. Some have a mixture of full- and part-time contracts, with flexibility designed to give principal players greater freedom to pursue solo and other ensemble work. Other orchestras run on a freelance sessional basis. They may have a fixed membership, but no minimum level of guaranteed work, and each player is only paid for the work they do. There are also orchestras with no fixed membership that operate on a casual basis. If in doubt about the nature of employment being offered, you can seek advice from organisations such as the Musicians' Union.

As well as many of the great twentieth-century scores, contemporary scores increasingly include piano, organ, celeste or harpsichord. There is therefore a growing need for pianists who can work as orchestral players.	Some orchestras maintain an 'extras' list and it is possible to write to the orchestral manager to audition for the list; in other cases, word-of-mouth recommendation from members of the section gets extra players invited. Initial experiences in orchestral playing often result from playing as a substitute for a regular player, or playing an additional part in larger repertoire for which the orchestra has no regular player.	

Classical music – soloists and chamber musicians

Description	Skills/qualifications required	Employment type
A few musicians achieve an exclusively solo career as a recitalist and soloist with orchestras. Opportunities are scarce and the field is highly competitive. There tend to be more opportunities for pianists and violinists than, for example, for wind and brass players. Soloists may specialise in particular areas of repertoire and become particularly known for this. Others actively engage in extending the diversity of their work, and often include commissioning new pieces as part of this. Many soloists play a lot of chamber music as well, and some musicians work pretty much exclusively in small ensembles. A solo career invariably involves a lot of touring internationally, and most soloists will have agents and/or managers. Giving concerts is balanced with making recordings when possible,	Soloists require exceptionally high instrumental and interpretative skills. Having done well in national and international competitions is also pretty much essential in order to be able to launch a career, as this kind of success brings both wide recognition and often specific performance opportunities. Success in competitions is also likely to be beneficial in securing representation from an agent, and in getting radio exposure or recording contracts. Soloists and chamber musicians all need intense dedication to their work, quite often at the expense of other interests in their lives. Nothing else can really take priority. As well as having strong musical personality, they must be self-reliant socially and able, for example, to spend long periods of time touring, away from family and close friends, which can be quite a lonely	Soloists and chamber musicians are almost always self-employed. Fees tend to be much higher than for orchestral players, but usually have to cover travel, accommodation and subsistence expenses. Few successful soloists are able to operate without an agent or manager, as these provide both international contacts for securing work and strong negotiating skills for their clients. Big artists may be signed to a record label, with a contract to produce a series of CDs. This, however, is an area of work that is gradually decreasing.

| and schedules are often planned several years in advance. | experience. Musicians in chamber ensembles require sophisticated social skills that enable them to spend long periods of time travelling, etc., with their colleagues. An analogy is often drawn between the relationships in a string quartet and marriage! | |

Commercial recording sessions

Description	Skills/qualifications required	Employment type
Commercial recording sessions are used, for example, to record music for advertising and film. Recording usually takes place in a dedicated studio. Depending on the material, it may require musicians to record a track individually, wearing headphones and working with a click track.	You will need excellent instrumental, musical, ensemble and sectional skills, especially technical and sight-reading skills. The ability to deliver an immaculate performance on the first take and then repeatedly and on demand is important, since studio time is very expensive. Professional reliability is essential. Musicians who are late for sessions are rarely booked again. Some sessions may also involve a lot of waiting around while recording problems are solved or other parts of the music are recorded. This requires an ability to be patient and to deal with boredom.	This kind of work is almost always paid on a sessional basis, and requires musicians to have self-employed status. The work is often considered lucrative, particularly compared with regular orchestral playing. Many session musicians are also working as orchestral or chamber music players. The work tends to be controlled or 'fixed' by a few managers, and many musicians begin session work by being introduced to one of the fixers by a colleague.

Accompanists, répétiteurs and rehearsal pianists

Description	Skills/qualifications required	Employment type
The term 'accompanist' is becoming more and more difficult to define, perhaps happily so as practically all 'solo' pianists also work within the collaborative spheres. Professional accompanists	Excellent piano skills and particularly sight-reading skills, along with an ability to learn and assimilate new repertoire quickly, are key. Fine listening – always keeping an ear on that third	Accompanists work almost exclusively on a freelance basis. Some music schools and conservatoires offer full-time or part-time permanent contracts for pianists.

will turn their fingers to any collaborative work: being the official pianist for instrumental or vocal auditions and competitions, for assessments, for lessons, classes, courses and masterclasses.

There are pianists who almost only play for song or instrumental recitals. These are few and far between, but the song repertoire is still often recognised to be a specialised field. Here the ability to coach singers is often considered to be part of the job.

Those training to be répétiteurs are aiming, at least initially, to work in an opera company. Among other tasks they would be expected to:

- prepare singers before rehearsals begin
- work with them during production to bring a particular conductor's or director's interpretation to life
- play for rehearsals
- take notes during rehearsals
- play continuo or orchestral piano in performances
- conduct off-stage choruses.

This role of conductor is one that many répétiteurs aspire to. Indeed they may become répétiteurs as a stepping stone towards that goal.

(and fourth…) line so that you can quickly adapt to whatever is happening in the moment – is also essential.

Accompanists need to be personable, easy to get on with, and flexible in matters of interpretation. In the case of a rehearsal pianist, it is important to have a reassuring and helpful manner, and the ability to calm nervous candidates with whom one needs to make an instant rapport. They must also have sure stylistic and musical knowledge, which would include baroque styles (e.g. continuo playing), music theatre and lighter music, and contemporary extended techniques. Other useful keyboard skills may include being able to transpose at sight and read from chord symbols. For those wanting to specialise in song repertoire, then a working knowledge of various languages and an understanding of how the voice works would be needed. You would be expected to work both as a partner and a coach, and an understanding of the song world, of the poetry and of the period in which both words and music were written is part of this. Networking will be essential to survive, together with a willingness to work at short notice, particularly when starting out.

Pianists who, for example, play for ballet classes, need some understanding of ballet, together with skill in improvisation and then remembering the

It is an uncertain career path, and alternative ways of making money are important. This most usually involves teaching, coaching singers or working as a soloist. Some pianists also work as conductors, music directors in music theatre, or even play another instrument professionally.

There are some lucrative prizes to be won, which are helpful financially as well as giving a young pianist exposure. Many pianists will also develop their own concert series. There are a few places on agents' books for accompanists, but most often the work comes through the vocal or instrumental partners.

A diary service can be helpful, as sometimes diary services are asked to suggest someone, especially at short notice.

For répétiteurs a mixture of short-term contracts and full-time permanent work in opera houses is available.

Many répétiteurs may use this work as a means of getting into conducting.

improvisation and repeating it. Ballet teachers demand very particular styles and structure of pieces, which they then require to be repeated, reduced, altered or expanded upon.

There is no set career path. At the start of a career, an accompanist will probably happily explore anything that involves the piano. A recognised leader in the field may be able to be more specialised, command higher fees, and play with more famous partners and in more prestigious venues.

For répétiteurs, fluency at the keyboard is essential, allied to quick learning skills. Pianistic subtlety is not as important as an ability to create orchestral textures in the playing. A love of working with singers and of the operatic repertoire is taken for granted, along with a good working knowledge of the core operas.

Some knowledge of languages is needed – primarily Italian, French, English and German, although Russian and Czech are handy – and a fine ear for coaching singers, which implies an understanding of the way the voice works, as well as sure stylistic and musical knowledge.

An ability to work well with the large personalities often found in the opera world and an ability to work in a team to produce a performance are vital. It is also important to bear in mind that you may not always be a part of the final performance itself.

| | Many répétiteurs in the UK begin their careers through various courses at conservatoires, the National Opera Studio or through the Jette Parker Young Artists Programme at the Royal Opera House. These courses in many ways run as supervised work experience and are excellent first steps. Thereafter lies the world of auditions for a variety of small and large companies. In the early stages of a career you may expect tasks with less musical responsibility, but senior répétiteurs become vital assistants to conductors in major opera companies. | |

Performing as a jazz musician

Description	Skills/qualifications required	Employment type
Working as a jazz musician first and foremost involves performing in a wide variety of venues. This is likely to include touring in a similar way to the work undertaken by performers in other musical genres. Equally, jazz musicians often combine performing with related activity, such as composing, arranging, directing bands, recording, score setting or copying, teaching privately (for a music service, in schools or in higher, further or continuing education), promoting gigs, arts administration or music journalism. Jazz musicians can also be strong candidates for music therapy training, given their	An extremely high standard of instrumental and performing skills is required, together with relevant associated skills (e.g. for teaching). An excellent knowledge of jazz genres and repertoire is also essential. Professionalism is another essential part of success – poor time management or unreliability, for example, are recipes for disaster. Excellent social skills, self-awareness, patience, determination, realistic expectations, facility with IT and self-management skills may be equally important. In the early stages of a career, performing work may well be less prestigious or poorly paid, with the expectation being that it is	Most jazz musicians combine freelance work (such as performances) with some part-time employed work (such as teaching or music administration contracts). Working in jazz is not usually well paid, and private or alternative income will be extremely helpful. Funding and professional bodies can be sources of support and invaluable information, for example: Jazz Services, the Arts Council or the Musicians' Union.

| existing skills as improvisers, provided they have an undergraduate degree or equivalent academic experience. | valuable to do the work for 'the experience'. Similarly, roles such as assistant teacher, assistant director or conductor, assistant sound engineer may be common in the early stages, and many jazz musicians also take on some work that is not specifically related to jazz in order to make a living. | |

Performing as a pop musician

Description	Skills/qualifications required	Employment type
Most pop musicians include performing as a part of their work, in bands or as a solo artist, and many also compose their own material. Live concerts take place in diverse venues and may well be part of a tour, particularly for more established artists.	Unlike the 1960s, 1970s and 1980s, when being a character was important, the modern pop industry demands that people be highly organised. There is little tolerance for the wild behaviours that were not just forgiven in the past but even encouraged. The majority of participants in the pop music field will have come through the traditional path of forming a band with friends, getting better, making contacts and expanding their horizons. Some will have undertaken formal training, either through vocational training organisations or through universities and conservatoires. What are essential are the abilities developed as a musician, rather than having a formal qualification. Determination is key, along with being prepared when opportunities arise. Developing and maintaining a fan base is also very important.	There is almost no salaried work available for pop musicians, although some opportunities exist in the academic world. Most pop musicians will undertake a portfolio of freelance activities, often including playing in several bands. As well as performing and composing, many pop musicians take on work as agents, promoters, managers, publicists or programmers (of music in sequencing applications). They may also be involved in 'aggregation' (where musical intellectual property is exploited in other media, such as placements in TV or film, as ring tones for phones or inclusion in websites), or in sound production for live performance, lighting, staging, tour management and catering. It is not uncommon to find popular musicians working in audio engineering or audio production roles.

Having distinctive points artistically, as well as similarities with other acts that are currently successful, seems to be the winning combination.

Agents and managers tend to be more necessary once a degree of success has been attained, as is the case with major record company and publishing contracts.

In the recording world, newcomers will frequently do a lot of 'demo' recordings, often replaced by more experienced players for the final versions. In live performance settings, pay-to-play gigs are common, where a band or group of bands will have to pay for the venue's public address (PA) system, security and bar staff, and sometimes also the advertising.

Performing as a traditional (folk) musician

Description	Skills/qualifications required	Employment type
There is a wide range of work related to performing traditional music. The successful traditional (or 'folk') musician often pursues and develops a portfolio career, and may be involved in live performance and touring, including: • solo and/or ensemble work • composition (own projects and commissions) • recording and producing for outputs such as commercial albums and digital downloads	Musicians working in the field of traditional music must be particularly skilled in learning by ear and performing from memory, and need to be able to articulate through practice the deep-seated link between instrumentalism and song. A good working knowledge of relevant languages and traditional dance-steps helps for the purpose of contextualisation and interpretation; as do collaborative skills and a comprehensive understanding of the potential of using PA resources as they apply to	Most traditional musicians are self-employed and pursue a portfolio career with a range of concurrent activities. Alongside performing, they may be involved in all kinds of other work in music, such as teaching, composing, broadcasting, journalism, administration, promoting artistic events and producing.

• teaching in either classroom, peripatetic or informal contexts, such as festival or voluntary sector projects • festival organisation and arts administration • marketing • journalism. If concentrating on performance, an emerging professional will often focus a great deal of attention on touring and live performance and on building up a profile among festival organisers, promoters, agencies and record producers. More experienced professionals often develop a particular specialism, such as producing the studio-based work of others, being an artistic director for festivals or youth gatherings, or continuing to develop performance skills in a range of solo and/or ensemble contexts.	folk ensemble and a mature sense of stagecraft. Breaking through and developing a profile or portfolio as a professional traditional musician, as in many fields of music, involves perseverance, patience, doggedness, diplomacy, and a good knowledge of the roles and responsibilities that make up the industry. In addition, traditional musicians cannot succeed without summoning and refining a sense of enterprise and an ability to think critically and creatively, and to know how to market their products.	

Playing on cruise ships

Description	Skills/qualifications required	Employment type
Musicians give a number of performances on board ship during the course of a cruise, as a soloist or ensemble player. The nature of these performances can be extremely varied: a recital, a lecture-recital, background music or accompaniment for dancing.	High-level instrumental and performing skills are important, together with an ability to communicate with the audiences through introducing repertoire and building a rapport with them. In some cases, a social element to performers' duties may also be stipulated in addition to the performances, e.g. through hosting dinner tables.	Recitalists are often engaged for just one or two cruises at a time and will typically give around four to six performances in a two-week cruise. Bands and background musicians may be required to play every day and are often contracted for periods of several months. Recital work is usually arranged through agents who are contracted by the cruise line to supply performers, and who receive a percentage of the performers' fees.

Military bands		
Description	**Skills/qualifications required**	**Employment type**
This work involves playing in military bands and smaller ensembles on state occasions, to entertain troops and on private-hire engagements. Most posts are for wind, brass and percussion players, although there are some opportunities for other instruments. Continuing musical training is provided on principal and (usually) second study instruments, in theory and musicianship and in specific skills such as arranging and conducting. Some basic military training is included at an early stage in a career, and you could potentially be called upon to support troops in a conflict zone. Training for civilian qualifications (including a music degree) may also be available.	Entrance is by audition. You can apply to join at various standards, and the period of training will vary accordingly. The minimum standard for a recruit would usually be Grade 8.	This is usually based on a full-time contract. Bandsmen and women are ranked personnel in the armed forces and military strictures apply. The terms and conditions vary between different areas of the military. See for example: • www.army.mod.uk/music • www.royalmarinesbands.co.uk • www.rafmusic.co.uk

Organists		
Description	**Skills/qualifications required**	**Employment type**
Organists usually work in cathedrals, churches and synagogues, playing for services including weddings and funerals, sometimes training and conducting a choir, and giving recitals. As well as performing on a regular basis, the work may involve recording. Organists are also needed for some orchestral music in concert halls, although this is relatively rare.	Organists are skilled musicians, who often started off as pianists and then developed additional skills in playing the organ. No formal qualifications are usually required, but many organists will have developed experience over a long period of time, and the best are likely to have held specialist apprenticeships, for example as organ scholars at university.	Some cathedral organists have permanent, full-time posts. Many more are employed part-time or casually and are self-employed.

Organists who are also directors of music in a cathedral or church will almost certainly be involved in conducting and training the choir. They therefore need all the skills of a conductor as well as their skills as a player (see also the section on conducting, below).

Where organists are working in contact with children under the age of 18, they will be required to have an enhanced CRB check.

Music theatre – singers and instrumentalists

Description	Skills/qualifications required	Employment type
The West End of London has the most music theatre performances in the UK, but shows also get produced 'off West End', in theatres outside London and on tour. Most shows put on eight performances per week.	For singers, acting and dance skills are likely to be needed in addition to vocal ability. The emphasis depends on the demands of the show. Not all music theatre singers are required to read music, but it can be an advantage. Instrumentalists require excellent instrumental facility, musical awareness and a good ear. They are frequently required to 'double': play several related instruments. Good sight-reading skills can be very useful in the early stages of production. The band often plays in a theatre pit. West End shows can run for years and the parts remain the same! An ability to cope with the repetitive nature of the work is important.	Most musicians in this context are self-employed and working on short contracts (typically rolling, with a two-week notice period). Rates of pay are often lower away from the West End. In addition, when on tour performers may need to find 'digs' in each town. There is usually a contribution in the fee towards subsistence, but it may not always easily cover costs. Doubling on another instrument usually increases the fee. There are sometimes opportunities to deputise for the regular player on a show.

Music theatre – musical director (MD)		
Description	**Skills/qualifications required**	**Employment type**
The MD conducts performances and rehearsals of music theatre shows, frequently from the keyboard. The MD usually has a say in auditions and casting, and is frequently required to edit and arrange scores.	Excellent keyboard skills are required (both as a pianist and in reducing scores, transposing, etc.). Many MDs work as rehearsal pianists as a way into the field. The ability to conduct and arrange scores is essential, as well as being able to work in an environment where acting is as important as singing. MDs also require good administrative and people skills. Note that assistant MDs are often keyboard players within the band.	MDs tend to be self-employed and work on short contracts (typically rolling, with a two-week notice period). In addition to the performances, an MD will continue with daytime rehearsals in order to manage cast substitutions and ensure that 'swings', who are able to cover several parts, are kept fully rehearsed during the run. Options to send in deputies vary. Often there is an assistant MD, who will deputise for one or more shows each week and who will also watch and note the performance.

Singing, including opera, oratorio, as a recitalist, in choirs		
Description	**Skills/qualifications required**	**Employment type**
At the highest level, a solo singing career is commonly centred around opera, but equally it may focus on, for example, singing oratorio and – in a small number of cases – art song. In the early stages of a singing career, operatic roles are likely to be smaller and to be combined with singing in the chorus or understudying major parts. Other solo work is most likely to be available, perhaps as a soloist for choral societies or as a concert singer and recitalist for music clubs. In addition, there is a growing interest among promoters in developing cross-arts projects and building innovative	It is inevitable that the quality of your voice – its inherent colours, flexibility, range and power – plays an important role in determining how successful you might become. But that is only a starting point. Indeed, some singers have had high-flying careers with voices that could not conventionally be described as beautiful. What matters is how they use them. So imagination, a spark in performance, that ability to communicate words and music with honesty and individuality are paramount. Of course, even for the most naturally gifted singer, a strong vocal technique is crucial: without it, no career	Full-time employment is generally rare in the singing profession – an opera-company chorus is one of the few examples of full-time singing work in the UK. The majority of singers will be freelance, employed on short-term or one-off contracts. There are programmes for young artists, which pay a stipend (in opera companies, the major vocal ensembles and broadcasting organisations), but these tend not to last more than a year or two. The likelihood for most singers is that early on they will sing for free at charity concerts or in self-promoted

contexts for classical music, so imaginative, innovative singers are also finding themselves in increasing demand outside the conventional concert arena.

Session work (singing for TV or film soundtrack recordings, for instance) is a common constituent of the singer's 'portfolio' career, along with corporate entertainment (singing at company functions – or even leading workshops in communication for business people), working as a cruise-ship musician or maybe as a singer on- or off-stage in theatrical productions. These more commercial avenues can often form the financial backbone of a career as a singer.

In choral and ensemble singing there is work in churches, as a lay-clerk in cathedral choirs, singing regularly (sometimes daily) for services, or as a 'dep', standing in on an occasional basis. The top professional choirs have busy concert schedules and can be a consistent source of work for the best ensemble singers.

Throughout a singing career, a key consideration is choosing repertoire that is appropriate for the voice. Since the voice changes as you grow older, some of that repertoire will change too. So, for example, certain grander, larger-scale works will probably be off-limits in the early stages of a career, and many singers find that they are not ready to take on major operatic roles in large venues until their thirties.

will last. Technique will help to give you vocal consistency, stamina, the ability to perform under pressure and the facility to adapt to different musical demands.

Strong musicianship skills are important, too. If you are able to learn repertoire quickly (preferably by yourself) and accurately, you will have more opportunities for employment. Opera singers also require strong acting skills, and good sight-reading is expected in the choral sphere. At every level you will need to be able to respond with ease to different conductors, fellow soloists, orchestras and venues, which means knowing about musical styles and how to switch from one to another.

Most practically, you will need good time management and a reputation for reliability (lose that reputation and you are in trouble). Persistence will help you get ahead, but so will excellent collaborative skills and the ability to work easily and positively with colleagues, making friends across the profession. You will want to keep fit so that you are physically able to cope with performing, and if you can drive a car, that journey home after concerts can be much easier.

There is no requirement for formal qualifications, but in the early stages of a career, some organisations (choral societies or music clubs) will set store by your place of study, and, of course, music education institutions will

concerts, with the hope that these might lead to paid work in the future – there are more singers than there are concert opportunities, so at the base of most career ladders, a willingness to perform for little financial reward can pay dividends later.

An agent can undoubtedly be helpful, certainly once you are past the initial career 'break', to deal with contractual issues, to help negotiate on your behalf and to help in the process of finding performing opportunities. Some larger organisations – opera companies and concert promoters – are unlikely to consider you unless you have been put forward through an agent (although there are other routes to being heard by promoters), so being on an agent's list is one way into the business. But through personal contacts and your own publicity and initiative, there are plenty of alternative routes to a successful career, even without an agent early on.

For choral work you will want to be on 'depping' lists for churches and professional choirs – standing in for someone is often the way towards a more permanent position. And both as a soloist and as an ensemble singer a good website is becoming ever more essential, allowing you to control your own publicity and to reach a wide audience, if you are entrepreneurial enough.

Many singers work in other fields, both musical and

For many singers, the early stages of a career demand the most flexibility as far as musical styles and performing contexts are concerned: a *Messiah* in a town hall one night, a selection of favourite opera arias at a corporate dinner the next. Solo work will tend to be in smaller venues, possibly with amateur instrumentalists, and often it will be something that you have had to set up yourself, with all the demands of promotion and event management on top of performing. As the career develops, you will be known for, and associated with, certain types of work, so you might find yourself becoming increasingly specialist.

On the other hand, some singers establish themselves by developing in a particular repertoire niche, e.g. Early Music or contemporary repertoire. In this scenario, the work early on is likely to be specialised and only later, once you are more widely known, does the range of options become broader.

allow you to make contacts that you might otherwise struggle to find.

non-musical, particularly while establishing a career. Teaching is a common option, and a good way to develop skills that will be useful throughout your career (and often helps to clarify areas of uncertainty about one's own singing). There are opportunities in music administration; and freelance writing (perhaps of programme notes or reviews) can provide useful parallel work. Anything is possible, as long as it does not put too much of a physical strain on you and it allows you the time to practise and be flexible enough to say yes when performing work comes along.

Conducting

Description	Skills/qualifications required	Employment type
Conducting offers opportunities to work across a huge range of music, including ballet, opera, symphonic and chamber orchestra music, choral music and smaller-scale new music. Conducting for music theatre (musical director) is covered above. Conductors are also	In the UK, no particular training in conducting is required of music teachers, although this is not the case in the USA for choral conductors. Conductors come from many different backgrounds, and may develop at different ages. Significant experience in practical	Some conducting positions with ensembles may be salaried, usually for a fixed-term period. A few cathedral posts are full-time. The majority of conductors, however, are self-employed and develop a portfolio of short-term, hourly-paid and one-off contracts.

required in diverse contexts, such as working with youth orchestras and amateur ensembles as well as with professional groups.

Choral conducting ranges from choirs in schools to fully professional church choirs, choirs associated with orchestras to local choral societies and other amateur groups. In cathedrals a choral conductor is usually expected to be an organist, and trained primarily as such, although this is beginning to change.

A conductor holds responsibility for the overall performance of the music, and sets the tone both musically and interpersonally. As well as keeping an ensemble together, the conductor brings an overarching idea about the piece and its interpretation. In making a performance, this then involves finding effective solutions in bringing the score and the players together, and combining these with their own musical vision of a piece. In rehearsal, conductors are continually making decisions in the moment about how to shape the music, solve technical issues, and bring the best out of the other performers. This requires quick responses, the ability to analyse what is going on, and considerable flexibility, for example avoiding getting bogged down with particular instrumental difficulties, and knowing when to give a strong musical lead and when to follow what members of the ensemble are doing.

music-making, however, is extremely important, as this brings a real understanding of how instruments work and how musicians think.

Conductors all need to have an excellent and highly trained ear. Perfect pitch can be an advantage but is not essential. The ability to read scores, including all the different clefs, and to deal with transposed lines is vital. Practical understanding of harmony, rhythm and musical form are core to being able to get on the inside of a score and its complexities. Technical skills in the physical movements of conducting are important, particularly when working with professional ensembles. A conductor working with new music needs to be confident in beating many different patterns, that often also continually change within a short period of time.

The ability to be highly focused and to embrace the intensity of the mental space required to develop interpretation of large-scale pieces is essential. This requires dedicated study, often alone, and a willingness to embrace the autonomy of such an artistic vision. Conductors must also then be able to convey their conception to an ensemble through their conducting and rehearsal process. This requires confidence to work with people, share musical ideas and enthusiasms, and make quick decisions about who can be persuaded to do what when there is not time to work in

Within education, independent schools are likely to appoint a 'director' of music, assuming that the person in this role will direct the major ensembles. In a state school, it is likely that a 'head' of music is appointed, and the role will focus first and foremost on curriculum, with conducting being a secondary part of the role.

Agents are extremely hard to get, particularly before a significant reputation has been built up. Conductors will often, therefore, have to find their own work and negotiate fees, considering all the additional costs needed to prepare a performance (including purchasing scores), travel, etc.

It is possible to combine conducting with a wide range of other work. Typically, conductors may also be instrumentalists or singers, and at times may direct an ensemble from their instrument. Many combine conducting with, for example, teaching, composing or examining.

In the early stages of a career, conductors are most likely to put on their own concerts and ask their friends and colleagues to perform.

detail on particular issues. This kind of focus involved in conducting is quite particular, and is different from the focus of, for example, domestic life; it can be challenging to combine them effectively.

There are some Masters-level courses in conducting, but experience is usually considered more important than qualification in gaining work. Many conductors also learn by watching their peers, asking advice from more established conductors, and preparing their work with their sights set on rather higher musical demands than the immediate context may provide.

There are few formal training opportunities for budding choral conductors in the UK, although there are some Association of British Choral Directors' courses available. Many will develop skills through, for example, being an assistant organist in a cathedral/church or through working with amateur groups.

Conductors also need considerable skills of diplomacy, enabling the relationships within the ensemble to function as well as possible and, for example, taking care of some things that members of an ensemble may not be able to say directly to one another. In addition, they require good problem-solving skills, for example in situations where the wrong music turns up or players have different editions.

5. INSTRUMENT BUILDING AND MAINTENANCE

Instrument makers and repairers represent a small and highly specialised group of musicians. Most have some prior expertise as players and then undergo specific training or apprenticeship in the technical craft.

TABLE 9.5: CAREERS IN INSTRUMENT BUILDING AND MAINTENANCE

Piano technician		
Description	**Skills/qualifications required**	**Employment type**
A piano technician may be involved in manufacturing instruments (largely factory based), marketing and selling them (primarily in showrooms) or servicing them (moving, tuning and maintaining them and specialist concert work). Some technicians will be trained in all areas – able to build a piano from scratch, to individually customise the sound or touch to suit pianists' specific requirements, or to run a company selling new pianos and restoring quality pianos.	Traditionally, apprenticeships were available with piano makers or retailers. However, numbers of piano makers in the UK have gradually dwindled, and there are currently none. Training is now extremely difficult to obtain, with only one formal programme available in Newark. It takes three years to become a basic piano tuner and a further two years of 'improver' training before taking the professional trade examination to become a Member of the Piano Tuners' Association. Becoming a good piano tuner requires excellent hearing. A natural dexterity for using tools and manipulating them with ease and precision is also vital, along with terrific powers of concentration. Tuning a piano is best learnt young. It becomes more difficult every year over the age of 25 and practically impossible over the age of 35, even for people with excellent hearing and a good musical education.	Some companies, such as Steinway, employ piano technicians on a full-time or part-time basis. Many people, however, prefer to be self-employed, as once a business is built up, a reasonable living can be obtained from it. By and large, tuners are independently minded people, who work by themselves most of the time and frequently do not like the rigid, inflexible structures of larger establishments. Many of the people in the piano trade come into it through a love of music and pianos. A number, therefore, combine work as a technician with playing.

The best route in is straight from school. No formal qualifications are necessary if the required hearing level, manual dexterity and powers of concentration are there.

Financial resources to cover the training period are essential, as an income cannot begin in this area for the first two or three years.

Instrument maker and repairer

Description	Skills/qualifications required	Employment type
Making instruments from raw materials – billets of wood and sheets of metal, together with design and manufacture of the tooling required to undertake the making processes – requires a considerable range of skills. These may include programming and operating lathes and milling machines, both manually controlled and increasingly computer numerically controlled (CNC), and will almost certainly require finely tuned craft skills. Manufacturing processes can usually be broken down into distinct stages, each of which may take a considerable period of time. In some cases, a maker may specialise in one part of the process; in others, a maker may be responsible for the complete process. Repairing tends to need a more generalist skill set. Someone who has broad experience from working in a production environment will have plenty of skills and	Many of the tasks do not require musical skills, although many makers/repairers are musically active. The facility to assemble a plastic modelling kit meticulously gives good insight into the sort of manual dexterity needed. There are few structured routes for developing expertise. Natural aptitude with craft processes and experience are the essential ingredients. A few courses are available (e.g. in Germany there is a rigorous instrument-making master-craftsman system), but in many cases, staff are trained in-house through direct apprenticeship. Given the complexity of the tasks, it can take a couple of years or more before someone is up to speed commercially. It may be possible to gain some initial experience alongside an experienced technician/craftsman as holiday work, or by working in some aspect of the manufacturing side.	Opportunities are varied. In general, repairers tend to be self-employed. A few will be under contract with specialist firms in each field, although terms vary between companies, and with some there may be a commission/bonus element as well as a basic salary. This work demands a great deal of patience! Many of the skills as either a maker or repairer are about being meticulous if they are to be done well. Financial support will help, particularly in the early stages of building up skills to a commercially viable level.

understanding of instrument design, but will have to apply them differently to work as a repairer, since it can be a lot easier to work with new materials than with bent or worn parts. Conversely, anyone with some repairing experience should easily pick things up in the production environment, but will need to learn to refine a smaller set of skills to suit the tasks in hand.		

6. SOUND PRODUCTION

Music production covers sound engineering and recording, and sound production for live events.

TABLE 9.6: CAREERS IN SOUND PRODUCTION

Sound engineer		
Description	**Skills/qualifications required**	**Employment type**
Sound engineers plan, set up and operate sound equipment (such as microphones, monitors and mixing desks) for live performances, broadcasts and recordings. They are responsible for balancing sound levels of different instruments/voices when amplified. Similarly, they will determine the quality and level of sound achieved for a recording, and for example whether a single microphone or multiple microphones are used. Sound engineers may also be involved in editing recordings to provide a master copy.	Sound engineers frequently have a specialist sound recording or 'Tonmeister' degree or similar degree-level qualification. In any context, they require a high level of understanding of acoustics, electronics and digital sound processing. They also need to be sensitive to a wide range of artistic considerations in order to make effective technical decisions. Equally, good communication skills are vital, as it is these that help to put performers at ease to get the best out of them in pressurised situations. When dealing with classical music, sound engineers will also need to be good score-readers. It is possible to start without formal qualifications. In this case, people often take on the role of a technical assistant. Work can be at quite a basic level and there are no guarantees of progression, but it does provide an opportunity to build up skills in sound engineering. Positions are often described as 'runner' or 'gaffer'; some applicants write to studios expressing an interest in these posts.	A few posts are contracted within big record companies or venues, and there are some opportunities in higher education institutions. Many sound engineers, however, work on a freelance basis. Further information can be found through professional organisations: • the Association of Professional Recording Services (www. aprs.co.uk) • the Audio Engineering Society (www. aes.org) It is not uncommon to find popular musicians working in audio engineering or audio production roles for large-scale live events.

	The sound engineer and producer are sometimes the same person.	

Record producer		
Description	**Skills/qualifications required**	**Employment type**
A record producer is responsible for making artistic decisions on the editing and production of a recording in collaboration with the artist(s). This will most likely also involve ensuring that the various takes made during a recording session have covered all the required material to a sufficiently high standard. In popular music sessions the producer will frequently be arranging and writing material in collaboration with the artists, and even possibly playing for the sessions too.	Record producers require an excellent ear, and a broad and deep knowledge of music. In addition, a firm basic understanding of the technical aspects of recording is essential. With classical music, good score-reading is also a vital skill. The sound engineer and producer are sometimes the same person.	As with sound engineers, most record producers work on a freelance basis or on short-term contracts.

7. MUSIC THERAPY

Music therapy is a growing area of practice, where music is used as a tool towards a therapeutic end, helping to treat a range of mental and psychological conditions, such as depression, dementia and post-traumatic stress syndrome. It is also used widely with children with a range of emotional, communication and developmental difficulties.

TABLE 9.7: CAREERS IN MUSIC THERAPY

Clinician linked to NHS, education or residential settings, or in private practice		
Description	**Skills/qualifications required**	**Employment type**
Music therapy uses improvisation, incorporating a range of musical styles, as the core technique to facilitate the interactions with clients. It can take place in group settings or one-to-one with individuals. Music therapists may work with adults and children of any age, and of any musical ability. They may aim to help people with, for example, learning disabilities, mental health problems, dementia, communication problems, addiction, eating disorders, and emotional and behavioural difficulties. They can find themselves working with very vulnerable or challenging client groups. Music therapy may be organised in a range of places, including hospitals, schools, day centres, hospices, care homes and within the prison service.	Music therapists must have a qualification from a registered Masters degree programme, and they must register with the Health Professions Council (HPC). Applicants to training programmes are expected to have a first degree. Many applicants are music graduates, but graduates in other subjects are equally welcome, provided they have a high level of instrumental skill and communicative capacity on their instrument(s). They also need to display creativity and the potential to develop as an improviser. Admission is by audition and interview. For most music therapy programmes, an interactive group experience is also part of the selection process. Training as a music therapist is personally and musically challenging, and applicants need to be sufficiently grounded emotionally and psychologically to handle this – and eventually to provide support to clients.	Contracts vary greatly; many are part-time and for a fixed term. Traditionally, music therapists have worked in psychiatric hospitals and special schools, as well as a wide range of voluntary sector settings. Growth areas for music therapy work in recent years have been hospices and mainstream schools. For further information, contact the British Association for Music Therapy (www.bamt.org).

8. MUSIC PUBLISHING AND LIBRARIES

This field covers publication of new music, editions of existing repertoire, together with the maintenance and hire of scores and parts for performers and ensembles.

TABLE 9.8: CAREERS IN PUBLISHING AND LIBRARIANSHIP

Music publishing		
Description	**Skills/qualifications required**	**Employment type**
Music publishers play a vital role in the development of new music across many genres, including songwriting, world music and Western art music. They produce notated copy of musical work in a form that can then be used for performance and/or study. Looking after the business side of creating new music, they are responsible for protecting the work that songwriters and composers produce and for making it widely available. This depends on having a robust copyright framework, which enables initial investment in artists and their work to be recovered. Music publishers may cover all aspects of the business or may specialise in one or more areas: • promoting songwriters and composers, and supporting their development of performances, recordings and broadcasts	Music publishers must have a love and appreciation for music. They will usually be formally trained in music notation or as a performing musician. Many will have extensive composing experience, and will be fluent with the various software packages available for composers and songwriters. Successful publishers have an ability to spot talent and new work that is likely to have an appeal. They are also creative in coming up with interesting ways to promote the work they publish. In addition, being a music publisher requires an ability to communicate well with others. The relationships established between a music publisher and songwriters/composers/performers underpin their success. For anyone working with musicians from other countries, a good understanding of languages is extremely helpful.	The large publishing houses offer some full-time and part-time permanent contracts. Increasingly, there are also opportunities to work on short-term contracts with smaller publishers, and some composers and songwriters publish their own work. Experience may also be gained through internships.

- dealing with the legal aspects of publishing, including negotiating contracts and registering copyright
- commissioning new work, and the detailed preparation of manuscripts ready for publication
- marketing and sales
- working on the financial aspects of the business, including negotiating fees and royalties.

Orchestral librarian

Description	Skills/qualifications required	Employment type
Music librarians are found in a variety of contexts, for example: • within a public library, servicing a community's needs for music recordings and materials for performances, school assignments and private lessons • in an orchestra, sourcing, preparing and maintaining the music required for performance • in higher education, servicing the needs of staff and students both academically and in terms of performance • for an audio archive, setting up online resources and digitising materials.	Music librarians usually have a degree in music and will also require detailed knowledge of library science. Knowledge of music and history, for example, are essential in being able to guide other people who are seeking musical information. Good IT skills are also essential, not least in using industry-standard software for composing (such as Sibelius) and library database management. Knowledge/interest in areas of music other than classical music (jazz, popular, world) may be extremely beneficial, as these are the fastest-growing areas in many music libraries. Some positions require a Masters-level qualification in either library sciences or music, or both – especially in academic settings.	The market for music librarians is relatively small. The majority of positions, however, are full-time or part-time permanent contracts. There tend to be rather few progression routes for librarians, although some librarians move sideways into another type of position, such as from being an orchestral librarian to working in higher education libraries. Internships are often available to help get started in the field.

A music librarian may select and catalogue books, journals and music collections and recordings, archive material, and help others to locate particular musical sources. An orchestral librarian will work with a conductor to ensure that parts are marked up appropriately before rehearsals for a performance start. They will also be responsible for distributing music to players for rehearsals and performances, and will travel with the orchestra when on tour.	Librarians usually require neat handwriting, and must be well organised, with good interpersonal skills. An orchestral librarian will also need to be skilled in copying musical markings into parts, and assisting conductors when they have decided on particular markings or changes to a score required for a performance.	

9. RESEARCH

Research in music covers musicology and performance studies, music psychology, philosophy, music education, performance science, and increasingly practice-based research, where research is undertaken through creative practice or performance as well as through analysis of them.

TABLE 9.9: CAREERS IN RESEARCH

Research in higher education		
Description	**Skills/qualifications required**	**Employment type**
The nature of research in music varies with the specific field. Musicologists, for example, tend to work with scores and texts at a theoretical and analytic level. Performance scientists are more likely to undertake experiments where they work directly with musicians and devise ways to measure physical and mental aspects of their practice. Practice-based researchers include composers, and will do research that takes place through the creative process of composing or performing. Researchers are usually based within higher education institutions. They are therefore linked to formal progression structures from research assistants to lecturers and finally professors. Senior researchers have a responsibility to demonstrate a significant profile nationally/internationally, to attract external funding and partnerships, and to provide a role model for more junior staff. They tend to lead on major research	A doctoral degree is almost always required, and for more senior posts a proven track record within higher education, including high-quality research outputs and/or a transformational approach to teaching. For research assistant posts, the area of expertise usually needs to align closely with the specified project, at least in terms of the type of research being undertaken (depending on whether this is e.g. musicological; in performance studies; creative, practice-based research; music education; music psychology; ethnomusicology). Researchers need an eye for detail, and an interest in exploring things in real depth, as well as imagination and an ability to identify interesting lines of enquiry. They need to be able to express themselves clearly, verbally, through the written word and through music where appropriate. As interdisciplinary collaboration grows, researchers also require strong interpersonal	Contracts are a mixture of full- and part-time, fixed-term and permanent. Professors usually have tenured positions, while research assistants are usually fixed-term (from six months to three years).

projects, often overseeing several other more junior researchers and doctoral students. They are often responsible for the final outputs, including writing journal articles and books and disseminating their work, for example through conference presentations. Increasingly there is an emphasis on large collaborative and interdisciplinary research.

Most researchers are also required to teach. Generally, the more senior the post, the more flexibility there is for an individual to reduce this teaching load. More junior posts often carry a heavier teaching load, but there are nevertheless expectations of producing significant research outputs.

Research assistants (often postdoctoral) are usually given responsibility for co-ordinating research projects, doing desk research, contributing to the detail of research design and/or methods, gathering and undertaking analysis of data, drafting reports and research outputs. They may also be involved in public dissemination: conference presentations, publications or performances.

skills and need to be able to make sense of multiple perspectives on a particular question or idea.

10. BROADCASTING AND JOURNALISM

Broadcasting and journalism cover aspects of news reporting, reviewing, writing programme notes, and producing features on specific musicians or issues. The work spans different media, including newspapers, journals, websites, radio and television.

TABLE 9.10: CAREERS IN BROADCASTING AND JOURNALISM

Music journalist and broadcaster		
Description	Skills/qualifications required	Employment type
Music journalism covers a variety of writing, audio and video broadcasting media. Typical outputs include features about general issues in the music world, opinion pieces, interviews with musicians, news reporting, and reviewing of live events and recordings. Generally, music journalists specialise in a particular genre – classical, jazz, world, rock and pop – with an increasingly dominant emphasis nowadays given to the latter in the newspaper media. The range of possibilities is wide for those who are willing to be flexible. Reviewing work involves listening to/watching recordings and writing about them, or attending live events. Daily newspapers tend to review things on a performance-by-performance basis. Sunday papers and weekly magazines are more likely to give a brief to cover two or three events in one article, drawing the experiences together	Musical knowledge is vital, although many journalists who do not specialise in music can still write successfully on the subject – part of being a journalist is being able to write to order on a variety of topics. Most important is the ability to express yourself well via the written word, or through broadcast media. Journalists need to be aware of their readers, and to tailor their material to what can be understood and appreciated by the target readership. Those seeking an editorial role will need an excellent command of written language and a keen eye for spotting mistakes. For critics, it is important to have an open mind and to be able to express oneself strongly without being opinionated. When pitching for work, confidence and doggedness are enormous assets, as nine times out of ten, ideas are rejected. Being overconfident, however,	Most music journalists work freelance, being paid for what they do on the basis of regular copy rates that vary according to the publication. In general, national newspapers pay better than specialist magazines and local newspapers. Editors may well have a staff contract with the organisation for which they work. Journalists who write regularly for particular organisations (e.g. music critics) may have a wordage contract with the publication, which guarantees a monthly sum in return for a certain number of words published each year. When starting out, a journalist may join a specialist magazine as editorial assistant, where they are largely responsible for administrative tasks with a certain amount of copy-editing, depending on the structure of the office, and later progress to deputy editor or editor, where they will take responsibility for commissioning material, etc.

thematically. Daily newspapers require the reviews to be filed (sent to the relevant editorial desk) in the morning following the event, or in some cases the same night. Features and interviews often require substantial research. When interviewing an individual, for example, asking the right questions can make the difference between a dull account and a lively encounter.

In newspaper press, jobs include: commissioning editor (responsible for commissioning the paper's content on specific issues), reviews editor and arts editor. Many papers also have a chief music critic, who is the lead reviewer for music, and a number of other regularly commissioned critics.

In broadcasting, the work is split between researchers, who contact contributors, set up interviews and put together material; producers, who establish what a particular programme will contain and who it will involve; and presenters who may take a more or less active role in creating the content of the transmission (many presenters now are expected to write their own scripts).

In classical music, many journalists also write books and programme/sleeve notes for concerts and recordings.

can give an impression of arrogance!

Most music journalists are graduates of one kind or another, though not necessarily music graduates. Journalistic qualifications may help in certain contexts, but are not generally seen as necessary or desirable.

Reliability is vital. It is all very well being brilliant and radical, but if someone is not dependable, the chances are that an editor will look elsewhere. The first priority of an editor on a regular publication is to get copy that will fill the space.

The competition for regular reviewing roles in the main newspapers is extremely high, and young journalists can spend years trying to get a foot in the door and still not get anywhere. Nowadays, most aspiring critics will have some presence on the web, either through one of the reviewing websites, or through their own sites and blogs.

A career as a music journalist can be approached from many directions. A number even start after retiring from some other career. Since experience is the main prerequisite for getting work, and it is very easy to set up your own site, those wishing to pursue a career in this area can do no better than to get out and about and start writing about the music they hear.

Music journalism can be combined with a career in performing or conducting, but if the journalism involves critical writing, then there will be a clear conflict of interest. Teaching music, if the journalist is suitably qualified/gifted, is another option.

Music journalism is in most cases not well paid! For those who are very successful, with activities encompassing a wide range of publications and broadcasting, it may be necessary to have an agent.

Overall, musicians have a wide variety of career choices, providing many different kinds of opportunities. The extent to which these are attractive may change over time in relation to other demands or changes in aspirations. Being prepared to adapt and accept new challenges is important in being able to take advantage of these opportunities.

CHAPTER SUMMARY: CAREER OPTIONS

There are a range of career options within music.

Each career has different opportunities and ways of working.

Increasingly, musicians have portfolio careers.

Decisions about which careers to pursue depend on specific skills, interests and practical considerations about work patterns and lifestyle.

There are opportunities in:

- arts management
- music education and creative learning
- composing
- performing (including conducting)
- instrument building and maintenance
- sound production
- music therapy
- music publishing and libraries
- research
- broadcasting and journalism.

FURTHER READING

Baskerville, D. and Baskerville, T. (2010) *Music Business Handbook and Career Guide*, London: Sage. This is a comprehensive guide to different fields of work in music and to the business aspects of building a successful career.

Bolles, R.N. (2008) *What Color is your Parachute? A practical manual for job-hunters and career changers*. Berkeley, CA: Ten Speed Press. This book offers all kinds of practical and interesting ways to think about your skills and interests and how to match these to career possibilities. It is as useful for people at the start of a career as it is for those mid-career, who are wondering about making changes.

NOTES

1. Bennett, D. (2008) *Understanding the Classical Music Profession: The past, the present and strategies for the future*. Aldershot: Ashgate.

2. Bennett, D. and Hannan, M. (eds) (2008) *Inside, Outside, Downside Up: Conservatoire training and musicians' work*. Perth: Black Swan Press.

3. Solbu, E. (2007) 'What is excellence in higher music education?' Presentation for the Seminar *Trends in the Music Profession in Europe: Lifelong learning and employability* (DVD Lectorate and Polifonia: Dialogue in Music), Lectorate Lifelong Learning in Music. Prince Claus Conservatoire, Groningen, Royal Conservatoire, The Hague and Erasmus Thematic Network for Music, Polifonia, 3. Online. http://tinyurl.com/dxw6zc9 (accessed 11 April 2012).

4. Fine, L.G. (2009) *The SWOT Analysis: Using your strengths to overcome weaknesses, using opportunities to overcome threats*. London: Kick It, London Learning Consortium.

CHAPTER 10
GETTING YOUR CAREER STARTED

INTRODUCTION

This chapter focuses on professional skills that support career development. It:

- provides examples of different approaches to beginning a career
- sets out an overview of professional services and the nuts and bolts of running a small business
- offers tips for common situations, such as auditions, job interviews, pitching for funding or putting on a gig.

Starting a career is often a transitional process rather than an overnight change. Many musicians start professional work while studying. Whether pursuing a single path or more of a portfolio career, musicians usually find that the professional skills covered in this chapter are vital to them at some stage or other.

There are no definite rules to getting started in music. As one musician suggested:

> There is no one route in music. Everyone that you meet will have come some crazy route and started at the bottom somewhere and moved on and found their own way. You have to keep on looking out for opportunities and be prepared to do whatever people want you to do. And work bloody hard!

What comes out clearly in stories of success, however, are the strength of musical skills, passion, a willingness to be proactive and to set achievable goals, self-belief, a feeling for what is distinctive about their musicianship, and flexibility to adapt to the opportunities that arise.[1,2] Case Study 10.1 provides some examples.

COMMUNICATION, NETWORKING AND INTERPERSONAL SKILLS

Many musicians are attracted to music precisely because they find that they are most at ease when communicating through music. Nevertheless, being able to communicate well, for example in conversations and through written

CASE STUDY 10.1: MUSICIANS GETTING STARTED AND GOING DOWN UNEXPECTED PATHS

Jazz performer

'When I was a student, I'd go to the professors' gigs and hear them play. Eventually, Billie Jenkins came and did a workshop with us and he recognised me from gigs I'd been to at the Vortex, and in the last ten years I've done two tours and two albums with him. He picked me up from seeing me around and absorbing me into the scene.'

Drummer and teacher

'I answered ads in *NME* for drummers…I always had to look for work. Most of the money I made on drums in London comes back to one call I got from Upstairs at the Gatehouse to do a musical, where the MD and guitarist got me work.'

Arts administrator

'Be prepared to start at the very bottom – literally make tea for people. I did a music degree at Sheffield, moved to London, did summer playing piano at the Edinburgh Festival – and then nobody wanted to know! So I came back to Sheffield. I saw an advert looking for [a] full-time employee at a club night I used to go to. I was on £9k, basically flyering – distributing publicity materials. But through that, I was given the opportunity to set up a small agency which sent out musicians – often world musicians – to schools, and got a job as the first-ever ethnomusicology officer at Sheffield City Council.

'To be a successful artist, you have to be prepared to be poor, and be young! One friend in a band has to pay rent and Council Tax and lives with [his] girlfriend, so he has a job. But that means the band can't go off on a tour, so they can't get an agent.'

material, is a huge asset, and it is a skill that can be developed. These skills will in fact be used all the time, for example in:

- interviews
- presentations
- introducing concerts and gigs
- teaching
- running workshops
- talking to sponsors, promoters and publishers
- negotiating with agents.

Some important aspects of effective communication are given in Tips and Reminders 10.1.

TIPS AND REMINDERS 10.1: FUNDAMENTAL ASPECTS OF EFFECTIVE COMMUNICATION

- Consider who you are talking to and what may interest them.
- Know what you want to communicate and what you want to achieve from it.
- Listen actively to others, as well as communicating your own ideas.
- Be sensitive to non-verbal communication (in face-to-face situations this usually accounts for about 70 per cent of what is received, while verbal content accounts for only 10 per cent and tone of voice 20 per cent).
- Seek and respond to feedback on your work where appropriate, for example when talking to employers and audiences. This can provide invaluable information and spark new ideas.
- Check to see what people have understood from your communication and be open to their response.
- Tune in to a situation and what may or may not be possible at that time.
- Where appropriate, be ready to summarise and reframe a conversation as a vital step in identifying priorities and next steps.
- Be prepared to suggest following up a conversation at a later date with a meeting, email contact, etc.

BUILDING NETWORKS

Networking enables you to create productive relationships with different organisations and individuals, exchanging information and support. They are an essential part of building a career.

Books on the subject, courses and gurus abound![3,4] A lot of time and effort can be saved simply by thinking about what this is all for in music. Networks may be used to:

- build an audience
- promote, disseminate and sell work
- provide personal and professional support, including advice, coaching and mentoring, access to professional services
- make contact with other professionals and establish collaborative partnerships
- explore new professional avenues and entrepreneurial ideas – creativity is usually a collaborative process.

The business of getting out there, talking to people, exchanging knowledge and experience, finding interest and support is inevitably something that some people find easier than others. This, in part, is connected to personality type: extroverts are generally happier in social situations that require them to initiate conversation and introduce themselves. A lot is common sense, however, and networking needs practice and organisation, like any musical skill. While many people feel anxious or resistant to the idea, once there are some objectives and a structure to work within, the process often becomes less daunting and even quite satisfying when the good results start to show (see Case Study 10.1 and Exercise 10.1).

Professional organisations offer ready-made networks and may provide networking opportunities that bring members together face-to-face or online. Considering which professional organisations to join is an important step.

EXERCISE 10.1: STEPS TOWARDS BUILDING A NETWORK

You already have a network, although you may not think of it in these terms. The aim of this exercise is to help you plan how to activate your network for mutual benefit and to help build your career.

If you find the whole subject of networking daunting, you may want to build up the habit by starting small and getting support by working on this exercise with someone else.

1. Think about all the people you know who might be useful to you professionally in some way, or whom you might be able to help professionally. Make a database of them and consider what information to include, e.g. names, email and postal addresses, phone numbers, areas of expertise and spheres of influence, which of your events they have attended. A spreadsheet is usually a good way to do this. Make it searchable, so that you can easily pull out all the people with a particular area of expertise, for example.

2. Identify specific objectives where you want help, whether this is with a task such as building a website, or more generally with finding employment of a particular type. Similarly, identify specific objectives where you might be able to offer something to others.

3. Plan a detailed strategy for meeting each objective. Who do you need to approach? How can you best approach them (email, personal meeting, inviting them to an event, etc.)? When should this happen? How will you need to follow up on initial contact? In each case, think about how the benefits can be reciprocal – this is what is most likely to make your ideas successful.

4. Update the contact list regularly. Where there are important gaps, how could you fill these? Plan opportunities where you can make new contacts.

5. Think through how you want to communicate in any particular setting, bearing in mind the fundamental aspects of communication outlined above and the value of mutual benefits. Take relevant materials to networking events. These might be business cards and/or publicity materials. It may not be easy to give out hard copies of materials, but this can provide the perfect excuse to follow up a conversation with an email or letter, with other materials attached. Finding an appropriate and timely way to continue contact after an initial conversation to see where it can develop is often key.

6. Reflect on how you are using your network and what more you can do.

DISCIPLINE-SPECIFIC ASSOCIATIONS AND PROFESSIONAL ORGANISATIONS

Joining one or more professional associations or organisations can be important in establishing professionalism and in supporting the development of a career. In the UK, the Musicians' Union (with over 30,000 members) and the Incorporated Society of Musicians, for example, provide membership of a professional network and access to a range of services, such as legal advice, guidelines for copyright protection, fee levels and recovery of unpaid fees, and health and safety issues.[5]

Discipline-specific organisations can also be extremely valuable for networking and continuing professional development opportunities. Examples include the British Voice Association, the European Piano Teachers Association, the International Clarinet Association, or Jazz Services.[6,7,8]

WORKING IN PARTNERSHIP – COLLABORATION

Increasingly in the music industry, a lot of professional work is being undertaken through partnerships, both in terms of identifying and planning relevant projects and in delivering them. This can be exciting, opening up all kinds of opportunities. Working in partnership also brings significant challenges that require particular skills and an understanding of, for example, the amounts of time that may need to be invested.

In the field of music education, the complexity of the different elements involved in making partnerships work effectively has been identified:

> Effective partnership working takes account of context; requires good communication, time, leadership, mutual trust, clarity of roles and responsibilities and the support of senior management. Training needs must be identified and addressed. Planning, monitoring and evaluation are crucial and a shared ethos and sense of purpose are essential.[9]

In order to be successful working in this way, detailed planning and ongoing attention to the partnership – as well as to the content of the work being undertaken – is needed.

Effective interpersonal interaction is also particularly vital. This is likely to involve:

- empathy
- trust
- respect and being non-judgemental

- active listening, and acting on other points of view
- reading body language
- honesty and integrity
- taking on different roles at different times within a team
- having the confidence to share one's vulnerability
- using language flexibly, so that it resonates with the context
- problem-solving and managing conflict.[10]

PROFESSIONALISM AND UNDERSTANDING ETIQUETTE IN DIFFERENT CONTEXTS

The transition to employment means becoming a professional – or does it? What makes a musician a professional? This is a complex question, particularly as the music industry contains lots of subcultures and genres. Aspects of professionalism are not always aligned between them. Dress codes, for example, vary considerably, as do expectations of timekeeping. Being alert to these differences and being able to fit in can be essential for survival.

Nevertheless there are some basic aspects of professionalism without which most musicians will struggle to succeed. These include:

- mutual respect and tolerance for colleagues
- integrity, authenticity and sensitivity to the cultural differences and the interconnections between personal and professional identities
- commitment and enthusiasm for maintaining and extending musical and professional knowledge and skills; this often requires planning time for practising, keeping up with the latest research and development in the sector, or undertaking further professional development to develop new skills
- being adequately prepared for the work, for example having studied parts and scores, or having planned the structure and content of sessions when in a leadership role
- personal demeanour, being appropriately dressed and in a positive frame of mind and focused on the work in hand
- effective diary management and timekeeping – being reliable
- being willing to interact with colleagues, work as a team and help out where appropriate, even if this involves something relatively

mundane, such as making the tea, or something which might appear to fall outside a given remit

- the ability to ask for and act on constructive feedback, and the resilience to cope with negative feedback and professional setbacks.

It is always possible to seek advice from experienced colleagues. Tips and Reminders 10.2 takes orchestral playing as an example of a professional culture, and offers some do's and don'ts.

TIPS AND REMINDERS 10.2: ORCHESTRAL ETIQUETTE – 'BEING ABLE TO PLAY AND KNOWING HOW TO BELONG'[11]

- Be on time and be prepared. Know the music, know your part, and have the right equipment with you. Ability, combined with modesty and charm, is much appreciated.
- Listen and learn from colleagues. Appreciate their successes (there may be ways in which this is traditionally shown). Do not practise someone else's solo in public, and do not draw attention to yourself by practising concerti backstage.
- Look after and maintain your own playing, particularly when there is a gruelling schedule. Slipping standards affect everyone.
- Be open to conductors' ideas, respect their approach, but do not allow insensitive comments to undermine your self-confidence and ability to perform.
- Do not stare at someone when they are playing a solo, and avoid looking round when someone makes a mistake – it will be your turn next!
- Never show disapproval, even of your own performance, and avoid appearing to know better than colleagues.
- Respect colleagues and their strengths. Tolerate everyone's weaknesses, including your own. Acknowledge the different qualities that younger and more experienced musicians may have.
- When tensions arise, avoid angry outbursts, and sort out disagreements in private. Publicly discrediting a colleague disturbs the working atmosphere. Humour is often the perfect balm for tricky situations.

TIPS AND REMINDERS 10.3: AUDITIONS AND INTERVIEWS

- Only apply for a job if you really want it. It is easy to see when someone's interest is actually elsewhere or they are half-hearted.

- Focus on what is required to get an interview/audition in the first place. Ensure that your CV is targeted to the job specification and is easy to read. Underpin what you say about yourself in an application with evidence from your qualifications, achievements and professional experience. Any covering letter should be short, and should highlight both what you can bring to the role and why you are applying for it.

- Be prepared. While this sounds obvious, it is amazing how many people turn up without really knowing what they are doing.

- If you are not prepared for an interview/audition or are unwell, it may be better to cancel it, or postpone. It is essential, however, to let people know that you will not be coming. Simply not showing up wastes time and money and is likely to affect your professional credibility.

- Think through what you are going to wear and how your appearance will communicate. Consider whether the panel will expect more formal or informal dress.

- Plan your time carefully on the day. Leave plenty of extra time for travel. Arriving late will immediately lower the panel's estimation. Arriving at the last minute will increase your own anxiety. Be prepared to meet other candidates whom you may already know, and treat them with respect, making sure that you do not infringe on their preparation time or undermine them in other ways. Remember that other candidates are your colleagues even though you may be competing at that moment.

- How you walk into an audition or interview room and greet the panel speaks volumes about your professionalism and suitability for a post. Generally panels are desperately hoping that candidates will do well. They also understand that you may be nervous. Smiling and making eye contact is likely to help break the ice and establish rapport. Being grounded and open in your body language will help to present a feeling of confidence and enthusiasm, and will help you to avoid getting too tense. Do not attempt to shake hands with the panel unless one of them initiates it, as this may seem overbearing.

- All musicians face rejection and everyone has some bad experiences with auditions and interviews! If you do not succeed at an audition this is not necessarily an indication of your ability. Remember that the next audition will provide a different situation and set of musical and professional priorities. If you can get feedback, take it seriously and use it constructively within your own development trajectory, but do not let each piece of feedback send you off in a different direction. It may be helpful to debrief with a trusted mentor to get things in perspective. Consider what went well, what not so well, and what you would like to change next time. Then let it go!

TIPS FOR AUDITIONS AND INTERVIEWS

Just about everyone finds themselves having to do auditions and interviews, and most of us find ourselves daunted by them in some contexts. A lot may be at stake, and often a lot of ground is covered in an unnaturally short space of time. No wonder anxiety levels rise. The first thing to remember is that everyone on the panel has had to audition or interview for a position themselves, and they may well have to do so again in the future. The second thing is that for this kind of intense situation, preparation is everything. It provides the best chance of being able to do yourself justice when it comes to the actual event. Tips and Reminders 10.3 offers tips for both auditions and interviews, while 10.4 focuses in further on auditions, and 10.5 on interviews.

TIPS AND REMINDERS 10.4: FOCUS ON AUDITIONS

- For auditions, have several suitable audition pieces in your repertoire ready to play at any time, including the ones that are often requested. Auditions can be called at short notice, and being prepared with standard repertoire will mean you can spend available time on things you do not know, such as more unusual extracts. Where you have some choice about repertoire, choose material that is contrasting and shows off your strengths.

- Auditions often present challenging conditions, such as poor acoustics or limited warm-up and rehearsal time. You may have only a few minutes in which to prove your worth. Giving an assured musical performance is a top priority, and is more important than tackling the most difficult repertoire. Make sure that what you choose is well within your capability and does not have a very difficult piano accompaniment. If an accompanist is struggling with an obscure and difficult part, it will only put you off and detract from the overall impression.

- If you have several pieces of music to play or sing, particularly if any of the music is photocopied, make sure that the parts are carefully ordered and that you can access each one quickly. Fumbling with paper will irritate the panel and do nothing for your confidence or concentration.

- Never turn up to an audition without having rehearsed pieces with piano accompaniment. It will be immediately obvious to the panel, particularly if the accompanist does not know a piece either. If you are required to play or sing extracts from a piece, make sure that you know the piece as a whole and have a detailed understanding of the immediate context: what is it about, what else is going on, who should you be listening to, etc.? Wherever possible, do some mock auditions and get feedback from mentors and friends you trust. Do not be despondent if your first attempts feel terrible. Auditioning is an art and it takes practice.

- An official accompanist is usually provided. Use this accompanist unless there is a compelling reason to use your own, such as playing unknown and difficult repertoire. Make sure that: any music you give to the accompanist is easy to navigate; pages cannot get into the wrong order; and cuts, repeats and points of rubato are clearly marked. Do not insert music into transparent plastic envelopes, as these can make it difficult to read when light reflects onto them. If you have a chance to rehearse, use this time to set tempi and to cover tricky corners for the ensemble. If there is no time for rehearsal, be clear about the tempi as you start each piece within the audition, and take the lead in showing the musical contours where needed.

- Be comfortable and ensure that clothes and shoes do not impede your ability to play or sing. If in doubt, ask advice from an experienced professional in the field. Avoid hair covering your face, as it means that panel members cannot see you properly.

- Auditions particularly can seem to fly past at an incredible speed, and during them you are likely to have to move from one piece of music and style to another much more quickly than in regular performances. This requires supreme concentration and flexibility. Slow practice and relaxation techniques may help you to prepare, calming you down and encouraging you to focus on detail in the moment.

- In situations where an audition is undertaken behind a screen, be aware that even more relies on the musical personality that you project.

- Take time to settle yourself in the space. Arrange instruments, music and equipment so that they are ready to hand. Take in the physical space and, if possible, for example while tuning, notice the acoustics. Wait for the panel to indicate that they are ready for you to start.

- Above all, remember that you are there to give a performance, even if the material is short extracts. Panels will be looking for personality as well as facility. Do not be concerned if you are asked to stop before completing a piece. The reasons are more likely to do with time pressures and wanting to cover a range of repertoire than to do with your ability. If a member of the panel asks you to play something again, listen carefully to the instructions they give and do your best to respond, whether or not you agree with them. Demonstrating your flexibility as a musician is important.

- If things go wrong, do not dwell on them. Keep a positive attitude, by concentrating on the moment and on what you are trying to convey. It is a myth that mistakes are fatal. Panels are usually much more interested in overall ability and potential than in individual slips. If sight-reading is included, remember that establishing the pulse and keeping going, come what may, are the first essentials.

TIPS AND REMINDERS 10.5: FOCUS ON INTERVIEWS

- Research the organisation, its outlook and priorities. Find out how this job fits into the structure and what it really requires.

- If you are asked to make a presentation, address the brief carefully, drawing on your particular skills/experience and linking your vision/aspirations to what you know about the needs, values and strategic direction of the organisation. Ask whether a PowerPoint presentation is expected. If the presentation is for fewer than ten people, it is probably better to do without it. Practise the presentation and get feedback on content and communication. Time it so that it fits the allocated time. Use handouts only if they really add to the presentation.

- Take time to settle yourself in the space. Make sure that you can communicate easily with all the panel members, and organise any materials for a presentation before starting to answer questions.

- Listen carefully to the questions that you are asked. If you do not understand something, ask for clarification, rather than attempting a shot in the dark. Be conscious of how much time you are spending on responses and notice the reactions. If the panel seems to be losing interest, be brief and to the point. If you are unsure about continuing in more detail, check whether they would like you to do this.

- Prepare any questions that you may want to ask the panel. Time is usually allocated at the end of an interview for this, and having some appropriate questions will emphasise your interest in the job.

MANAGING PROJECTS

As the music industry evolves increasingly to a world where individuals and small groups work entrepreneurially to devise new ideas, the skills of project management, finding sponsorship and pitching for funding are becoming a regular part of the portfolio.

PROJECT MANAGEMENT

Project management includes all organisational aspects of a project – from conception to completion. Once the big building blocks of a project are in place, such as dates, venue, participants and overall purpose, a project manager is responsible for:

- fleshing out detail
- producing and following a timeline
- identifying and solving all practical issues
- drawing up and managing the budget and liaising with key people.

A project manager may also be responsible for publicity, print, project evaluation and even ticket sales. It is a hugely influential role.

Project management requires complex organisation and communication skills and can only be learnt by doing it. The detail is beyond the scope of this book (there are plenty of books and online resources dedicated to this[12,13]), but the most important skill in any situation where you are responsible for organising things is to plan ahead, thinking through every step of the way and deciding how it can best be managed.

SPONSORSHIP AND BIDDING FOR GRANTS

Raising sponsorship relies on finding a match between a project and an individual or corporate desire to raise the philanthropic profile, entertain clients or VIPs, reach a particular target audience, or to be associated with the qualities of the project and its social context.

Key questions to think about when considering who to approach are what you have to offer, what is distinctive and successful about the enterprise, and how this might meet the needs of the sponsor. Careful research of potential sponsors is therefore essential. Once individuals or companies have been identified as possible sources of sponsorship, the approach may need to be direct, but more likely it will need to be developed gradually over time. Stages of engagement have been described as: moving from ignorance on the part of the sponsor, through awareness, interest, commitment and finally to ownership, where the sponsor supports on several levels and almost certainly through financial contribution.[14]

The overall pitch that you make to the potential sponsor, whether in person or in writing, needs to be compelling. It will certainly:

- include a clear outline of the project – its purpose, why it is important, what will happen, who will be involved, when and where, and what will be achieved
- profile previous work of the group or individuals leading the project
- identify the opportunity and benefits to the sponsor
- identify the contribution that the sponsor might make.

Fundamentally, the same things apply when making grant proposals, although these tend to require more elaborate paperwork and may not offer the same opportunities for slowly building a relationship.

Sponsorship does not only need to focus on hard cash. Giving in kind is often just as valuable, whether in providing a venue, business expertise or publicity. Whatever is involved in sponsorship, it requires a personal interest in what is being supported, which is why building up commitment to the work through several stages of engagement can be so important.

PUBLICITY AND PROMOTIONAL MATERIAL

The ways in which publicity and promotional material can be effectively handled are changing dramatically, particularly in the context of the growing capacity of the internet. Increasingly, people seek to get their message across, promote their work or engage with their audiences through social networks and websites, as well as through print and traditionally established routes. Information technology skills, being internet-savvy, and having the ability to design the right materials for each situation are invaluable.

Types of publicity and promotional material include:

- press releases
- printed fliers and posters
- e-fliers
- promotion through radio, television or websites
- promotion through social networking and online interest groups
- pre- or post-event interviews or features in press, radio, television
- quotes from reviews and blogs.

No amount of promotional material will really make a difference to success until people start to know something about the quality of the work. If promoters see a brochure for an artist or an ensemble, and this rings no bells with them, they will probably put it in the bin. If, on the other hand, it reminds them of great things they have already heard about the artist or group, then something may happen. Getting stories told about the work that you do is key. When you have a significant piece of work to show, this should be a top priority. Is there anything about the work, the event or the participants that might be of particular local interest? If so, try, for example, to get local and national press and radio engaged.

EXERCISE 10.2: GETTING HIGH-QUALITY NARRATIVES WRITTEN ABOUT YOUR WORK

Decide whether you are going to work on a single event/group of events, or whether you are more concerned with creating a website and an overall strategy for developing your profile. This is likely to depend on how established your work is and how much promotional material you already have. Below are some questions to consider:

- Brainstorm the kinds of stories that would be useful. Which of these might be feasible, how would they be structured (text, pictures, interview, etc.) and who would need to be involved?
- Identify key people to invite to an event well in advance, and consider them to be VIPs. How and when will you approach them? What would they gain from being involved? Can you ask them in advance to review the work?
- How can you best look after the VIPs? What reminders and information do they need? How can you make it a high-quality experience for them? Make sure that invitations communicate the practical details clearly and concisely, and also convey the overall concept of the work/event.
- Steward VIPs through the event, making sure that someone greets them, offers them a drink, introduces them to other relevant people, shows them to their seat, and so on.
- If a VIP is going to write a review or provide some kind of feedback, what information do they need (about length, style, deadline, and so on) to inform what they produce? Should you document an event through photographs and audio/video recordings to support reviews?
- How will you thank VIPs after an event? How will you make sure that they do produce the stories you need?
- What will happen to the stories? Where will they be published? Who else should be told about them? How can they be used to support your work further?

All this can feel like attention-seeking, and many musicians think that this is not at all what they want to do! It is certainly the case that highly successful musicians sometimes have a professional publicist or an agent who will deal with this part of their professional profile. It is unlikely, however, that musicians have this service at the start of their career, and, increasingly, many people are largely taking care of promotion for themselves. If you are in this situation, working with a colleague can really help, so that you can encourage one other, offer feedback or even do the work for each other. It may well be easier to promote someone else rather than yourself.

PRESENTING INFORMATION IN WRITTEN FORM AND VERBALLY

In general the use of words is most successful when presented in bite-size chunks, for example in press releases or web announcements. It is always possible to indicate where further, more extensive material can be found (usually online). Bite-size information should be factual – the who, what, where, when and why of an event. It should avoid technical jargon, especially if appealing to a wider audience, and should avoid hype. All paragraphs should be short. A press release, for example, should never extend beyond a single A4 page. A high-quality photograph should be included only if it makes the story more compelling. All text should be proofread, preferably by someone who has not seen it before, as they will be better placed to notice important omissions and pick up on errors.

When publicity is a verbal announcement or short interview, many of the same principles apply. It is particularly important to make sure that you do not forget key information and that you communicate clearly. A good rule of thumb is to think in terms of condensing and clarifying information into just three points. Also think carefully about whether you want a script or to have your points as a set of prompts. A script can certainly enable you to be clear, but may make you sound wooden. Having no script may lead to stumbling or to vital information being left out. Practise this kind of communication, get people to listen and give you feedback until you find what works for you.

PUBLICITY BROCHURES AND PROMOTIONAL PACKS

Publicity brochures and demo CDs/DVDs are often described as a 'must-have', particularly for performing musicians embarking on a career. However, the timing of putting these together is critical, not least because they usually involve investment. It is much better to record a demo CD/DVD once a group has been playing together for a while; one made at the start of a collaboration is unlikely to be as good. Printed material that includes quotes from reviews packs a stronger punch than material that has none.

The essential questions to ask when planning such materials are:

- What is the purpose?
- Are they being targeted at a single audience or are they multi-purpose?
- What is the quality of the content available?
- How does this match the purpose?

Note that all printed publicity materials can easily be put together by musicians themselves, and indeed this may be the only available option. Professional design, however, can transform their overall impact, and it is well worth considering the returns that investment of this kind may bring in different situations.

For sound recording for acoustic instruments, the quality that can now be achieved with hand-held devices is of sufficiently good quality that musicians may well be able to make their own demo CDs/DVDs. This can be a major advantage, given the costs associated with bringing in professional sound engineers to do the job. Particular issues to consider in order to maximise the quality are set out in Background Briefing 10.1.

The decision about when to go for a professional recording should be driven by its purpose. Who will see or listen to it? What expectations of recording quality will they have? To what extent will the impression of the performers and/or material be enhanced by the quality of the recording? (For example, music with intricate textures and lots of dynamic variation will suffer more from a poor recording than music with simpler textures.)

The packaging of a demo CD/DVD also has an impact, and again professional design and presentation can make a difference. Before making a decision about how to produce a demo CD/DVD, careful budgeting must be done, as hidden costs often accumulate. Consider:

- costs of venue hire
- fees for sound engineer/producer and recording equipment
- fees for musicians
- hire of instruments
- costs of editing and producing a master copy
- costs of copying CDs/DVDs
- costs of packaging, including costs of design and print for covers and inserts.

BACKGROUND BRIEFING 10.1: GUIDELINES FOR MAXIMISING THE QUALITY OF A RECORDING MADE WITH A HAND-HELD DEVICE

Room choice

Choose the room with the best natural acoustic you can find, with some natural resonance. If the room sounds good, your recording is much more likely to sound good. A quiet space is also important, so that extraneous noises (e.g. traffic noise, air conditioning) do not interfere with the recording.

Mounting your recorder

The most flexible and unobtrusive solution is normally to mount the recorder on a microphone stand. If this is not possible, try placing it on a music stand or other flat surface, but ensure that you place it as close to the front edge as possible, to minimise sound colourations caused by reflections from that surface.

Choosing appropriate settings on your recorder

Gain

It is vitally important to check the meter levels, to ensure that the gain is set correctly and you are recording at a good level. If possible, run through the loudest section of the music to be recorded. Here you want these levels metering as high as possible without reaching the end of the meter scale. Levels too high will cause the signal to 'clip', causing audible distortion. If the levels are too low, the signal may get buried in the 'noise floor' of the recorder. On playback, turning this signal up to a usable level will also turn up this noise floor, resulting in hiss on your recording (recording at 24-bit rather than 16-bit would lower this noise floor, reducing any hiss).

File format

Many portable recorders will give you a choice of recording formats. It is normally a good idea to use 44.1 kHz, 24-bit WAV, if that is an option – unless you need more recording time, in which case you can use 44.1 kHz, 16-bit WAV.

Some recorders will allow you to record to MP3, which gives you smaller file sizes at the expense of sound quality – consider this if you need even more recording time, or you need the resultant file to be small (e.g. if it has to be emailed). The MP3 bit rate you choose, measured in kilobits per second (kbps), will control this trade-off; choosing a lower bit rate will reduce both the file size and the sound quality.

Set the correct date/time

Make sure that your recorder has the correct date/time set, as this will help you to identify your recordings in the future.

Placing your recorder

Two important things to consider are the *balance of direct to indirect sound* and the *balance between instruments*.

The balance of direct to indirect sound

The direct sounds are your sound sources (when recording live music, this will be the musicians), whereas the indirect sounds are everything else – most notably the reflected sounds that make up the natural reverberation (or 'reverb') of the room, as well as any applause, air conditioning, traffic noise, etc.

Moving the microphone closer to the musicians will favour the *direct* sounds, giving a *less* reverberant, *'drier'* sound with greater rejection of outside noises. Moving the microphone further away from the musicians will favour the *indirect* sounds, giving a *more* reverberant, *'wetter'* sound and any outside noises will also be brought up in volume.

An understanding of this fundamental principle will allow you to control the amount of room sound on your recording, meaning that you can reject an unfavourable acoustic, choose the most appropriate balance of a nice-sounding acoustic, and control the level of other indirect sounds in your recording.

Balance between sound sources

Placing your recorder closer to an instrument will favour that instrument relative to the other instruments. If you are recording a solo instrument, then the same principle applies (on a smaller scale), but the elements you are balancing are the different parts of that instrument.

For example, when recording an acoustic guitar, consider the balance between the body and neck of the instrument. Placing the recorder closer to the body will pick up a deeper, more resonant sound, whereas putting it closer to the neck will give a brighter, more percussive sound. Choosing a position between these two positions should allow you to find an appropriate balance.

When recording a soloist with piano accompaniment, consider placing your microphones such that they are picking up a balanced sound of the piano with an appropriate amount of room 'reverb'. Now add the soloist and listen to the balance between the soloist and the piano. Moving the soloist towards/away from the recorder should allow you to find an appropriate balance. In ensembles involving a grand piano that is too loud, you can consider putting the lid at half-stick to help achieve the desired balance.

Make test recordings

It is highly recommended to make some test recordings and listen back on headphones. Doing this allows you to test that the gain is set correctly, and that the overall sound quality is good. Try experimenting with different microphone placements in your test recordings, to really get the most out of your recording space.

WEBSITES

A website can be a good place to start in terms of making general publicity available. Websites can be relatively easy to put together at low cost, and most importantly they can be regularly updated. It is easy to refer people to a website where they can find full details of biographies, work already undertaken, recordings, publications, forthcoming events, etc.

More and more people are creating their own websites, and learning to do this need not be all-consuming. A range of publications offer practical guides and there are plenty of short courses available.[15,16]

Critical points to consider include the following:

- Overall design of the website makes a strong statement, so make this reflect the core purpose and values of the work.

- Budget for the costs of hosting a website, initial design, ongoing management of content and development of the site.

- Functionality of the website should be thought through before you start. Plan ahead for how much material you may want to host and of what kind. Consider whether the site will, for example, need interactive functions, space to host tracks or videos, the ability to sell merchandise or stream events live.

- Updating a website regularly is essential, and must be built into the plan.

CVS AND BIOGRAPHIES

The best CVs and biographies present the necessary information for the reader in the most concise and compelling form. This means that a CV should be carefully tailored towards the particular audience for which it is intended. It can be helpful, however, to build up a general CV, from which the most relevant information for any particular occasion can be extracted.

A CV generally covers:

- basic personal information (name, address, telephone numbers and email contact, specialism/instrument where appropriate) – nationality and marital status are normally requested on an application form and should *not* be included on a CV
- education and qualifications (in reverse order, starting with the most recent qualification)
- additional points of recognition, such as competition successes, awards and professional memberships
- employment history (in chronological order starting with your most recent employment)
- hobbies and interests
- references (normally two) – ask referees for permission each time before submitting a CV, as there can be embarrassment and frustration if an employer requests a reference from someone who is not prepared for it.

Often people do not read beyond a single page of a CV. It is essential, therefore, to be able to condense a CV and present it so that the most important information stands out. For example, if applying for an orchestral job, education and qualifications are relatively unimportant. Professional experience and evidence of achievement as a player are the top priorities. Having studied with particular teachers may also be important. If applying for a teaching job, performing experience will be much less important, but teaching experience, qualifications, evidence of interest in and commitment to teaching will all feature strongly. Stick to facts and avoid all temptation to exaggerate achievements. The music business is a small world – inaccurate information is soon discovered, and trust can be lost and a reputation irrevocably damaged.

An indication of hobbies or inclusion of a personal profile is rarely important. In general, selection for an interview shortlist or audition will be made on the strength of qualifications and professional experience, with aspects of personal qualities and interests becoming more important in the last stages of choosing the most suitable candidate for a job. Many applications, however, request a personal statement or a statement about overall suitability for a post. In these cases, the most valuable points to focus on are those of your individual strengths that fit the job description and where there is evidence of how they have been demonstrated in previous work. In addition, it can be useful to highlight how opportunities that the job offers coincide with your current aspirations and professional development objectives.

Overcrowding the page of a CV is a disaster and means that nothing will get read. It should be possible to scan it and get the most relevant information out of it in a few seconds. If a CV does run onto two or more pages, make sure that each page is numbered and has your name on it. CVs should never be accompanied by a photograph, unless this is specifically requested.

Biographies tend to be read at greater leisure. These are less about capturing the attention of an audience and more about giving more information to people who are already interested. Biographies come in all shapes and sizes, often dictated by the requirements of the context. They should cover essential information about professional profile, highlighting distinctive elements, achievements and future work. A biography may well be accompanied by a photograph, which should capture something distinctive.

PROFESSIONAL SERVICES AND BEING SELF-EMPLOYED

DIARY SERVICES, AGENTS AND ARTIST MANAGEMENT

Acquiring an agent or manager may be a symbol of real success in some careers, although the type of service and quality of managers and agents vary considerably. With the increasing ease of international communication and potential for self-promotion, it may not always be the most beneficial solution. A full list of reputable agents and their areas of activity is available through the International Artist Managers' Association.[17]

In selecting an agent, things to consider include:

- the extent of the agent's contacts, nationally and internationally, and particularly in relation to relevant specialist areas of work
- the agent's track record
- to what extent a new artist taken on by the agent will be in competition with others on their books
- terms and conditions, for example expectations of exclusivity in the collaboration, and commission rates (likely to be 10–20 per cent, or for example in the United States even higher).

Agents and managers select their artists in different ways, but few artists find an agent through sending in unsolicited publicity materials. Personal recommendations can play a part, and most importantly agents select through seeing musicians' work. The success of having an agent will depend on your collaboration, and it is important to spend time discussing objectives and ways of working before signing a contract.

Diary services are a good option for freelance performers working in orchestral music, sessions and shows. A diary service will not actively promote individual musicians or handle publicity materials, but will manage your diary and you will authorise it to accept work offered to you. A diary service is a reliable point of contact for fixers and orchestral managers, who can also ask about the availability of several musicians at once, rather than having to make individual phone calls. Some fixers will only use these services and will not contact individual musicians. The service is also useful to musicians in enabling a fast response when work opportunities come up, in picking up opportunities when other musicians are not free, and in reducing the workload of answering phone calls and emails. Diary services usually charge a flat rate per quarter for the service.[18]

TAX, NATIONAL INSURANCE AND VAT

In the UK, individuals are responsible for their own taxation affairs and for making a return to Her Majesty's Revenue & Customs (HMRC) each year, if appropriate. Similarly, individuals are responsible for ensuring that they are up to date with National Insurance (NI). Failure to register as self-employed with the local HMRC tax office within the first three months of trading can lead to penalties.

Musicians' employment can be quite complex. In the UK, some musicians operate an entirely freelance career and are self-employed. They charge gross fees for every piece of work they do, and no income tax or NI are deducted before the fees are paid. The musician is responsible for calculating and paying the tax and NI. Self-employed musicians are required to pay Class 2 NI contributions, which have a fixed monthly or quarterly rate, and Class 4 contributions which are calculated according to profit over a certain level.

Certain expenses, such as travel, professional clothing, instrument maintenance and repairs, can be subtracted from the gross fees before the tax liability is calculated. For the computation of tax, these musicians are on what is called 'Schedule D'. Many musicians in this category will have an accountant to help prepare the submission to HMRC each year. They will also have to keep detailed records of all income and expenditure relating to their work, and to keep receipts and payment slips/invoices as evidence.

Some musicians are salaried by a single employer, and tax and NI (in this case Class 1 contributions) are deducted at source. For the computation of tax, these musicians are on 'Schedule E'. This is a relatively straightforward situation, but these musicians may also find that they are doing some freelance work in addition to a salaried post. In this case, they will require 'dual status', where part of their income is on Schedule E and part on Schedule D. Increasingly, many musicians have dual status, as employers who used to pay gross fees, for example schools using instrumental teachers for a few hours per week, now have to consider them as part-time employees.

All self-employed musicians can register for Value Added Tax (VAT) on a voluntary basis. When gross income reaches a threshold level (in 2011 this was £70,000 per annum), registration is compulsory. All musicians registered for VAT will have to charge VAT on their services, for example for every performance they do, as this will be levied on their income. They can, however, then also claim back VAT paid on business expenses where VAT is charged, for example on the purchase of new instruments.

Tax, NI and VAT need to be dealt with professionally, as stringent investigation and fines can be imposed if there is any suspicion of evasion or inadequate record-keeping. There are plenty of accountants who specialise in musicians' affairs, and a good one should be easy to find by asking colleagues. In addition, professional organisations such as the Musicians' Union and the Incorporated Society of Musicians provide guidance.

CONTRACTS

Some parts of the music industry operate without written contracts for freelance work, others use them as a matter of course. Contract law, however, indicates that a contract does not always have to be in writing to be enforceable. Nevertheless, this is an area that is worth considering, particularly in situations where a lot of income is made through individual pieces of work or work with a small group. It is perfectly possible for performers to draw up contracts of service to use, for example, with festivals and promoters. Templates and advice are readily available through professional organisations.

In addition, contracts are usually signed between, for example, an agent and an artist, a record company and an artist, or a music service and a teacher. Once signed, these contracts are legally binding. If in any doubt about the details, seek legal advice.

COPYRIGHT

Copyright law is designed to protect composers, authors and creators of material. In general this means that anything subject to copyright cannot be reproduced or performed in public without permission – and in some cases without paying fees to the copyright holder. This can include, for example, using a photocopy of a score for a performance, although a single photocopy of a piece of music is permissible for private study. Copyright law is extremely complex and subject to change. There can be substantial legal repercussions if someone fails to comply with it. Be informed and check detail in particular situations. Music librarians often have expertise, and professional organisations will be able to advise.

For anyone producing new material, understanding and ensuring copyright protection is essential. It is wise to seek professional advice on an individual basis at a very early stage, as a lack of clarity about intellectual property and copyright when material is first developed, particularly where several people might have a claim, often leads to disputes later on. In general, copyright arises automatically for an eligible person when a work is recorded either in writing or through a sound recording.

INSTRUMENT INSURANCE AND PUBLIC LIABILITY INSURANCE

All self-employed musicians are responsible for their own insurance relating to the protection of their instruments. They are also responsible for their own public liability insurance, which provides legal cover for accidents that may happen, for example, to a child during a lesson at a teacher's home, or to a member of the public attending a performance.

Failure to have the relevant protection can lead to highly problematic situations, and it is essential that these matters are carefully considered. Professional organisations can advise, and in some cases may offer discounted cover.

You may also want to consider health insurance (essential if you are working in a country without statutory health provision), life insurance that makes provision for your dependants in case of your death, and critical illness insurance that replaces some income for a period of time if you are unable to work through ill health.

CHAPTER SUMMARY: GETTING YOUR CAREER STARTED

Starting your career is likely to be a transitional process – there are no rules about how it happens.

Be proactive and flexible, and set realistic goals.

Know yourself and your strengths and weaknesses.

Be passionate and believe in yourself.

Develop good communication skills.

Take opportunities to network and to work collaboratively.

Be professional and learn the etiquette of the environments that you are working in.

Develop your interview and audition skills.

Learn how to gain sponsorships and to manage projects.

Develop skills relating to publicity and promotion.

Make use of professional services when required.

FURTHER READING

Bailey, M. (2009) *Building a Web Site Using a CMS (in 90 Minutes)*. Brighton: Management Books. This is a good place to start for anyone who knows nothing about building websites.

French, A., Lillya, D. and Johnston, S. (2010) *Directory of Grant Making Trusts 2010/11*. London: Directory of Social Change. This is a comprehensive list for the UK, updated annually.

Noken, S. and Kelly, S. (2007) *The Definitive Guide to Project Management: The fast track to getting the job done on time and on budget*. London: FT Prentice Hall. This is an essential resource for anyone who is going to be involved in organising projects in music.

Zack, D. (2010) *Networking for People who Hate Networking: A field guide for introverts, the overwhelmed and the underconnected*. San Francisco: Berrett-Koehler. This is a useful practical resource to help you get started in the process of networking, particularly for those who find the idea of it really difficult.

NOTES

1. Bennett, D. (2008) *Understanding the Classical Music Profession: The past, the present and strategies for the future*. Aldershot, Hants: Ashgate.

2. Smilde, R. (2009) *Musicians as Lifelong Learners: Discovery through biography*. Delft: Eburon Academic Publishers.

3. Zack, D. (2010) *Networking for People who Hate Networking: A field guide for introverts, the overwhelmed and the underconnected*. San Francisco: Berrett-Koehler.

4. Sosinsky, B. (2009) *Networking Bible*. Indianapolis: Wiley.

5. Online. www.musiciansunion.org.uk; www.ism.org (accessed 26 February 2011).

6. Online. www.british-voice-association.com (accessed 24 May 2011).

7. Online. www.epta-uk.org (accessed 26 May 2011); www.clarinet.org (accessed 16 April 2012).

8. Online. www.jazzservices.org.uk (accessed 26 February 2011).

9. Hallam, R. (2011) 'Effective partnership working in music education: Principles and practice'. *International Journal of Music Education*, 2, 155–71.

10. Renshaw, P. (2010) *Engaged Passions: Searches for quality in community contexts*. Delft: Eburon Academic Publishers, 66–7.

11. Ludlow, J. (1996) 'The orchestral musician' in Ford, T. (ed.), *The Musician's Handbook*. Guildford: Rhinegold Publishing Limited, 37–42.

12. Noken, S. and Kelly, S. (2007) *The Definitive Guide to Project Management: The fast track to getting the job done on time and on budget*. London: FT Prentice Hall.

13. Billingham, V. (2008) *Project Management: How to plan and deliver a successful project*. Plymouth: Studymates Ltd.

14. Beeching, A.M. (2010) *Beyond Talent: Creating a successful career in music*. Oxford: Oxford University Press, 281–3.

15. MacDonald, M. (2009) *Creating a Web Site: The missing manual*. Sebastopol, California: O'Reilly Media Inc.

16. Bailey, M. (2009) *Building a Web Site Using a CMS (in 90 Minutes)*. Brighton: Management Books.

17. Online. www.iamaworld.com (accessed 26 February 2011).

18. Online. www.maslink.co.uk; www.morgensternsdiaryservice.com (accessed 26 February 2011).

CHAPTER 11
LEARNING FROM YOUR EXPERIENCES

INTRODUCTION

This chapter focuses on how you can learn from your experiences. It focuses on a range of practical approaches, including:

- developing your capacity for reflection, and connecting this to future planning
- identifying, describing and analysing critical incidents
- developing systematic reflective processes
- gathering focused and constructive feedback, for example through asking specific questions of peers/mentors, or reviewing audio and video recordings of your own work
- developing creative cycles of planning, undertaking and evaluating work.

REFLECTION AS A MEANS OF GENERATING CHANGE

The ability to monitor progress, reflect and learn from experiences is essential for professional musicians – as it is for professionals in any field. It is perhaps particularly important where feedback from others is not built into the formal working structure and is not always readily available informally. Many years of having one-to-one tuition can encourage dependency on a teacher, rather than stimulating the development of a wide repertoire of skills in reflecting and learning from engagement with others.[1,2]

In addition, the ongoing pace of change within the creative and cultural industries and the diverse projects that musicians are likely to engage with during their careers mean that successful musicians can never think about 'business as usual', but are always evaluating their work and working on new ideas (see Case Study 11.1 and Case Study 11.2).

CASE STUDY 11.1: LEARNING AS A LIFELONG PROCESS

Drummer and teacher

'There are masterclass teachers who are on hundreds of albums telling students how much they still practise, and about all the projects they have on. It's inspiring for most students to realise you've never finished. Some students – mostly when they start – think that you do a music degree and that means you're a professional musician, it gives you what you need. I'll do the degree, then I'll be ready. Part of our role as teachers is to say that's not necessarily the case; that's not the point. I'm not here to give you the answers to everything, but to show you how to keep on asking the right questions and finding the answers.'

CASE STUDY 11.2: PLANNING AHEAD AND ORGANISING TIME

Recent conservatoire graduate

'I've always been busy, ever since school with after-school clubs and things. You need to learn to be productive in the time you have. Make lists. Use your diary and put everything you have to do in it; get a "week to view" [diary], so you know what's coming up.'

Two key elements have been identified by Schön in relation to reflecting on learning:

- reflection-in-action
- reflection-on-action.

Reflection-in-action can be described as 'thinking on our feet'. It relates to situations that are unfolding, connecting with our feelings and building new understandings of situations to inform our actions. As Schön puts it:

> *The practitioner allows himself to experience surprise, puzzlement, or confusion in a situation which he finds uncertain or unique. He reflects on the phenomenon before him, and on the prior understandings which have been implicit in his behaviour. He carries out an experiment which serves to generate both a new understanding of the phenomenon and a change in the situation.*[3]

(Schön, 1983: 68)

In some situations, decisions have to be made quickly and there may not be time for reflection. Then individuals draw on their internalised repertoire of strategies, based on previous experiences which may have become automated. In order for these to change and develop, we need to reflect on our actions after the event.

EXERCISE 11.1: USING A PROCESS OF ALTERNATING IMPROVISATION AND CONVERSATION AS A WAY OF REFLECTING AND SOLVING PROBLEMS

If you are working on a particularly intractable problem relating to your career development, it is worth exploring the following discussion format with a friend or mentor:

Both of you should have the problem in mind but not, initially, discuss it directly. Begin with a short free improvisation (5–10 minutes), then talk briefly about its striking features or any critical incidents that you experienced. At this stage it is better not to talk about the problem in hand. Do several further rounds of improvisation and then conversation, each lasting anything from 10 to 40 minutes. Finally, reflect together on the particular problem, drawing on whatever from the session seems relevant.

Reflection-on-action, which is undertaken after the event, enables us to explore why we acted as we did, what was happening in the situation and how we might change things for the future. This can lead us to increase the possible strategies that we have for dealing with particular situations. The space afforded by thinking, recording or having conversations about our actions can support us in changing our behaviour. It enables us to frame situations in different ways, as sometimes we respond to situations inappropriately because the way we are viewing them is flawed.

Musicians in general use these reflective processes as a matter of course in their work. This is particularly the case in ensemble playing, where individuals constantly respond to one another in the moment, adjusting their own actions in relation to what they hear, see and feel. There may also be discussion during rehearsals or post-performance, to evaluate what has happened and to consider how to develop further. Schön's language of reflection may not be used in these contexts, and indeed much of the process may be tacit. Nevertheless, the practice is clearly there.

This kind of reflection, at which musicians are adept, tends to relate to an immediate situation – a piece being studied or a current performance. It is less likely to deal with longer-term thinking and visioning for the future. In terms of individual learning and career development, however, it is extremely important to include such longer-term reflection in connection with planning for the future (see Case Study 11.3). In addition, the fact that much musical reflection, particularly reflection-in-action, is non-verbal has both advantages and disadvantages. On the one hand it can move fast and deal effectively with issues that are hard to put into words or become constricting when verbalised; on the other hand it can mean that we find it hard to pin down what the critical issues really are, or simply do not become conscious of them. A balance is needed, and developing reflection as an integral part of artistic practice and long-term personal development is an art.

Musical improvisation can provide a powerful tool within such reflective processes. This is partly because of the conversational nature of some improvisation forms that give them strong parallels with a verbal conversation: a powerful communicative exchange between participants. It also relates to the way in which improvisation can enable (or require) us to let go of rules and protocols that are most familiar in our practice. This opens the way for unexpected actions and insights. We move away from our fixed habits and ways of thinking. Unconscious, as well as conscious, thoughts and impetus can surface, so enabling reflection to reach a different level, to move beyond our current expectations and to provide a different perspective on what we do.

CASE STUDY 11.3: CHANGING PROFESSIONAL DIRECTION

Self-taught composer who worked professionally in information technology (IT)

'The opera was staged and then I stopped writing for two years, because...well, doing the opera was so stressful, especially because the schedule was very tight. I was also working through the day [in another field] whilst I was composing and during most of the rehearsal period. After that I think I just burned out... and I couldn't write anymore... then I got really tired of working in IT and realised it wasn't what I wanted to do...so I put in a very late application to study composition full-time.'

Considered in this way, improvisation provides a specific mode of reflection-in-action. In order to use it really well as a reflective tool, free improvisation in particular can be combined with reflection-on-action, through conversation or individual reflective writing. Moving between free improvising and then reflecting verbally on, for example, 'critical incidents' (see below) within the playing can yield surprisingly powerful insights.

CRITICAL INCIDENTS

Critical incidents can provide an important focus for reflection. A critical incident need not be a dramatic event, but it has significance for the individual. It raises questions and can lead to a reconsideration of beliefs, values, attitude or behaviour. In some way it has a significant impact on personal and professional learning.

In music, a critical incident might include:

- an aspect of a performance that went particularly well or particularly badly
- an aspect of technique or repertoire that proved particularly difficult to master
- an activity that increased awareness or challenged understanding

- an interaction with someone that made a particular impression on you
- an incident involving conflict or criticism.

EXERCISE 11.2: LEARNING TO WORK WITH OTHERS

Think of a recent musical situation with colleagues where a discussion about musical interpretation did not go the way that you wanted. Briefly describe the incident. How did the discussion start? What were the differences between you? Could you have presented your case more persuasively? Was the discussion really about interpretation, or were there issues relating to power within the group? Are there other members in the group who you could discuss this with? They might have a different perspective. Try to think of a range of alternative ways in which you could have approached the situation. Write them down, so that you don't forget them. When you next find yourself in this situation, try some of these alternative approaches. Note whether they work or not. Make sure that you take particular account of the reactions of others.

To learn from a critical incident requires asking questions about it. These might include the following:

- Why did I view the situation like that?
- What assumptions did I make about the situation?
- Are there other ways I could have interpreted the situation?
- What other action could I have taken that might have been more helpful?
- How can I change the way that I react if faced with a similar situation in the future?

EXERCISE 11.3: ANALYSING CRITICAL INCIDENTS

You can do this exercise alone, writing down your responses, or you might wish to work with a friend, talking through the issues. Identify a critical incident in your life. Describe the context of the incident. Describe the actual incident in detail. Explain why the incident was critical or significant for you. Explain your concerns at the time. Describe what you were thinking and feeling as it was taking place, and afterwards. Mention anything particularly demanding about the situation. Explain how the incident will impact on your learning. Explain how it will impact upon your future role as a professional musician.

DEVELOPING SYSTEMATIC REFLECTIVE PRACTICES

Students are often asked to undertake written tasks that demonstrate their ability to critically reflect on their work, as this practice encourages learning at a deeper level and supports personal growth, professional development and meaningful change in behaviour.

Reflection can develop an individual – morally, personally, psychologically and emotionally, as well as cognitively. It helps you to:

- better understand your strengths and weaknesses
- identify and question your underlying values and beliefs
- acknowledge and challenge possible assumptions on which you base your ideas, feelings and actions
- recognise potential bias
- acknowledge your fears
- identify possible inadequacies or areas for improvement.

Taking time to reflect can help you identify approaches that have worked well, so that you can adopt them again. It also helps you to identify what doesn't work, so that you don't repeat it.

REFLECTING ON LEARNING AND PERFORMANCE

For musicians, it is crucial to be able to monitor and enhance performance constantly. This requires critical reflection on both the process of learning and on performances themselves. Chapter 3 explored ways in which you can reflect on practice through the use of recordings. Clearly it is possible to do this with performance, although this may be problematic if you are playing in a group, as others may not wish to record the performance.

An alternative is to ask for feedback from your colleagues or from someone who acts as a mentor. This process may not be easy for either party. Being honestly critical requires particular skills, which offer support while suggesting ways in which improvements can be made. Receiving criticism, even when it is constructive, can be difficult and can engender emotional responses that need to be managed. Any such relationship therefore requires trust and respect between the two parties involved. This relationship may develop with a teacher or mentor, but if it does not, it is worth finding someone who can act as what is sometimes known as a 'critical friend'.

BEING (OR WORKING WITH) A 'CRITICAL FRIEND' OR MENTOR

> A critical friend can be defined as a trusted person who asks provocative questions, provides data to be examined through another lens, and offers critiques of a person's work as a friend. A critical friend takes the time to fully understand the context of the work presented and the outcomes that the person or group is working toward. The friend is an advocate for the success of that work.[4]

If you can identify a colleague who can act as a critical friend, while also becoming a critical friend yourself, this can be invaluable in supporting you to develop as a musician. Acting as a critical friend to someone else develops your evaluative and communication skills and gives you insights, which you can apply to your own learning and performance.

Mentors fulfil a similar role to that of a critical friend, but are usually more experienced. Mentors provide expertise to less experienced individuals, to help them advance their career, enhance their education and build their networks. A teacher may often fulfil this role, but where this is not the case, try to find someone else who can. Mentoring entails informal communication over a sustained period of time, usually face-to-face, although it can take other forms. Some professions have mentoring programmes, in which newcomers are paired with more experienced people, who advise them and serve as examples as they advance. However, this is rarely the case in the music profession.

There are a number of models of mentoring. These include:

- **the cloning model** – where the mentor tries to produce a copy of himself or herself
- **the nurturing model** – where the mentor becomes a parent figure, creating a safe environment in which the 'mentee' can learn and experiment for himself or herself
- **the friendship model** – which involves peers working together; this model lacks a hierarchical element
- **the apprenticeship model** – which focuses on professional relationships.[5]

EXERCISE 11.4: WORKING WITH OTHERS IN A SUPPORTIVE, CRITICAL RELATIONSHIP

Identify a colleague who might be interested in developing a mutual 'critical friend' or mentoring relationship. Set aside time to work together. Using recordings or live performance, work with each other to identify particular strengths and weaknesses and strategies to improve. Try to meet on a regular basis, so that trust and mutual respect are enhanced.

Explore with several colleagues setting up a support group, which meets regularly to perform to each other with a view to offering a supportive environment that is constructively critical.

The five most common techniques adopted by an experienced mentor are as follows:

- **Accompanying** – involves committing to taking part in the learning process alongside the learner.
- **Sowing** – includes preparing the learner for change at a point prior to them being ready for it. It is necessary at a point in time when learners may not understand or accept what needs to be raised, even though they will come to terms with it in the long run.

- **Catalysing** – occurs when change reaches a critical level of pressure. The mentor challenges the learner and provokes change, leading to a different way of thinking, a change in identity or a reordering of values.
- **Showing** – involves demonstration and modelling.
- **Harvesting** – is where the focus is on creating awareness of what has been learnt through experience and drawing conclusions.[6]

DEVELOPING CREATIVE CYCLES OF PLANNING, ACTING AND EVALUATING WORK

For reflection to have an impact, it has to influence behaviour. Kolb[7] developed a useful model through which to develop evaluative skills. This is sometimes known as the 'experiential learning cycle'.

The cycle comprises four different stages of learning and can be entered at any point. However, all stages must be followed in sequence for successful learning to take place. The learning cycle demonstrates that it is not sufficient to have an experience in order to learn. It is necessary to reflect on the experience, to make generalisations and formulate ideas which can then be applied in the future. This learning must then be tested out in new situations.

Figure 11.1 sets out the key elements of the cycle. Brief descriptions of each element are given below.

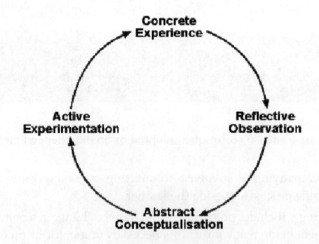

Figure 11.1
Kolb's experiential learning cycle[7]

CONCRETE EXPERIENCE

Concrete experience involves doing or having an experience. This may be any element related to being a musician, including practising, rehearsing with others, performing, composing, and so on.

REFLECTIVE OBSERVATION

Reflective observation (reviewing/reflecting on the experience) involves analysing and making judgements of events and the learning that occurs as you share your experiences with others. People tend to reflect naturally on new experiences, particularly when they lack confidence or when things have gone badly. To be useful, these reflections need to be more systematic, so that we remember what we learnt and use it in the future. This might be through keeping a log or journal, but might also include feedback that you get from colleagues or a 'critical friend'. You will also get feedback from assessments and external critiques of performances.

ABSTRACT CONCEPTUALISATION

Abstract conceptualisation (concluding/learning from the experience) involves drawing some general conclusions about what we have learnt. This may also be supplemented by what we read or actively research.

ACTIVE EXPERIMENTATION

Active experimentation (planning/trying out what you have learnt) involves acting on the conclusions that we have drawn, planning and implementing things that will change, and improving on what we were doing previously. This active experimentation then feeds into our experiences and the whole cycle begins again. It is important to use the cycle in relation to both short-term and longer-term planning, so that reflection is an ongoing process, which supports you in developing and managing your career.

FROM REFLECTING TO ESTABLISHING PRIORITIES AND ALLOCATING TIME

When reflection is effective, the outcome can be real change in what you do and how you approach your work. This is often exciting and also challenging.

The process of turning intentions into practice and establishing new habits requires persistence.

A key part of this can be taking a careful look at, and reorganising, how your time is allocated to different activities, ensuring that you are following your priorities and that your expectations are realistic. A common difficulty that musicians encounter is not being able to say 'no' to offers of work or new projects, so that the quantity of things to be done becomes hugely stressful, or even unmanageable. No one really wants to be in this situation, but it can easily creep up and start to affect the quality of your work and your well-being. Saying 'no' is an important thing to be able to do. It may be something that takes a bit of practice, if you are not used to it. Critically, it is something that is much easier to do when you are clear that, for whatever reason, it is not sufficiently high on your list of priorities to take on. The key is being able to identify where it does lie within your priorities, and taking the time to do this before making a definite response (see Case Study 11.4).

CASE STUDY 11.4: SAYING 'NO'

Professional singer

'Although as a freelancer you can't say "no" all the time, there are times where you have to say "no", and it's a really good idea to say "no". Learning where you are in the scheme of things and whether you can afford to say "no", and how to read that…I think it's really important to say "no" if saying "yes"' will mean that you will do all the jobs you are trying to juggle quite badly…There is a limit to how much you can take on and…work well. I'm not always good at knowing where that point is…I've learned through taking on too much, and really struggling at points to fulfil the expectations. And also realising what a cost that has, what a cost it has just personally, when you're run ragged…I still have that problem. I'm just so thrilled when I'm asked to do things.'

One helpful tool in evaluating current priorities and how these align with medium- and long-term goals is to construct a life-balance wheel, as shown in Figure 11.2.

Figure 11.2
Example of a life-balance wheel

BECOMING A SUCCESSFUL MUSICIAN

To be a successful musician over the lifespan requires flexibility and resilience. The music profession is constantly changing, and what is learnt while training or during the early years of a career is unlikely to be sufficient to sustain a career throughout the lifespan.

Musicians need to evaluate their work constantly, to be open to change and new ideas and not be afraid to implement them. This requires confidence and a willingness to take risks and reflect on the outcomes of doing so. Developing positive relationships with colleagues who can act as mutual critical friends or as mentors supports this process.

Developing resilience – the positive capacity of people to cope with stress and adversity through adapting their behaviour[8] – is crucial. Resilient individuals are able to reframe their thinking, so that they see problems as challenges and opportunities.

EXERCISE 11.5: USING A LIFE-BALANCE WHEEL TO ARTICULATE AND REALIGN PRIORITIES IN YOUR LIFE

This exercise can often crystallise where things are going well and where you want to focus attention. The process is as follows:

- Draw a small circle, and around it a slightly larger circle (circle A). Divide the outer ring into segments, to represent in rough proportions the major activities in your life. These might include things such as studying, professional work, networking and developing a professional profile, leisure pursuits, family commitments, social time, maintaining health and fitness.

- Draw another larger circle (circle B), around the two inner ones, and extend the segment divisions from circle A to circle B. Within each segment create further subdivisions in circle B to show the main activities within each of the areas you outlined in circle A.

- Create one more larger circle (circle C), with the same segment divisions as circle B. In each segment consider how you are doing with this activity and its level of priority in your life. Does the activity have about the right level of activity and take up an appropriate amount of time? If not, do you want it to be more or less of a priority (mark this with a + or – symbol).

Having done this, consider what you will need to do to make the changes you want, in order to get activities aligned with how you have prioritised them. Which changes are likely to have the most impact for you overall? Who or what could help you? It should be fairly easy at this stage to group things into bands of priority – from the most critical to the least important. You can then work from these bands of priority to create specific goals for the short and medium term.

CASE STUDY 11.5: STRATEGIES FOR DEVELOPING RESILIENCE AND MANAGING THE NATURE OF THE MUSIC INDUSTRY

Professional singer

'I've become more clear about what works for me in the last five years…I've become much better at depersonalising, and personalising, the business of seeking work as a freelancer – you're constantly having to chase work. That can be soul-destroying. I've become a little better at seeing it in a context, and seeing that in the end there is a space to fill, and it's how you fit the vision of that space. It's not overall either an acceptance or rejection of what you have; it's how you fit what someone is looking for at that time. So that's something that has really helped, I think, in that I don't really know what they're looking for really, whether it's a role, or a gig on a film. [There will] be a little thing that they need to fill there, and you don't know exactly what that is. So the rejection or acceptance isn't so much about everything that you have to offer, but it's what they're looking for in that particular job, and what they happen to notice in you on that day.'

There are generally considered to be ten ways to support the development of resilience:

- making connections
- avoiding seeing crises as insurmountable problems
- accepting that change is a part of living
- moving towards your goals
- taking decisive actions
- looking for opportunities for self-discovery
- nurturing a positive view of yourself
- keeping things in perspective
- maintaining a hopeful outlook
- taking care of yourself.[9]

Musicians who are able to take these into account in their everyday life, and who also continue to maintain and enhance their musical skills, are likely to have long, successful, interesting and diverse careers.

CHAPTER SUMMARY: LEARNING FROM YOUR EXPERIENCES

Reflecting on your experiences will support your personal and professional development.

It is important to learn from reflection, and change your thinking and actions.

Finding colleagues to act as mentors or critical friends supports evaluation of your work and enhances your development.

Reflection is a lifelong process, which can help you to manage your career in response to the changing external environment and can enable you to develop resilience.

FURTHER READING

Cameron, J. (2007) *The Complete Artist's Way: Creativity as a spiritual practice*. London: Penguin. This book offers a wide range of creative approaches to reflecting on personal and professional development, particularly from an artistic point of view.

Lloyd, C. (1997) *Creating a Life Worth Living: A practical course in career design for artists, innovators, and others aspiring to a creative life*. New York: HarperPerennial. This book is written in an easily accessible style, and provides lots of practical exercises to help reflect on experience and build a creative vision for the future.

Megginson, D. and Clutterbuck, D. (2009) *Techniques for Coaching and Mentoring*. London: Elsevier. This book suggests practical approaches to coaching and mentoring, many of which apply equally to the process of critical friendship or to co-mentoring.

NOTES

1. Gaunt, H. (2008) 'One-to-one tuition in a conservatoire: The perceptions of instrumental and vocal teachers'. *Psychology of Music*, 36(2), 215–45.

2. Lebler, D. (2007) 'Getting smarter music: A role for reflection in music learning'. Unpublished thesis, Queensland University of Technology, Brisbane.

3. Schön, D. (1983) *The Reflective Practitioner. How professionals think in action*. London: Temple Smith, 68.

4. Costa, A. and Kallick, B. (1993) 'Through the lens of a critical friend'. *Educational Leadership*, 51(2), 49–51.

5. Buell, C. (2004) 'Models of mentoring in communication'. *Communication Review*, 53(1), 56–73.

6. Aubrey, R. and Cohen, P. (1995) *Working Wisdom: Timeless skills and vanguard strategies for learning organizations*. San Francisco: Jossey-Bass, 23, 44–47, 96–97.

7. Kolb, D.A. (1984) *Experiential Learning: Experience as the source of learning and development*. New Jersey: Prentice Hall.

8. Rutter, M. (2008) 'Developing concepts in developmental psychopathology'. In J.J. Hudziak (ed.), *Developmental Psychopathology and Wellness: Genetic and environmental influences*. Washington, DC: American Psychiatric Publishing, 3–22.

9. American Psychological Association (2010) *The Road to Resilience: Ten ways to build resilience*. Online. www.apa.org (accessed 10 June 2011).

INDEX

This index is in word-by-word order taking account of spaces between words, so 'art music' files before 'artist'. Page numbers in **bold** indicate case study boxes, and those in bold with the suffix '*ex*' indicate exercises. *Italic* page numbers indicate diagrams.